Service Management and Marketing

Issues in Organization and Management Series
Arthur P. Brief and Benjamin Schneider, *Editors*

Employee Ownership in America: The Equity Solution
Corey Rosen, Katherine J. Klein, and Karen M. Young

Generalizing from Laboratory to Field Settings
Research Findings from Industrial-Organizational Psychology, Organizational Behavior, and Human Resource Management
Edwin A. Locke, editor

Working Together to Get Things Done
Managing for Organizational Productivity
Dean Tjosvold

Self-Esteem at Work
Research, Theory, and Practice
Joel Brockner

Implementing Routine and Radical Innovations
A Comparative Study
Walter Nord and Sharon Tucker

The Outsiders
Jews and Corporate America
Abraham Korman

Organizational Citizenship Behavior
The Good Soldier Syndrome
Dennis W. Organ

Facilitating Work Effectiveness
F. David Schoorman and Benjamin Schneider, editors

Futures of Organizations
Innovating to Adapt Strategy and Human Resources to Rapid Technological Change
Jerald Hage, editor

The Lessons of Experience
How Successful Executives Develop on the Job
Morgan W. McCall, Jr., Michael A. Lombardo, and Ann M. Morrison

The Invisible Powers
The Language of Business
John Clancy

The Processes of Technological Innovation
Louis G. Tornatzky and Mitchell Fleischer

Pygmalion in Management
Productivity as a Self-Fulfilling Prophecy
Dov Eden

Service Management and Marketing
Managing the Moments of Truth in Service Competition
Christian Grönroos

Service Management and Marketing

Managing the Moments of Truth in Service Competition

Christian Grönroos

Lexington Books
D.C. Heath and Company/Lexington, Massachusetts/Toronto

Library of Congress Cataloging-in-Publication Data

Grönroos, Christian, 1947-
Service managment and marketing: managing the moment of truth in service competition/Christian Grönroos.
p. cm.
ISBN 0-669-20035-2 (alk. paper)
1. Service industries—Marketing. 2. Customer service. I. Title.
HD9980.5.G776 1990 658.8—dc20 89-29201
CIP

Published simultaneously in Canada
Printed in the United States of America
Casebound International Standard Book Number: 0-669-20035-2
Library of Congress Catalog Card Number: 89-29201

The paper used in this publication meets the minimum requirements of American National Standard for Information Sciences—Permanence of Paper for Printed Library Materials, ANSI Z39.48-1984. ∞™

Year and number of this printing:

90 91 92 8 7 6 5 4 3 2

Contents

Figures

Tables

Foreword

Philip Kotler

In 1977, Lynn Shostack, then a vice president at CitiBank, wrote an innocent-sounding article, "Breaking Free from Product Marketing." This article was to alter the course of our thinking about services marketing, if not general marketing itself. In her article, Ms. Shostack asserted that "New concepts are necessary if service marketing is to succeed. . . . Merely adopting product marketing's labels does not resolve the question of whether product marketing can be overlaid on service businesses. Could marketing itself be 'myopic' in having failed to create relevant paradigms for the service sector?"

When I first read the article, I was skeptical of its thesis. After all, banks, hotels, airlines, hospitals, and other service organizations need to manage the classic marketing mix, that is, the 4 P's of product, price, place, and promotion. True, the service customer comes in contact with a service provider who can substantially affect the degree of customer satisfaction with the service. And the service atmosphere of a bank or hospital can affect the customer's satisfaction. Should these and other factors be subsumed under product or investigated as additional dimensions of the marketing mix for services?

This and other facets of services marketing were subsequently researched and amplified by marketing scholars and practitioners. Eventually a self-conscious movement emerged advocating the separate development of theory and sound management practices for service industries. One of the earliest and most visible pioneers in this field was Christian Grönroos. Grönroos's approach is distinctive in two respects. First, he looks at services marketing in a much more comprehensive and systematizing manner. His goal is to forge a framework that ties together all of the issues in services marketing. Second, his approach is more conceptual and theoretical. He offers a tighter definition of terms and a more causal picture of relationships between elements in the services management and marketing system.

Having written over two dozen papers on services marketing since

1978, Professor Grönroos has brought all of his contributions together in this new volume. This is not a loose collection of publications but rather an integrated new text presenting the major concepts, tools, and techniques of services marketing. It is not only an odyssey through ideas but an exemplification of these ideas through the case studies, anecdotes, and quotations of the leading practitioners of services management.

Professor Grönroos is to be commended for his contributions to this field. His work, and that of others, raises basic questions about the current paradigm of marketing itself. Is the 4-P marketing mix an adequate paradigm for analyzing and planning marketing efforts? Does a marketing department actually increase a company's ability to serve its customers or does it cause other departments within the organization to lose sight of the customer, thinking this is the marketing department's job? These and other vexing questions will haunt marketing thinkers for the next decade. Hopefully newer and better frameworks for thinking about marketing phenomena will come out of the work of Christian Grönroos and others who are enriching our understanding of services marketing and management.

Philip Kotler
S.C. Johnson & Son Distinguished Professor
of International Marketing
J.L. Kellogg Graduate School of Management
Northwestern University

Foreword

Jan Carlzon

When I joined Scandinavian Airlines System a decade ago, it had just sustained a loss of $25 million. Somehow I managed to persuade the board of directors to let me spend another $25 million. All of it went into service improvements. And it really worked.

Some years later, as I was putting on paper some of my reflections on managing a service company, I realized that it was actually during the instant of contact between customer and staff that the future of the company hung in the balance. I called it the moment of truth; this may not have been wholly original, but it struck me with the force of a revelation.

Mine was a practical experience, in the heat of corporate rescue. From the academic point of view, Professor Grönroos has arrived at the same evaluation of customer/employee contact as a critical top management issue. I find his discussion of managing the moments of truth wholly admirable, containing many insights of great value to the manager or—as both he and I prefer to call the person in charge—the leader.

This is not a book exclusively for those of us who are active in service industries. As Professor Grönroos points out, the service component has also achieved vital importance for the manufacturing industry, and they can ignore it only at their peril. The arrival of the service economy will, when fully understood, be seen to have had social and economic effects fully comparable to those of the industrial revolution.

Jan Carlzon
CEO and Chairman
Scandinavian Airlines System

Preface

Most countries in the Western world have entered what is called a service economy or service society, or are about to do so. Services are becoming a critical source of wealth in many ways. First of all, the service sector is, to a growing degree, responsible for the increase in wealth and employment in the society. The percentages of GNP and total employment created by firms and organizations—private and public—in the so-called service sector are constantly increasing. In times of economic recession, the service sector has kept employment up. Moreover, on a micro level, the importance of services is constantly growing far beyond the boundaries of a "service sector." Every statistic defining such a sector is a gross understatement of the truth, since services produced by manufacturers of goods in so-called industrial sector are not included. If, for example, elevator service and maintenance is produced by a separate firm providing such services, it is considered part of service production. However, if the same services are provided by a manufacturer of elevators, it is the GNP of the industrial sector that grows. Hence, there is a large "hidden service sector." Today, service industries and manufacturing industries are to an increasing extent intertwined, and from a management perspective it is misleading to talk about management in service industries. The term "service industries" belongs to a time when services for manufacturers were a negligible part of their operations, without any significant strategic importance. Instead, one ought to be able to talk about managing services or service elements of the business irrespective of whether the organization belongs to what is traditionally called a service sector or to a manufacturing sector.

On the micro level, this "hidden service sector" becomes more and more important. For manufacturers of goods, services and service elements in the customer relationships are becoming an important means of creating a competitive advantage. The goods components get increasingly similar between competitors, and if a firm wants to avoid a devastating price competition, it has to find other ways of offering value added to its customers. Adding services or, for example, activating existing service elements like billing, customer training, and claims handling and deliveries, can be powerful means of differentiating the offering of a firm from that of the competition. There are numerous such "hidden services," and they offer great opportunities for managers of service organizations to develop a winning competitive edge.

However, competing in today's new situation, where from a competitive point of view services form the pivotal element of the offering to customers, is different from what most organizations—service firms and manufacturers of goods—are familiar with. Most management and marketing models are based on experience from competition with goods. The new situation where services are in focus demands new knowledge, on the strategic as well as on the operational level. Firms, and other types of organizations, face what can be termed a *service competition*, where traditional and familiar approaches and models may easily become pitfalls and poor guides to management. New frameworks and concepts geared to the characteristics of services and the nature of service competition are required. A solid *theory of service competition* is needed.

The present book offers a contribution to such a theory. Building upon modern research and practical experience from areas such as management and marketing, as well as operations and organizational behavior in service contexts, if offers a comprehensive body of knowledge on *service management*, that is, how to develop and execute a market-oriented service strategy. It takes the best of the Scandinavian management experience and the Nordic School of Service and incorporates it with North American management practice. The book is intended for managers in service firms and in manufacturing firms facing service competition, as most do today, as well as for students of service management and subareas of management such as services marketing. It is more a how-to-think book than a what-to-do book, although it also includes practical advice about how to cope with specific situations.

The literature on service management and services marketing is very scarce today, and very thin on theory. The present book offers a solid theoretical framework and practical advice on how to pursue a market-oriented service strategy and manage service competition.

Organization

The book is organized into twelve chapters. Chapter 1 describes the *service imperative* today. The growing importance of services is illustrated and the nature of a service strategy discussed. In chapter 2 we analyze the characteristics of services and the nature of service organizations, along with the issue of how customers perceive the quality of services. The concept of Perceived Service Quality and a model of *customer perceived service quality* is introduced. How to *manage service quality* is the topic of chapter 3. There, studies of facets or determinants of service quality are described and frameworks for analyzing and planning quality are illustrated.

In chapter 4 the issue of services as marketed objectives or offerings, that is, as *service products,* is discussed. A management-oriented model of services as marketed offerings, the Augmented Service Offering, which is geared to how customers perceive the quality of services, is presented. In chapter 5 the characteristics of a service strategy are discussed, and the pitfalls in using traditional guidelines from manufacturing are described. Finally, as a conclusion, some *principles of service management* are put forward.

In chapter 6 the issue of *marketing* is addressed. Since understanding services is very much related to understanding which benefits customers appreciate, a market orientation is implicit in service management. Because of the characteristics of services and the nature of service production and consumption, marketing cannot be viewed as a separate function for specialists as it has been traditionally. Instead, the marketing function is spread throughout the organization, and a large number of "part-time marketers," often many times outnumbering the marketing specialists, are responsible for how the customer relationships are developing. In service contexts marketing is found to be much more a top management issue. The role, scope, and content of the total marketing function is discussed in this chapter. In chapter 7 wee look at external market communication, and emphasize the importance of a *total market communication* approach. Problems and opportunities in managing corporate and local image are also described.

In chapter 8 problems related to how to *organize for services and market orientation* are covered. Traditional hierarchical organization structures easily create problems, because of the nature of service businesses. Moreover, because marketing takes place throughout the organization, not just within the domain of a separate marketing and sales department, traditional marketing departments may create or at least widen an existing gap between marketing and operations. Other types of organizational solutions are needed. This issue is addressed in this chapter. Furthermore, the resources required to generate quality—personnel, technology, physical resources, systems, and customers (because customers actively take part in service production)—are described and a model of service-generating resources is put forward. In this chapter we also discuss the concept of internal customers and the importance of providing *internal customers,* like external customers, with good service.

In chapter 9 the management of the *moments of truth* is discussed. Moments of truth (or, as they have also been called, "moments of opportunity") occur when customers meet and interact with the other quality-generating resources of the organization, that is, with personnel, technology, and physical resources and systems. A model of the consumption process is described and the customer's consumption process is integrated with the Service Production System. In this context the Service Production/Consumption Scheme is introduced as a means of managing the development of the service production process.

In chapter 10 the concept of internal marketing is addressed. Internal marketing is an umbrella concept for a range of internal activities in an organization aimed at enhancing a service culture and maintaining a service orientation among the personnel. It emerged in the research on services marketing, and is based on a notion that services cannot be successfully marketed to an organization's ultimate, external market if they have not first been properly understood and accepted by the employees of that organization. Hence, organizations have an internal market that must first be observed. Internal marketing is first of all a management philosophy that directs management's attention to the pivotal role and importance of people in service competition despite the indisputable impact of technology in service production. Second, it provides management with a set f tools and activities that typically can be used internally. Most of these tools are not new, and in fact have long been used, for example, training, internal communication, management methods, and recruitment and career policy. However, the notion of internal marketing provides a new way of making use of these and other tools in a more coordinated and effective fashion.

In chapter 11 the concept of corporate culture is described, emphasizing the importance to successful service organizations of a culture where producing good service—a service imperative—is a driving force. The characteristics of such a service culture are analyzed. Furthermore, prerequisites for a service culture and how to create such a culture are discussed. Chapter 12 offers a conclusion to the book. Once more, the issue of service quality is addressed, and a program for managing customer perceived service quality is presented. Finally, The Five Rules of Service are offered as guidelines for management to cope with the emerging service competition.

Acknowledgments

There are numerous people who have contributed to my thoughts about service management, services marketing, and the emerging service competition. Probably most important is my former colleague, who, one day in the spring of 1976, phoned and asked me to give a speech on the theoretical aspects of how to market services at a forthcoming seminar on services marketing for people in the hospitality industries. This telephone conversation was the beginning of my interest in first, services marketing, and later on, service quality, internal marketing, services in industrial marketing, and eventually service management and managing service competition. I might add that this seminar was later cancelled because of a lack of curiosity among the prospective participants; however, my own curiosity as a researcher remained.

My colleagues in Scandinavia and Northern Europe: Alf-Erik Lerviks, Gösta Mickwitz, Lars Lindqvist, Henrik Calonius and many others at the Swedish School of Economics and Business Administration in Finland; Evert Gummesson at the Center for Service Research at the University of Karlstad; Solveig Wikström at Stockholm University; and many others in Sweden have provided me with healthy criticism, good ideas, and encouragement over the years. My colleagues at Arizona State University; Stephen Brown, Lawrence Crosby, Ken Evans, Bruce Walker, and many others, as well as other American colleagues, of which I especially want to mention Leonard Berry, William George, Philip Kotler, and "Parsu" Parasuraman, have had an equally important impact.

My thanks also go to Benjamin Schneider and Arthur Brief who read previous versions of this book and have given me invaluable advice on how to improve the manuscript. Also, graduate students in my services marketing and management class at Arizona State University provided me with valuable comments on one version of the manuscript. I also want to acknowledge Karen Hansen, a former editor at D.C. Heath/Lexington Books, and Donna Vaillancourt, who provided me with support and important advice.

Finally, I want to extend my thanks to a large number of business executive whom I have had the fortunate opportunity to work with, to interview, or just to listen to. Their role in the development of a "theory of service" is fundamental. For example, my discussions with Jarmo Lehtinen and Lynn Shostack, both as much researchers as businesspersons, have always been creative. There are many representatives of Scandinavian management whom I want to acknowledge: Jan Carlzon, Kalevi Etelä, Allan Larsson, Leif Lundberg, Christian Ramm-Schmidt, Dan Rubinstein, Hans Åke Sand, Jan Wallander, and many others.

Last but not least I wish to recognize the encouragement I have received from family and friends. My wife Suvi has supported me in this endeavor, and she and my children, Henrika and Mickel, have shown an understanding for my work that I truly appreciate.

Christian Grönroos
Helsinki, Finland, and Tempe, Arizona

1
The Service Imperative: The New Competition of the Service Economy

We Live in a Service Economy

In the Western world we are already experiencing a *service society* or *service economy*. According to a frequently used definition introduced two decades ago, such an economy is characterized by the fact that more than half of the gross national product is produced in the so-called service sector (Fuchs 1968). Statistical data published by GATT (General Agreement on Trade and Tariffs) show that in 1984 the service sector of the economy counts for, on the average, 66 percent in the United States, whereas the figure for the EEC countries is 58. In two small European economies, Sweden and Finland, to give two examples, the percentages are 62 and 55, respectively.

The impact of the service sector on the U.S. economy has really been substantial. In the past three decades, the service sector has generated forty-four million new jobs; services have softened the effects of every recession since World War II; and they have also fueled every economic recovery (Heskett 1987).

Bell (1973) describes the service society as a "game between persons." Although this metaphor does not capture all of the characteristics of service activities, it seems to describe the essence of this postindustrial era as compared with the previous eras, which Bell labels "game against fabricated nature" (the time following the industrial revolution up till now) and "game against nature" (the time before the industrial revolution). In short, the "game against nature" is characterized by the struggle of humankind to cope effectively with nature, whereas the "game against fabricated nature" following the industrial revolution changes the relationship of men and women to work. A new relationship between people and machines emerged, and new forms of organizational solutions, coordination of job activities and management skills concerning, for example, overall management, marketing, and organizational behavior, were required (Bowen & Schneider 1988).

Today, in the "game between persons," the critical importance of managing the relationships between people—between service firm employees and their customers and among employees of service firms alike—receives a totally new and upgraded attention. As Normann (1984) in a straightforward manner puts it: "A typical feature of service companies is that one of their outputs is *new social relationships* and that they have to extend their organizing capability well outside their own company" (p. 16). We agree with this analysis, but at the same time we would like to stress the growing importance of managing technology as well.

We deliberately choose to use the expression *service economy* instead of the frequently used term *information society*. Although it is an easily observed fact that the amount of information has increased exponentially, and continues to do so, this is not a structural change in the economy. There has always been a flow of information; there is nothing fundamentally new. However, the growing size and increasing importance of the service elements in business and in the economy, as well as the birth of a range of new types of services, are a *structural change* in the economy. Many of these new kinds of services are related to information processing, but there is a lot more going on in this new society. It is a transition to a society characterized by a focus on new lines of businesses, a new form of competition, which we label *service competition* in the present book, new bottlenecks in management methods, and a new organizational logic in business, as compared to the industrial society. It is a transition of the same magnitude as the transition to the industrial society two hundred years ago.

However, a word of warning is necessary when interpreting the concepts of service economy and service society. These concepts may lead us to believe that services will be the only really important factor in the new economy and consequently that, for example, manufacturing will be of minimal importance to society and to overall wealth and therefore needs less or even marginal attention. This is, of course, not true. A solid, well-functioning, and competitive manufacturing sector is necessary to maintain wealth, in the same way a well-functioning agricultural sector was important to the wealth of the industrial society, and still is. Manufacturing and the industrial sector needs at least as much attention as before, but for most manufacturers, the nature of achieving and maintaining competitive advantage is changing as a result of the growing service society and the emerging service competition. Understanding services and what they can do for manufacturing and for establishing an ever-improving competitive position, on the domestic market as well as internationally, will be *the* critical issue, as much for manufacturers of physical goods as for service firms and institutions in the public sector.

When the service economy is mentioned, one first comes to think about the service sector as it is defined in national statistics. However, the statistical data produced by official sources all over the Western world are based on yesterday's society, when manufacturing was the main source of economic development and national wealth. Manufacturers of goods could rely more or less entirely on the technical qualities of their products. We had a seller's market, where manufacturers did not have to offer much in the form of services or other auxiliaries to their customers. They did not have to differentiate their offerings from those of their competitors in order to maintain market share and survive.

Originally we had markets for commodities only; but even with the emergence of the branded products—industrial goods and consumer goods—the technical solution itself was normally sufficient to create a competitive advantage. Services were produced only in the narrowly defined service sector consisting of banks and financial institutions in the public sector, and a range of numerous different service industries such as hotels and restaurants, professional firms, cleaning firms, and barber shops.

The "Hidden Service Sector" and the "Official Service Sector"

Today, service firms have come to realize that competition is now so severe that mere technical solutions offered to customers are not sufficient to create a competitive edge. In most cases, for instance, mere lodging, financial transactions, and transportation from one place to another are not a sufficient guarantee for success in the marketplace.

Most manufacturing firms in the so-called *industrial sector* of the economy have to offer their customers a variety of services as *an integral part of their total offerings*. A good solution in a technical sense only is not enough in an increasing number of situations today. To put it in a somewhat too simplified way: everybody can produce the goods. But the source for a competitive edge has to be found elsewhere. Services that can be added to the goods produced include, for example, technical service, repair and maintenance, customer training, consulting services, joint R&D programs, materials administration, deliveries, and a whole range of other services or servicelike auxiliaries. We will, of course, return to this in more detail later on. At this point it is sufficient to state that there is a substantial "hidden service sector" (Evans & Berman 1987, p. 618) alongside the "official service sector" and that the former must not be excluded in a discussion of service management and services marketing.

Everybody Is in the Service Economy

Now, and even more so in the future, it is difficult for a firm to produce better technical solutions in the shape of services or goods than its competitors do. What counts in more and more lines of business are the auxiliaries, various types of services firms can offer their customers in a competitive, marketinglike manner.

Manufacturers will have to realize that they, too, are part of the service economy, and thus will have to learn the new rules of service. As Sir John Harvey-Jones, retired chairman of the huge British chemical empire ICI Imperial Chemical Industries, says,

> "increasingly as the world becomes more and more competitive and as the skills of manufacture become more easily replicated, the selling of a defined product against a formula becomes, from a competitive point of view, a matter of cost and ability to command a market position. . . . It could be, and indeed it is my belief, that the chemical industry of twenty years hence will be more of a service industry and less of a manufacturing industry. One can already see trends in this direction. (Harvey-Jones 1989, pp. 59-60)

Indeed, such trends can be seen in other manufacturing industries as well.

Chase and Erikson (1988) state that the traditional view of manufacturing is to seal off production from the outside world ". . .by placing organizational buffers (marketing, product design, etc.) between the customer and the production system" (p. 191). They continue to argue that "there are, however, fewer and fewer markets that can be effectively served by this closed system philosophy. What is needed today [in manufacturing] is quite the opposite—an open system that includes the customer—one that can gather and act on information from the marketplace in real time" (p. 191). They introduce the term *service factory* for such an open manufacturing system (see Chase & Erikson 1988, pp. 194 – 195). To use the words of Heskett (1987): "Whatever your business, services have something to teach"(p. 118). Hence, the service economy is not only relevant for those firms that by definition today are labeled service firms. *Everybody is in the service economy.*

Because services are important in most parts of the economy, it may be less appropriate to distinguish between *service industries* and, for example, *manufacturing industries*. Agreeing with Gummesson (1987d), who suggests that "it may even be questioned whether it is useful at all to talk about 'service industries' and 'manufacturing industries'; it could be more reasonable to talk about 'service activities' and 'manufacturing activities' irrespective of the kind of organization in which they appear" (p. 6), we try to avoid using the term service industry in the present book.

The Importance of Services in Today's Society

A study published as early as 1983 by the Office of the U.S. Trade Representative showed that about three-quarters of the total value added in the goods sector was created by service activities within the sector (U.S. National Study on Trade in Services, p. 24) Giarini explains this in the following way:

> . . . if we look at all sectors of contemporary economic activity, we can easily find out that services of any sort represent the essential part of the production and delivery system of goods and services. A first fundamental fact to be taken into consideration is that for each product [good] we buy, be it an automobile or a carpet, the pure cost of production or of manufacturing is very seldom higher than 20 to 30 percent of the final price of these products. More than 70 to 80 percent is represented by the cost of making the complex service and delivery system work. Which means that the service functions have become the greatest part of concern and investment even within the most traditional industrial companies. (Giarini 1990 forthcoming)

He goes on to claim that the service economy is not in opposition to the industrial economy, but rather represents a more advanced stage of development in economic history.

Giarini's macro perspective can easily be supported by examples from the micro level. For example, Peters and Austin (1987) in their book on passions for excellence, list a number of firms that have achieved success through a service orientation. Chase and Erikson (1988), in their article on the service factory, add a few more examples (Frito-Lay and IBM) of the importance of service for manufacturers of goods:

> Most of their [Frito-Lay] snack products (potato chips and pretzels being prime examples) are indistinguishable from similar products (goods) sold by other manufacturers. Yet, Frito-Lay has over 50 percent of the market within most regions of the United States. *The noteworthy difference is service* [emphasis by the author]. IBM, another well-known example, has been renowned as a company that places customer service at the top of its list of corporate objectives. IBM, never noted for leadership in low prices or product innovation, depends on service to keep IBM's market share in excess of 50 percent in the United States and most other countries of the world. (p. 191)

However, Stigler's observation from 1956 that, in economics at least, there seems to be "no authoritative consensus on either the boundaries or the classification of the service industries" (Stigler 1956, p. 47) unfortunately holds true even today, over three decades later. Hence, old classifications and typologies describing the economy are still used. The official statistics concerning the size of the service sector are but a reminiscence of yesterday's industrial revolution. There is an ongoing change in the economic pattern observed by Regan as early as 1963, at which time he introduced the expression *service revolution* (Regan 1963). The economy has developed rapidly in the direction outlined by Regan since he coined the term. Today, in many speeches and books, services are considered the main output in the new economy, with major implications for sources of productivity and new product generation, and for organization of manufacturing systems and customer relationships (see Reich 1987 and Bowen, Siehl, & Schneider 1989). Davis (1987) argues that the intangibles, the service activities, that companies offer their customers may be the most important source of value added in the service economy.

This new wave, which has long since overrun the industrial revolution, is not evident in official statistics. Every figure describing the size of the service sector is an enormous understatement. This sector is in fact much larger and much more important to the society than it would appear. The lack of exactness—and even sense—in the statistical data is easily illustrated by the following example: If, say, a manufacturer of elevators takes care of the service, repair, and maintenance of their elevators, this increases the industrial sector's contribution to the GNP. If, however, an outside service firm provides the owners of the elevators with the same service, it is the service sector that grows!

However, even as narrowly defined, the service sector is a major factor in today's economy. In periods of economic contraction the service sector has kept total employment from declining, and in times of economic expansion employment within this sector has grown faster than within the manufacturing sector. As reported by Quinn and Gagnon (1986): "In the last two decades, employment in services has advanced on average 2.1 percent during economic contractions and 4.8 percent during expansions. In contrast, in the goods-producing sector, employment has declined an average of 8.3 percent during recessions and increased only 3.8 percent during expansions" (p. 96; see also Statistical Abstract of the United States 1984 and Heskett 1987). Also, as an entrepreneurial force, services are important to the economy. According to Zemke, 80 percent of start-up firms surviving the first two years are service-producing companies.

The service sector offers substantial contributions to the economy in other respects as well (Quinn & Gagnon 1986, pp. 95–96):

1. People value services at least as highly as manufactured goods. Services are not something one looks at after the good needs have been met.
2. The value added produced by service firms is very well comparable to, and even higher than, the value added produced by manufacturers of goods.
3. The service sector is at least as capital intensive as the goods sector, and many service industries have a high technology impact.
4. Service industries tend to be just as concentrated as manufacturing, and service firms tend to be sufficiently big in scale to be important and sophisticated buyers.
5. Service industries develop productivity increases that are big enough to support continuing real growth in per capita income.

However, people tend to view services in an ambiguous way. According to a Conference Board study in 1985, consumers predominantly believe that goods have high value, whereas services have low value.

Services, be they produced by service firms or by manufacturers of goods, interfere in several ways with the production of wealth today. As Giarini claims, "services are no longer simply a secondary sector, but they are moving into the focus of economic action, where they have become *indispensable production tools* to satisfy the basic needs and to increase the wealth of nations" (Giarini 1990 forthcoming). Heskett (1987) states that ". . . today service industries have assumed the mantle of economic leadership" (p. 118). In fact, one can go even further and state that without services, most goods produced within the industrial or manufacturing sector cannot contribute to economic wealth today. Services are real production factors at the same level as the material production itself. (Compare Giarini 1990).

There are, of course, substantial differences among industries, geographical markets, customer segments, and even specific situations. Nevertheless, every firm, irrespective of whether it is a service firm by today's definition or a manufacturer of goods, has to learn how to cope with the *new competition of the service economy* (Grönroos 1988a). Services have become so important to every organization—so-called service firms, manufacturers of goods, not-for-profit organizations and institutions in the public sector alike—that everyone faces a *service imperative* today.

Why Is the Service Economy Growing?

There are a number of reasons for the growth of the service economy—the narrowly defined so-called service sector and services produced by manufacturers of goods—seen during the last decades. Some of the reasons are related to the nature of the business; some of them are related to changes in the society, in the attitudes and life paths of people. These reasons are, of course, highly interrelated.

Cowell offers the following business-related driving forces: "Three of the main explanations . . . are:

(a) the lag in growth in labour productivity in services compared with the rest of the economy;
(b) the growth in intermediate demand from firms;
(c) the growth in final demand from customers" (Cowell 1984, p.12).

First, the volume of labor required to produce any given output has decreased more rapidly in sectors other than services. This would explain the relative growth of service industries as compared to other sectors. Today, labor productivity in service firms is increasing, of course, but because services lag behind, their importance for employment has grown. Moreover, the importance of services to employment, as well as to the production of wealth, is still increasing. This is because there is growing demand for more and new services.

The second reason for the growth we are seeing is the growing intermediate demands from firms, that is, demand for inputs for manufacturing and service production. Professional services, such as management consultancy, engineering services, market research, and so on are required to a greater extent than earlier, and such services are extensively provided by specialist firms established to carry them out. Previously, firms handled these activities themselves to a larger extent. Moreover, totally new services provided by newly established service firms are offered to and used by manufacturers and service firms. Such services are very often related to computer technology and information processing, but new types of environment-related services, such as pollution control, have emerged.

Finally, there is growth in a direct demand for services from customers. As society changes, people get wealthier, and a different attitude toward life develops, people turn to service expenditures. The marginal utility from goods diminishes, at least in a relative sense, and services grow in importance. The demand for leisure services, sports, travel, and entertainment, for example, increases, and in addition to this demands for totally new types of services emerge; for example, new types of health services and fitness services.

Behind much of the change described above are, of course, trends in society. Schoell and Ivy (1981) have explored this issue in some detail. In Table 1–1 their discussion is summarized. Increasing affluence, more leisure time, a higher percentage of women in the labor force, and greater life expectancy create a greater direct demand for various services, some of which have been around a long time, some of which are entirely new. Greater complexity of products, increasing complexity of life, and more new products fuel an increased demand for services. Things that firms or private persons never had to bother themselves with, or could take care of themselves, such as maintenance of goods or income tax preparation, have become so complex that the services of outside specialists are usually required. A greater concern for ecology and resource scarcity creates new services, or boosts the demand for existing services, such as use of public transit service instead of private cars.

Table 1–1
Reasons for the Growth in Service Industries

1. Increasing affluence	Greater demand for lawn care, carpet cleaning, and other services that consumers used to provide for themselves
2. More leisure time	Greater demand for travel agencies, travel resorts, adult education courses
3. High percentage of women in the labor force	Greater demand for day care nurseries, maid service, away-from-home meals
4. Greater life expectancy	Greater demand for nursing homes and health care services
5. Greater complexity of products	Greater demand for skilled specialists to provide maintenance for such complex products as cars and home computers
6. Increasing complexity of life	Greater demand for income tax preparers, marriage counsellors, legal advisers, employment services
7. Greater concern about ecology and resource scarcity	Greater demand for purchased or leased services, such as door-to-door bus service and car rental instead of car ownership
8. Increasing number of new products	The computer-sparked development of such service industries as programming, repair, and time sharing

Source: Schoell, W.F. & Ivy, J.T. (1981): *Marketing: Contemporary Concepts and Practices.* Boston, Mass.: Allyn and Bacon, p. 277. Reprinted with permission.

Is There a Problem with Services Today?

There are a lot of complaints concerning services today. In everyday discussion the services provided by insurance companies, repair and maintenance firms, banks, restaurants, plumbers, and motor vehicle bureau clerks are targets of attack. Moreover, prominent magazines and newspapers are focusing on the bad state of many services by publishing cover stories and columns by respected journalists. There seems indeed to be something rotten in the area of services.

In a 1987 cover story in *Time* Magazine (Pul-eeze! Will Somebody Help Me?, February 2) the writer together with "frustrated Americans wonder where the service went" (p. 48). Americans returning from abroad seem to get particularly upset by the deterioration of services. In the same issue of *Time*, its correspondent Edwin M. Reingold reflects after returning to Los Angeles from an eight-year assignment to Tokyo: "To a returning American grown accustomed to the civility and efficiency of modern Japan, the U.S. seems to have become a quagmire of bureaucracy, ineptitude, mean spirit and lackadaisy. In Los Angeles, New York and Miami and other cities, the repatriate is appalled and depressed by the lack of efficiency and of simple courtesy and caring" (*Time*, February 2, 1987, p. 55).

Such observations are usually reported by people returning from countries like Japan, well-known for efficiency and courteous manners. However, in a column in the *Mesa Tribune* in 1988, for example, Larry Pintak (former correspondent for CBS News) after spending the last decade in Africa and the Middle East, compares services in the United States to similar services in Kenya, Burundi, Italy, and Lebanon. He writes:

> In places like Bujumbura in Burundi, you expect airlines to be overbooked and cab drivers to get lost. But not in the U.S. Have you flown Continental lately? Or braved a New York cab? . . . And then there are the phones. From Beirut, I could dial direct to New York. But from Florida, if I want to call overseas, I have to go through an operator. Even within the United States, long-distance calling is an exercise in frustration. "Glad I could get through," says a relieved executive on the television commercial. (Pintak 1988, p. A7)

And he continues:

> It's not just the telephones. The Italian post office sells a $17 stamp that guarantees overnight delivery. But that's chaotic Italy, right? Here, the U.S. Postal Services spends millions advertising its $8.75 overnight service, but you're often told, "We can't guarantee it will be there tomorrow." "More for less" now means more costs for less service. (p. 7)

However, it is not only the United States that seems to suffer from such a decline in so many services. In a 1988 issue of the major daily paper in Finland, the *Helsingin Sanomat*, a cover story on the state of services in that small Western society was titled, "Services are wanted. Services decline, in spite of an increased number of service employees. In a welfare society you can't survive without a self-service instinct" (Sartti 1988, p. B1). This conclusion seems to be well justified. That services should decline in a welfare society is in many ways very sad and sounds like a paradox. When the society gets wealthier, and people, on the average, become better off and have more leisure time at their disposal, it becomes harder for them to get good service.

In a sense this is not true, of course. There are far more services available today than a decade ago, and, moreover, modern technology has improved accessibility to a lot of them. For example, a range of home computer–related services has emerged, and you can get information about flight connections and their availability on a certain day much quicker on line today, which was impossible not too long ago. However, in the final analysis, people still complain. They feel that services have declined. Because of escalating labor costs self-service procedures are forced upon customers even when they don't want them. Full-time employees who are skillful workers and who take pride in their jobs—for example, salespersons in retail outlets and waiters in restaurants—are disappearing more and more; and part-time employees with fewer skills and less interest in their jobs are replacing them. The somewhat ironic analysis in the *Helsingin Sanomat* cover story on services goes on:

> We live in a modern service society, where 1,300,000 Finns take care of services so that they don't work—at least not well. . . . In 1959, there were just 50,000 service employees. The service society can be recognized by the fact that everybody serves himself/herself—except in the grocery store, where he or she is served by a talking scale. . . . For a long time now, many have wondered what this service army is doing, as many services have either totally disappeared or deteriorated. . . (Sartti 1988, p. B1)

Similar kinds of criticism have been published in several countries, and not only in the Western world. In Singapore, and in the Pacific rim, concerns about the level of services are expressed as well. There are, of course, a range of decent service providers and even many excellent service firms. In the issue of *Time* Magazine featuring the state of services in the United States, excellent firm such as Nordstrom are recognized. In other contexts, IBM, for example, and Marriott, are often said to understand the importance of service. And there are a lot more of them. Internationally, firms like SAS (Scandinavian Airlines System) and Club Med are often mentioned.

However, even if we were not to go so far as to say that services, on the average, "stink," there are serious problems which service organizations will have to solve. Quinn and Gagnon in their 1986 *Harvard Business Review* article are concerned about the fact that American services may follow manufacturing into decline. In their analysis of the service sector, they find serious symptoms of deteriorating services. The importance of services to the economy and to the wealth of the nation grows continuously, but on the micro level there is a constant threat to maintaining good services, not to speak of creating service excellence. They conclude:

> It will take hard and dedicated work not to dissipate our broad-based lead in services, as we did in manufacturing. Many of the same causes of lost position are beginning to appear. Daily we encounter *emphasis on scale economies rather than customers' concerns,* and *short-term financial orientation* that earlier injured manufacturing. Too many service firms have been *slow to invest in the new market opportunities* and *flexible technology* available to them. They . . . have concentrated on *cost-cutting efficiencies they can quantify rather than adding to their value* by listening carefully and in a flexible manner providing the services their customers genuinely want [emphasis by the author]. (Quinn & Gagnon 1986, p. 103)

Managers of service organizations may be making a mistake in following methods similar to those used by their colleagues in manufacturing. Some have worked there, but some have not, as noted by Quinn & Gagnon. There is a *management trap* in services, which we are going to discuss in some detail in a subsequent chapter. In the analysis of good service firms in the issue of *Time* Magazine featuring services, it is observed that ". . . nearly all the experts agree that the way to improve America's service industry is to understand the lot of the frontline worker" (*Time*, February 2, 1987, p. 55).

This is certainly a valid observation. The employees who are in contact with the customers are a key resource in most service organizations, private as well as public, as will be discussed later on in the present book. The problem to be addressed is somewhat bigger than that, though. Managers also will have to understand the needs and desires of customers and how the customers perceive the total quality of the services, as well as the importance of new technology and of functioning systems and procedures, the role of flexible and encouraging rules, and the impact of leaders instead of mere technical managers. In short, managers will have to appreciate what the key issues in managing a service organization are, and understand the nature of the emerging competition in the new service economy. They must realize what works and what doesn't in service competition.

The Nature of the New Competition

What is this new competition? Is it sufficiently different to justify the term "new"? Indeed, for most firms a substantial change in the relation with the market has taken place, which in turn influences managerial thinking, the required organizational structures, the way of operating in the marketplace, and the division of responsibilities among the various functions in the firm. At least two sources for this change can be identified. The change is partly *market-driven,* partly *technology-driven.* First, the customers in the marketplace demand more than a mere technical solution to a problem by a service firm or a manufacturer of goods. Customers are gradually becoming more sophisticated. This demand by the market is constantly enhanced by the fierce competition in more and more industries. Firms have to take into account the new requirements by the market in order to add more value for the customer to the technical solution imbedded in a good or a service. Consequently, more services and servicelike auxiliaries are developed and included in the offering. Second, technological developments, especially within the area of information technology, enable firms to create new services easier. For example, successful implementation of a just-in-time approach to materials administration requires a high-power computerized information system.

When new elements are added to the goods and service components of customer relations, these relations are expanded. Traditionally, marketing hierarchically organized in a sales/marketing department has been responsible for the customer relationship. The other functions of the firm got involved but only to a very limited extent. As the relationship grows in scope more functions are in immediate contact with the customers: for example, bank tellers, technicians involved in technical service and maintenance of machines and equipment, telephone receptionists, and people in an R&D department. Responsibility for maintaining and developing customer relationships, that is, for what normally is called marketing, is no longer solely related to the marketing department and the vice president of marketing. In the organizational structure this new shared responsibility for marketing has to be recognized.

Finally, management has to accept this change intellectually and base its decisions and its involvement in executing the decisions on the truly new competition. The technical solution, irrespective of whether it is provided by a good or a service, is not the key to market success anymore. Services and other servicelike elements in customer relations—in a broad sense we can use the single term "service"—are the values and benefits that firms compete with. The technical solution is more or less taken for granted by the customers. And the tough competition of today gives them the right to do so.

Service Competition and the Moments of Truth

The new competition in the service economy requires a deep understanding of the nature of service production and consumption and the "rules" for managing in the competitive situation of today. Because understanding services is the key to success in this new competition, we may talk about *service competition.*

The key processes of adding the critical value to the offering are moved out from the factories to the *moments of truth*, to use a term introduced in the management literature by Norman (1984) and successfully used, for instance, by SAS Scandinavian Airlines System (Carlzon 1987). The moments of truth are the interactions between the representatives of the customer and the various resources of the firm: for example, when a piece of machinery is delivered to a buyer, when a restaurant guest is being served by a waiter, or when a person operates an automatic teller machine. Albrecht (1988, pp. 26–27) exemplifies typical moments of truth in an air-travel experience as follows:

1. Customer calls the airline for information
2. Customer books the flight with the airline representative
3. Customer arrives at airport counter
4. Customer waits in line
5. Ticket agent invites customer to the counter
6. Ticket agent processes payment and issues ticket
7. Customer goes looking for the departure gate
8. Gate agent welcomes customer to the flight, validates boarding pass
9. Customer waits in departure lounge for flight to depart
10. Boarding agent takes customer's ticket and invites customer on board
11. Customer boards airplane, is greeted by flight attendant
12. Customer looks for his/her assigned seat
13. Customer looks for a place to stow carry-on luggage

14. Customer takes his/her seat
15. Etc., etc.

To sum up, for everybody the services are the basis for effective differentiation between firms and, thus, an exploitable source of competitive advantage. As will be described in some detail in this book, this requires a new approach to management as well as to other business functions such as marketing, operations, personnel, and finance.

It is important to use a service-oriented language when service-related issues are discussed and planned. As already realized by Thomas in the 1970s, "if managers talk about services instead of products [goods], they also think about services and those characteristics that make services unique" (Thomas 1978, p. 165). Nevertheless, our images of work and the mainstream literature on, for example, management, marketing, operations, and organizational behavior remain highly geared toward the manufacturing of physical goods (Bowen & Schneider 1988, Gummesson 1987c and d, Mills 1986, and Schneider 1985).

In this book the term *product* is used as an overall concept of objects or processes that provide some value to customers. *Goods* and *services* are subcategories describing two types of products. Another such subcategory is *systems* of goods and service components, such as turnkey projects involving, for example, planning, construction work, deliveries and installment of production machines, and creation of maintenance systems.

Strategy Options

There are, of course, a range of strategical decisions which have to be made. A service-oriented strategy is only one of several options. In this section we are very briefly going to discuss four overall strategy options, which we believe cover at least most of the long-term possibilities available for the firm. These strategies are not mutually exclusive. Elements of several strategies may be included; however, only one of the strategies should guide overall decision making and execution of decisions once it has been agreed upon. There are, of course various ways of looking at strategies as well. Here we focus on the *competence* the firm intends to transfer to its customers. The four basic strategy options are:

1. Technical quality strategy
2. Price strategy
3. Image strategy
4. Service strategy

A *technical quality strategy* means that the development and maintaining of a superior technical quality of a good or a service is considered the cornerstone of the operations of the firm. The company mainly relies on the competitive advantage imbedded in the technical solution itself. The competence of the firm is due to an excellent technical quality of the products. This used to be a widely used strategy, especially for many manufacturers of industrial goods. It works well in situations where technical excellence demonstrated by the firm is in itself of critical value to the customer. The more the technical competence among competitors grows, the less powerful this strategy becomes. As many firms come to offer a similar technical solution, the technical excellence may no longer be the critical issue in the marketplace. Keiser (1988) reports a study of why customers change suppliers, where it was found that 68 percent cited indifference of employees as the reason for the change, whereas, by comparison, only 14 percent were dissatisfied with the product (goods).

As Lee Iacocca, Chairman of Chrysler Corporation, concluded in a paid advertisement *Fortune* (September 26, 1988): "A company with the best distribution system and the best service will win all the marbles. —because you can't keep an advantage in other areas for long." He is in the same context echoed by Caleb L. Fowler, President of CIGNA's Property and Casualty Group: "We can differentiate our products through the quality of our services associated with their delivery." This is not to say that an excellent technical quality would be less important than before, but it may be impossible, or too expensive, to differentiate the offering by developing the technical solution (a good or a service). A high level of technical quality is most probably still required, but success is not related to this factor only.

In a service firm we have, in principle, the same situation as in manufacturing firms. For example, just transporting a person by air from one place to another, at a given price, is not enough to create competitive advantages per se. The way in which this is done, that is, developing the transportation service according to the nature of service operations into a more sophisticated offering, differentiates the basic service in a way that creates competitive advantage for the service firm.

A *price strategy* means that the firm basically relies on its price level and specific price offerings as the competitive edge. To be the less expensive alternative to the customer is the specific competence of the firm. In many cases this is an attractive option (compare Porter 1980). This strategy is, however, seldom to be recommended in the long run. Using low price as a main argument does not help the firm in building up enduring relationships with its customers. Price remains the cornerstone of the relation, and when the price is not the lowest one anymore, there is not much left to keep the parties together. If the firm can expect to maintain its excellence as low-cost producer in the long run, this is probably a profitable strategy. Otherwise, it may become a strategic trap and should most likely be avoided. Low price normally equals less capital to invest in other elements of the customer relationship such as the technical quality itself and various services to the customer. Therefore, as a long-run overall strategy the price strategy may be dangerous. Of course, price, including low-price offerings when appropriate, should be used actively as a part of any leading strategy.

The term *image strategy* does not refer to the concept of corporate image, that is, the view of the firm that actors in the environment of the firm have. A corporate (or local) image is an asset for any firm. Here, image refers to an imaginative auxiliary to the good or service. Thus, applying an image strategy means that the competitive edge is based on the imaginative extra surrounding the goods and services, which is frequently created by advertising or other means of market communication. This strategy is in a sense equivalent to the price strategy, because something without real substance is added to the offering in order to achieve a competitive advantage. Following a price strategy you offer a low and thus competitive price. In this case, however, the image of the offering is enhanced in the minds of the customers through the use of a range of means from labels, brand names, and distribution channels to various means of communication. Typical examples of goods enhanced by an image strategy are jeans, cigarettes, and cosmetics. However, even durables like passenger cars and services like fast-food restaurants seem to rely on this as the basic strategy.

The fourth, a *service strategy*, means creating a range of services to enhance customer relations. Even turning the goods components of the customer relations into a service can be the cornerstone of such relations. Here the contents of a service strategy will not be dwelt upon, because this will be the main topic of the rest of the book. However, in short, it can be said that various types of services and servicelike elements in the relationships with customers are developed so that the customer relationship is strengthened. The specific competence of a firm can be seen in its ability to serve its customers in a competitive way, and thus create a differentiated offering to the market (compare Porter 1980). Moreover, for a manufacturer, developing service elements as part of the offering creates a goods support, which may operate as a *barrier to entry* in many industries (Lele 1986). Thus, *a service strategy not only enables the firm to differentiate its offering and create a value added for its customers, it also helps keep competitors away from its customer relationships.*

On the other hand, a service strategy can be a powerful tool for a firm that wants to enter a market and overcome the advantages held there by established suppliers (Bowen, Siehl, & Schneider 1989). Although a service strategy is always a valid option in any market, it may be predominantly powerful in mature markets in which it is difficult to attract new customers (compare Campbell & Cunningham 1983 and Bowen, Siehl, & Schneider 1989) and for more technically sophisticated goods such as cars, computers, and paper machines (Levitt 1972). Also, durable goods require, in general, more service support than nondurables which are bought frequently and consumed quickly (Kotler 1988).

Applying a service strategy does not mean that less interest is given to the technical quality of the solution or that price and image are considered unimportant. Instead, applying a service strategy implies that the main focus in the strategic thinking and in the decision making of management is service. In other words, *the key competence is service*. A competitive edge is created by offering values or benefits that are due to various services or service elements in the relationships with customers (or distributors or other interaction parties). Differentiation is achieved mainly by focusing on services and by a profound exploitation of the characteristics of services, irrespective of whether the organization is a service firm in the traditional sense, a manufacturer of goods, or an institution in the public sector. Service is considered a very broad phenomenon, and the term service is therefore used in a very broad sense, which will be further discussed in subsequent sections of the book.

The Need for Studying Services and Contemporary Efforts to Enhance the Knowledge of Services

In 1974, over fifteen years ago, Rathmell (1974), in the first book on services marketing published in the United States, observed that marketing concepts, models, and tools often seemed awkward when they were to be applied in a service firm, and he concluded that service-oriented frameworks were needed. Although a lot has happened since those days, we are still in the early phases of developing a "theory of service."

Recently, the ongoing change and the need for understanding services for service firms and manufacturers alike were summarized by Davis (1987): "In the same way that service businesses were managed and organized around manufacturing models during the industrial economy, we can expect that manufacturing businesses (and service firms) will be managed and organized around service models in this new economy" (p. 108). However, as Bowen and Schneider concluded in 1988, the marketing of services and the management of service organizations have been studied much less than the marketing of goods and the management of organizations that manufacture goods. The same can be said about operations and organizational behavior as well. The predominant image of work is still associated with the production of goods, and manufacturing firms remain the main focus of the organizational behavior literature (Bowen & Schneider 1988, Mills 1986, and Schneider 1985).

However, there has been an ever-growing interest in the area of services. Throughout the 1980s, respected authors have highlighted the role of services in the economy as well as in the management of organizations (see, for example, Ackoff, Broholm, & Snow 1982, Naisbitt 1982, Peters & Waterman 1982, and Peters & Austin 1987). Probably, services, as a separate phenomenon, has been studied most intensely within the area of marketing. Bowen and Schneider (1988) call this trend "a minor service revolution .. . . in marketing" (p. 44. The importance of services marketing has been recognized. The internationally well known and highly regarded marketing professor Philip Kotler considered services marketing an area of top priority in a seminar for top marketing executives in Europe in September 1988: "I have suggested that every business school should include in their curriculum internationalization, *services marketing*, and entrepreneurship as central and necessary new management disciplines, because the future of management is not anymore what it used to be" [emphasis by the author]. And more and more business schools all over the world are indeed adding services marketing courses to their programs. (In 1980 the author started a services marketing course at the Swedish School of Economics and Business Administration in Helsinki, Finland, most likely one of the first of its kind to be offered worldwide.)

Probably the first series of research-oriented workshops was started in Belgium in 1975, sponsored by the European Institute for Advanced Studies of Management with headquarters in Brussels. This was followed by two similar workshops arranged in France in 1977 by the Institute d'Administration des Enterprises in Aix-en-Provence and in England two years later by the London Business School.

In 1980 the first conference in the United States was arranged by the American Marketing Association, and this has been followed by a continuing series of such conferences on services marketing. The eighth was held in 1989 in Chicago. In Scandinavia, a series of Nordic conferences on services started in 1983 in Finland. A conference on services marketing and internal marketing was arranged by the Swedish School of Economics and Business Administration in Helsinki. After that, in line with the emerging research approach in Northern Europe, sometimes termed the "Nordic School of Services," the general theme of these conferences has changed to cover broader aspects of services than just external and internal marketing. The following conferences arranged in Sweden, and the fourth one in 1989 in Norway, have been called Nordic Conferences on Service Management.

In the area of operations management some special attention to services has emerged as well. Research-oriented meetings solely devoted to services as a special phenomenon were arranged in Belgium in 1987, sponsored by the European Institute for Advanced Studies in Management, and in 1988 as an international conference arranged at the University of Warwick in the United Kingdom. In 1988 an interesting type of multidiscipline symposium was arranged in New Orleans by the Freeman School of Business at Tulane University, where marketing and organizational behavior scholars met to take a broader look at research into services.

There have also been published a number of books on some areas of services during the last decades, most of them outside the United States, however. There are, of course, unpublished doctoral theses and books addressing specific service industries, but they are omitted here.[a] The list, obviously, is not intended to be all inclusive, even with most of the relevant books taken into account. So far, the largest number of books seems to be within the area of marketing. The first book (if unpublished doctoral theses are excluded) published in Europe on services marketing, considering services a specific area of interest, seems to be the one on professional services by Wilson from 1972. To date, other books in English on services marketing from Europe are from 1984: a textbook by Cowell (1984), *Marketing of Services,* and a more research-oriented book by Grönroos, *Strategic Management and Marketing in the Service Sector,* which was also published in the United States by the Marketing Science Institute the previous year (see Grönroos 1983a).[b]

Internal marketing is an area that developed as a result of services marketing research. Within this area there is one book in Swedish (by Arndt and Friman in 1983), one in Finnish (by Klemi in 1983), and one in Danish (by Lund et al. in 1986).

---

[a]Probably one of the first doctoral theses with a specific service perspective was the one by Robert Judd from 1963 on the structure and classification of the service market (see Judd 1965).

[b]There are also at least seventeen, probably more, books published in Europe in languages other than English during the period 1974-1989 (this list is by no means inclusive): four in Swedish (by Gummesson in 1977 and Grönroos in 1979a, 1980b, and 1987d), four in Finnish (by Grönroos in 1980c and 1983c and Lehtinen in 1983 and 1986), three in Dutch (by Tettero and Viehoff in 1983, Faes and Van Tilborgh in 1984, and one edited by Van Tilborgh starting in 1986), three in German (by Berekoven and Falk from West Germany in 1974 and 1980, respectively, and by Scheuch from Austria in 1982), two in Italian (by Cherubini in 1981 and by Vicare in 1983), and one in French (by Langeard and Eiglier in 1987). In addition, there are a large number of industry-specific books.

In the United States, Rathmell's book from 1974 was the first one (unpublished doctoral theses not included) to be published on services marketing. In the 1980s it has been followed by two case-and-reading books by Lovelock in 1984 and 1988, one textbook on professional services marketing by Kotler and Bloom in 1984, one textbook on services marketing by Johnson, Scheuing, and Gaida in 1986, and one text and readings on services marketing by the British researcher John Bateson in 1989.

Service management is an area that began to develop later than services marketing. The first book with a specific service-oriented approach to management that looked at services in general was probably Normann's book *Service Management* which was published first in Swedish in 1982 and then in English in 1984. In the United States the list of literature with a service management approach is growing. There is Albrecht and Zemke's book from 1985; Heskett's and Mills's books from 1986; Albrecht's book from 1988; Zemke and Schaaf's book from 1989; and Albrecht and Bradford's book from 1990. There is also Collier's book from 1987, which covers the management of customer service.[c] In the area of operations there is at least one book in the United States, the one by Sasser, Olsen, and Wyckoff published in 1978. Also, service aspects are entering the area of industrial or business marketing (see, for example, Hutt & Speh 1989).

There is also, of course, a growing number of proceedings from conferences on services marketing, service management, and service operations, as well as journal articles. These, however, will not be analyzed separately here. In spite of the rapidly growing number of books, articles in scientific journals, trade journal articles, and research reports on various aspects of services, this body of literature is only a small fraction of what is published on management, marketing, organizational behavior, operations management, and so forth. Moreover, the mainstream textbooks in these fields do not yet include more than a chapter, if anything, on services, and normally treat them as some marginal phenomenon (compare the analysis in Gummesson 1987d). In conclusion, there is a definite need for a book on service management and marketing of services.

---

[c]In Europe several books on service management have been published in languages other than English, especially in Scandinavia and Finland where the modern service management approach probably first developed. There are six titles in Swedish (by Norman in 1982, by Gummesson and Edvardsson in 1988, and by Edvardsson and Magnusson in 1988; as well as three books focusing on the public sector—one by Pihlgren in 1985, one by Fock in 1987, and one by Grönroos and Monthelie in 1988). There are two in Finnish (Lehtinen and Storbacka 1986; Grönroos 1987), two in Danish (Lund and Knudsen 1982; Clement 1985), and one in Norwegian, which focuses on the public sector (Reichborn and Vifladt 1986).

The Objective and Approach of the Book

The main objective of the present book is to describe the nature of market-oriented management and marketing in service competition, that is, in the new competition of the service economy, in an in-depth and innovative way. The title *Service Management and Marketing* implies, first of all, that the key focus is the impact of the service-dominated competition on management thinking and decision making. Secondly, it implies that the marketing function in service competition will be discussed in more detail than other business functions. In fact, because of the characteristics of services and the nature of service competition, the marketing focus is present throughout the text.

To a large extent the book is based on the Scandinavian management experience. Its basic approach is mainly the one of the so-called *Nordic School of Service*, which originally emerged in Northern Europe but is gradually being adopted in North America as well. The basic standpoint of the Nordic School has been discussed by Grönroos and Gummesson (1985b). The main characteristic of this approach is the notion that decisions concerning marketing cannot be separated from overall management decisions, and that the same principle applies to other business functions as well. Moreover, overall management decisions and decisions concerning business functions other than marketing cannot be made without taking into consideration the external implications, that is, the marketing effects, of such decisions. Also, the Nordic School approach relies more on qualitative research methods and makes extensive use of case histories, without excluding more traditional quantitative methods when applicable. This approach has clear interfaces with, for instance, modern approaches to industrial marketing, the Interaction/Network Model (Håkansson 1982 and Turnbull & Valla 1987), and quality management (Juran 1982, Crosby 1984, Ishikawa 1985, and Gummesson 1987a).

The Nordic School of Services is, in fact, more or less the research-oriented equivalent of another phenomenon which has become widely known in North America: the Scandinavian management approach. This approach is often referred to in connection with SAS Scandinavian Airline System. And there is a distinct Scandinavian management touch, which to a great extent is service oriented. As Ron Zemke, co-author of *Service America!*, says: "For the last decade, while American management gurus have been alternately claiming world dominance in the workplace or loudly gnashing their teeth over the 'Japanese miracle,' the Swedes, Norwegians, Danes, and Finns have been systematically carrying out a little management revolution of their own" (Zemke 1988a, p. 44).

The subtitle of the present book, *Managing the Moments of Truth in Service Competition,* describes what the author considers the main focus of service management and marketing, that is, the moments of truth of the buyer-seller interactions and the main reason for being interested in service management, that is, the transition from competition through mere technical solutions to service competition.

This book is not a services marketing text only in the traditional narrow sense of consumer packaged goods marketing. This follows from the fact that in the new service competition marketing cannot remain a separate function of marketing and sales specialists only, but becomes everybody's responsibility in one way or the other. This is the same as to say that marketing becomes a top management issue, much more so than it is normally thought to be. As long as marketing is the responsibility of the marketing department only, the head of that department can manage the total marketing function. However, as soon as a substantial part of the total marketing function moves out of the marketing department, and thus marketing becomes an interfunctional and interdepartmental issue, the person in charge has to be above the department level. Managing a marketing department has always been, and may still remain, the responsibility of the head of that department. However, *managing the marketing function is, today, the responsibility of top management.*

The present book is not intended for service firms only, or only for the customer service departments of manufacturing firms for that matter. Everybody experiences the consequences of the service economy and the new competition. Therefore, every firm, irrespective of whether it has traditionally thought of itself as a service firm or as a manufacturer of goods, has to get familiar with the rules of service and the nature of service competition. Hence, the intent of this book is to add to the knowledge of management of manufacturing firms and industrial marketing just as much as service firms. It is a book on market-oriented management, which in service includes marketing.

Since the present book uses a management approach and a strategy focus, tactical problems are discussed only briefly. Instead, the strategic issues of market-oriented management and marketing in service competition are dwelt upon in greater detail. It is not a what-to-do book, but a how-to-think book. Issues such as personal selling and pricing, which are typical parts of standard textbooks, are therefore not addressed here. Thus, to sum up, this book is about managing service strategy and service competition, that is, it is about *service management.*

2
The Nature of Services and Service Quality

Introduction

In this chapter we are first going to discuss the nature of services. After reviewing definitions from two decades we suggest as a synthesis one that takes into account as many as possible of the characteristics of services normally mentioned in the literature. We also present the characteristics themselves and illustrate briefly a number of ways of classifying services. Then, the issue of service quality is analyzed, and the concept of Perceived Service Quality is presented. Following, some major studies that include typical determinants or facets of service quality are described. Finally, as a synthesis, the Six Criteria of Good Perceived Service Quality are introduced.

What Is a Service? Attempts to Define the Phenomenon

A service is a complicated phenomenon. The word has many meanings, ranging from personal service to service as a product. The term can be even broader in scope. A machine, or almost any product, can be turned into a service to a customer if the seller makes efforts to tailor-make the solution to meet the most detailed demands of that customer. A machine is still a physical good, of course, but the way of treating the customer with an appropriately designed machine is a service. As Sir John Harvey-Jones, retired chairman of ICI, says, referring to some successful firms in the chemical industry, "they have developed an ability to provide a chemical service to customers, rather than selling a product in a bag" (Harvey-Jones 1989, p. 60).

Moreover, there are a variety of administratively used services, such as billing and handling claims, which in reality are services to the customer.

Because of the passive way in which they are handled, they remain "hidden services" for the customers. In fact, they are usually taken care of in such a way that they are perceived, not as services, but rather as nuisances. Obviously, this offers lots of opportunities to create a competitive advantage for organizations that can innovatively develop and make use of such "hidden services."

There are a range of definitions of services suggested in the literature. These definitions look very narrowly upon the service phenomenon, and include more or less only those services rendered by so-called service firms. Here are a variety of definitions from three decades:

> "Service—Activities, benefits, or satisfactions which are offered for sale, or provided in connection with the sale of goods" (American Marketing Association 1960, p. 21).
>
> "Services represent either intangibles yielding satisfactions directly (transportation, housing), or intangibles yielding satisfactions jointly when purchased either with commodities or other services (credit, delivery)" (Regan 1963, p. 57).
>
> "Marketed Services—A market transaction by an enterprise or entrepreneur where the object of the market transaction is other than the transfer of ownership (or title, if any) of a tangible commodity" (Judd 1964, p. 59).
>
> "For the consumer, services are any activities offered for sale that provide valuable benefits or satisfactions; activities that he cannot perform for himself or that he chooses not to perform for himself" (Bessom 1973, p. 9).
>
> "A service is an activity offered for sale which yields benefits and satisfactions without leading to a physical change in the form of a good" (Blois 1974, p. 157).
>
> "Services (are) separately identifiable, intangible activities which provide want satisfaction when marketed to consumers and/or industrial users and which are not necessarily tied to the sale of a product or another service" (Stanton 1974, p. 545).
>
> "A Service is an activity or a series of activities which take place in interactions with a contact person or a physical machine and which provides consumer satisfaction" (Lehtinen 1983, p. 21).
>
> "Services are any intangible benefit, which is paid for directly or indirectly, and which often includes a larger or smaller physical or technical component (Andresen et al. 1983, p. 6).

> "A *service* is any activity or benefit that one party can offer to another that is essentially intangible and does not result in the ownership of anything. Its production may or may not be tied to a physical product" (Kotler & Bloom 1984, p. 147 and Kotler 1988, p. 477).
>
> "The meeting of customer expectations in the course of selling and post-sales activity through providing a series of functions which match or better the competition in a way which provides an incremental profit for the supplier" (Free 1987, p. 75).
>
> "Services is something which can be bought and sold but which you cannot drop on your foot" (Gummesson 1987b, p. 22; referring to an unidentified source).

Every one of the definitions above has its benefits, but also its drawbacks. The most obvious criticism is that in one way or the other they are too limited. (The last definition introduced by Gummesson is actually more of a criticism of attempts to find a definition that could be agreed upon by everyone than an explicit definition in itself.) However, it points out one of the basic characteristics of services, that is, that they can be exchanged although they often cannot be experienced in a tangible sense.

If we were to offer a definition of service here, it would be a blend of the ones suggested by Lehtinen, Kotler and Bloom, and Gummesson above. Hence, we propose, however reluctantly, the following definition:

> *A service is an activity or series of activities of more or less intangible nature that normally, but not necessarily, take place in interactions between the customer and service employees and/or physical resources or goods and/or systems of the service provider, which are provided as solutions to customer problems.*

Most often a service does involve interactions of some sort with the service provider. However, there are situations where the customer as an individual does not interact with the service firm. For example, when a plumber using the main keys of an apartment complex goes into an apartment to fix a leakage when the tenant is out, there are no immediate interactions between the plumber or his or her physical resources or systems of operating and the customer. On the other hand, many situations where interactions do not seem to be present nevertheless do involve interactions. For instance, when a problem with a car is taken care of at a garage, the customer is not present and interacting with anybody or anything. However, when the car is taken in by the garage and later delivered to the customer, interactions occur. These interactions are part of the service, as will be shown later on. Moreover, they may be extremely critical to how the customer perceives the garage. The customer probably cannot properly evaluate the job done in the garage, but can, however, evaluate the garage based on the interactions that occur at both ends of the service process. Consequently, in services, interactions are usually present and of substantial importance, although the parties involved are not always aware of it. Furthermore, services are not things, they are processes or activities, and these activities are very intangible in nature.

However, there does seem to be an increasing awareness among researchers, and certainly among practitioners, that it is probably impossible, and, moreover, even unnecessary, to continue to debate service definitions. In earlier books from 1979 and 1983 we suggested that it would be more fruitful to look at the characteristics that seem to be common to most services (Grönroos 1979a and 1983a). In the next section we are going to discuss the characteristics of services.

What Are Services? Some Common Characteristics

A whole range of characteristics of services has been suggested and discussed in the literature (see, for example, Grönroos 1983a, Lovelock 1983, Normann 1984, and Zeithaml, Parasuraman, & Berry 1985). Usually services are compared with physical goods. In Table 2-1 we have summarized the most frequently mentioned characteristics of services and physical goods.

Table 2–1
Differences between Services and Physical Goods

Physical Goods	*Services*
Tangible	Intangible
Homogeneous	Heterogeneous
Production and distribution separated from consumption	Production and distribution and consumption simultaneous processes
A thing	An activity or process
Core value produced in factory	Core value produced in buyer-seller interactions
Customers do not (normally) participate in the production process	Customers participate in production
Can be kept in stock	Cannot be kept in stock
Transfer of ownership	No transfer of ownership

For most services, four basic characteristics can be identified:

1. Services are more or less *intangible.*
2. Services are *activities* or a *series of activities* rather than things.
3. Services are at least to some extent *produced and consumed simultaneously.*
4. The customer *participates in the production process* at least to some extent.

A service is normally perceived in a subjective manner. When services are described by customers, expressions such as experience, trust, feeling, and security are used. These are highly abstract ways of formulating what a service is. The reason for this, of course, lies in the *intangible* nature of services. However, many services include highly tangible elements as well: for example, the food in a restaurant, the documents used by a forwarding company, and the spare parts used by a repair shop. The essence of a service, however, is the intangibility of the phenomenon itself. As a matter of fact, the intangibility characteristic is probably the most often cited criterion of services. Because of the high degree of intangibility, it is frequently difficult for the customer to evaluate a service. How do you give a distinct value to "trust," or to a "feeling," for example? Therefore, it is often suggested in the literature that one should tangibilize a service for the customer by using concrete, physical evidence, such as plastic cards and various kinds of documents (e.g., Shostack 1977).

Because a service is not a thing but a *series of activities* or processes—which, moreover, are *produced and consumed simultaneously* (this is also called the "*inseparability*" characteristic), at least to some extent—it is difficult to manage quality control and to do marketing in the traditional sense. There is no preproduced quality to control in advance, before the service is sold and consumed. Of course, situations vary, depending on what kind of service we consider. A hair stylist's service is almost totally produced when the customer is present and receives the service, that is, consumes it. When delivering goods, only part of the service production process is experienced and, thus, simultaneously consumed by the customer. Most of the production process is invisible. However, in both cases, one should realize that it is the visible part of production activities that matters in the mind of the customer. As far as the rest is concerned, he or she can only experience the result; but the visible activities are experienced and evaluated *in every detail.* Quality control and marketing must therefore take place at the time and place of simultaneous service production and consumption. If the firm relies on traditional quality control and marketing approaches only, the part of the production activities where the customer is involved may go uncontrolled and include negative marketing experiences for the customer.

The fourth basic characteristic of services points out that the customer is not only a receiver of the service; the *customer participates as a production resource* as well. Because of this and the previous characteristics it is not possible to keep services in stock in the same way goods are. If an airplane leaves the airport half-full, the empty seats cannot be sold the next day. They are lost. Instead, capacity planning becomes a critical issue. Even though services cannot be kept in stock, one can try to *keep customers in stock*. For example, if a restaurant is full, it is always possible to try to keep the customer waiting in the bar until there is a free table.

Furthermore, many definitions imply that services do not result in *ownership* of anything. Normally this is true. When we use the services of an airline, we are entitled, for example, to be transported from one place to another, but when we arrive at our destination, there is nothing left but the remaining part of the ticket and boarding card. When we withdraw money from our checking account we may feel that the bank's service resulted in our ownership of the money withdrawn. After the service process, we undoubtedly have the sum of money in our hands and we own it. However, the bank's service did not create this ownership. We, of course, owned the money all the time. The bank just took care of it for us for some time and used it in exchange for interest. On the other hand, retailing is a service, and after using the services of, say, a grocery store, the customer undoubtedly own the groceries. And the goods, more exactly the assortment of groceries as well as the individual goods, are part of the service offered to the marketplace. In this case, the consumption of the service of the service firm, the grocery store, does result in ownership of tangible goods.

Finally, because of the impact of people, either personnel or customers or both, on the production and delivery process, a "*heterogeneity*" aspect follows from the basic characteristics. A service to one customer is not exactly the same as the "same" service to the next customer. If nothing else, the social relationship between the two situations is different. And the service a customer receives by using an ATM may differ from the "same" service received by the next customer, because, for instance, the second person has a problem understanding the instructions on the screen. The heterogeneity of services creates one of the major problems in service management, that is, how to maintain an evenly perceived quality of the services produced and rendered to customers.

Classification Schemes for Services

There is, of course, a diversity of services; some services are in one way or another extremely far away from each other. For example, the highly personal touch-intensive service of a hair stylist is very different, indeed, from the technology-intensive service of a long-distance telephone operator. Lovelock (1988) summarized most of the classification schemes proposed in the literature some years ago (see Table 2–2). Four additional schemes which do not appear in Lovelock's original summary have been added. These schemes help the reader to understand services. First of all, they demonstrate the diversity of services. They also show how important it is in a specific situation to carefully analyze the detailed nature of the service operation at hand. However, this should not make the reader believe that a specific service is so special that general, fundamental principles of managing services do not apply. The general characteristics of services discussed earlier are almost always universally true, irrespective of the nature of the business.

If, for example, the service is maintenance to a machine, or financial planning for a private person, or hair styling, the customer is always a person (or several persons), the service is perceived more or less intangibly, some kind of interaction between the customer and some parts of the production system of the service provider—including personnel, technology, or both—always occurs, and some kind of input from the customer is always required in the process. However, the importance of various aspects of the service, what type of resources should be used, and how the process should be managed vary, depending on the nature of the service and the interface with the customers. In order to be able to make the best decisions in these respects, the manager can learn from identifying his or her service in one or several of the classification schemes in Table 2–2.

Research into Service Quality

In the previous sections we illustrated how complex most services are. Consequently, the quality of services has to be very complex, too. The quality of goods is traditionally related to the technical specifications of the goods, although, even in a goods context, a firm using an image strategy, for example, tries to add to the quality of the goods component by creating imaginative auxiliaries like fashion, status, or lifestyle.

Services that are a more or less intangibly experienced series of processes, where production and consumption cannot be totally separated, and where the customer often actively participates in the production

Table 2–2
Summary of Proposed Schemes for Classifying Services

Author	*Proposed Classification Schemes*	*Comment*
Judd (1964)	1. Rented goods services (right to own and use a good for a defined time period) 2. Owned goods services (custom creation, repair or improvement of goods owned by the customer) 3. Nongoods services (personal experiences or "experiential possession")	First two are fairly specific, but third category is very broad and ignores services such as insurance, banking, legal advice and accounting.
Rathmell (1974)	1. Type of seller 2. Type of buyer 3. Buying motives 4. Buying practice 5. Degree of regulation	No specific application to services—could apply equally well to goods.
Shostack (1977)[a] Sasser et al.[a] (1978)	Proportion of physical goods and intangible services contained within each product "package"	Offers opportunities for multi-attribute modeling. Emphasizes that there are few pure goods or pure services.
Hill (1977)	1. Services affecting persons vs. those affecting goods 2. Permanent vs. temporary effects of the service 3. Reversibility vs. nonreversibility of these effects 4. Physical effects vs. mental effects 5. Individual vs. collective services	Emphasizes nature of service benefits and (in 5) variations in the service delivery/consumption environment.
Thomas (1978)	1. Primarily equipment-based a. Automated (e.g., car wash) b. Monitored by unskilled operators (e.g., movie theater) c. Operated by skilled personnel (e.g., airline) 2. Primarily people-based a. Unskilled labor (e.g., lawn care) b. Skilled labor (e.g., repair work) c. Professional staff (e.g., lawyers, dentists)	Although operational rather than marketing in orientation, provides a useful way of understanding product attributes.
Chase (1978)	Extent of customer contact required in service delivery a. High contact (e.g., health care, hotels, restaurants) b. Low contact (e.g., postal service, wholesaling)	Recognizes that product variability is harder to control in high contact services because customer exert more influence on timing of demand and service features, due to their greater involvement in the service process.

Table 2–2 *continued*
Summary of Proposed Schemes for Classifying Services

Author	*Proposed Classification Schemes*	*Comment*
Grönroos (1979a)	1. Type of service a. Professional services b. Other services 2. Type of customers a. Individuals b. Organizations	Notices that the same services, e.g., insurance and financial, may be rendered to both individuals and organizations.
Kotler (1980)	1. People-based vs. equipment-based 2. Extent to which client's presence is necessary 3. Meets personal needs vs. business needs 4. Public vs. private, for-profit vs. nonprofit	Synthesizes previous work, recognizes differences in purpose of service organization.
Lovelock (1980)	1. Basic demand characteristics – Object served (persons vs. property) – Extent of demand/supply imbalances – Discrete vs. continuous relationships between customers and providers 2. Service content and benefits – Extent of physical goods content – Extent of personal service content – Single service vs. bundle of services – Timing and duration of benefits 3. Service delivery procedures – Multisite vs. single site delivery – Allocation of capacity (reservations vs. first come, first served) – Independent vs. collective consumption – Time defined vs. task defined transactions – Extent to which customers must be present during service delivery	Synthesizes previous classifications and adds several new schemes. Proposes several categories within each classification. Concludes that defining object served is most fundamental classification scheme. Suggests that valuable marketing insights would come from combining two or more classificaion schemes in a matrix.
Lovelock (1983)	1. The nature of the service act a. Tangible actions to people or things b. Intangible actions to people or things 2. Relationships with customers a. Continuous delivery b. Discrete transactions c. "Membership" relationships d. No formal relationships	Provides a series of classifications which together illustrate the complex nature of services and provide useful background information for managerial purposes.

Table 2–2 *continued*
Summary of Proposed Schemes for Classifying Services

Author	*Proposed Classification*	*Comment*
	3. Customization and judgment in service delivery a. Judgment exercised by customer contact persons b. Customization of services 4. Nature of demand in relation to supply a. Extent to which supply is constrained b. Extend of demand fluctuations 5. Methods of service delivery a. Single or multi-site delivery b. Service delivered on provider's or customer's premises	
Schmenner (1986)	1. Degree of interaction and customization a. Low b. High 2. Degree of labor intensity a. Low b. High	Recognizes that some services may be more customized and involve a higher degree of labor intensity, and may help the reader to understand the strategic and tactical options available.
Vandermerwe & Chadwick (1989)	1. Degree of consumer/producer interaction a. Lower b. Higher 2. Relative involvement of goods a. "Pure" services b. Services with some goods or delivered through goods c. Services embodied in goods	Recognizes the importance and role of goods components in service businesses.

Source: Lovelock, C.H. (1983): "Classifying Services to Gain Strategic Marketing Insight." Reprinted from *Journal of Marketing*. American Marketing Association, Summer, pp. 11-12. Some classification schemes have been added.

[a]These were two independent studies that drew broadly similar conclusions.

process, are bound to be perceived as extremely complex. However, in order to develop service management and marketing models, it is important to understand what customers really are looking for and what they evaluate. As was observed by Eiglier and Langeard in the early 1980s: "It is rather difficult to relate a good service idea to a stable, widespread, well identified customer benefit. And it is extremely difficult to implement the service idea as a well-structured offering of services" (Eiglier & Langeard 1981, p. 1562).

What is needed is a model of service quality, that is, a model of how the quality of services is perceived by customers. When the service provider understands how the services will be evaluated by the users, it will be possible to identify how to manage these evaluations and how to influence them in a desired direction. The relationship between the service concept, the service offered to customers, and customer benefits has to be clarified (compare Eiglier & Langeard 1981).

The interest in service quality has increased exponentially during the 1980s. In the services marketing literature a service-oriented approach to quality was introduced by Grönroos in English in 1982 (and in Scandinavia a few years earlier) with the introduction of the concept of *Perceived Service Quality* and the model of total service quality (see Grönroos 1983a and b, and 1984). This approach is based on research into consumer behavior and the effects of expectations concerning goods performance on postconsumption evaluations (see Grönroos 1983a for an overview of this research). The perceived service quality approach still seems to form the foundation of most of the ongoing service quality research and theory development in services marketing (for example, Lehtinen & Lehtinen 1982, Berry et al. 1985, Parasuraman et al. 1985, Lehtinen 1986, Crosby & Giacobbe 1986, Lewis & Klein 1987, Lindqvist 1987, Gummesson & Grönroos 1987 and 1988, Zeithaml 1987, Zeithaml et al. 1988, Lindqvist 1988, Crosby 1988 and Crosby et al. 1988). There are, however, attempts to study service quality from other perspectives, too (see Hedvall & Paltschik 1987 and Orsini & Meyer 1987).

In the area of service management the quality issue is addressed to some extent (for example, Normann 1984), as it is in service operations (for example, Wyckoff 1984, Johnston 1987, Haywood-Farmer & Stuart 1988, and Lyth & Johnston 1988). However, far less comprehensive model building seems to have taken place within these areas as far as service quality is concerned.

There is also an existing quality control establishment with roots that go way back in this century. However, as Gummesson (1989b) demonstrates, the traditional organizations are overwhelmingly devoted to issues related to goods quality. To prove his point, Gummesson shows how the 885-page proceedings of the 42nd annual conference held by the American Society for Quality Control (ASQC) in 1988 include only three papers out of 145 that mention services in the title (ASQC 1988), and how services are not mentioned at all in the titles of the 102 papers included in the 1,167-page proceedings of the 31st annual conference of the European Organization for Quality Control in 1987 (EOQC 1987). Because of the characteristics of services, much of the goods-related quality know-how is not relevant to, or at least not directly applicable in service organizations.

Of course, on the other hand, much of it is useful for services, too. This should not be forgotten, although in this and the next chapter we predominantly concentrate on what is unique with quality and quality management in service contexts.

In 1988 probably the first international symposium on service quality (the QUIS Symposium) was arranged in Karlstad, Sweden, by the Center for Service Research at the University of Karlstad in cooperation with the First Interstate Center for Services Marketing at Arizona State University and sponsored by SAS Scandinavian Airlines System. Twenty-five papers were presented, and an edited version of this material has been published in a proceedings volume (Brown et al. 1990).

Quality Is What Customers Perceive

Too often improving quality is mentioned as an internal goal without any explicit references to what is meant by service quality. To talk about better quality without defining what it is, how it is perceived by customers, and how it can be improved and enhanced is of limited value. Very often this is only paying lip service to service quality improvement. Basing their conclusion on the large PIMS (Profit Impact of Market Strategy) data base covering both manufacturers of goods and service firms, Buzzell and Gale (1987) state that ". . . quality is whatever the customers say it is, and the quality of a particular product or service is whatever the customer *perceives* it to be" (p. 111). This is in strict conformance with the models in the literature on services marketing (e.g., Grönroos 1983a and 1984, Parasuraman et al. 1985, Zeithaml 1987, and Zeithaml et al. 1988). Quality, and service quality in particular, is such a complex phenomenon that a much more detailed model than the ones normally used is needed. As Garvin puts it: "[Managers] must break down the word quality into manageable parts. Only then can they define the quality niches in which to compete" (Garvin 1987, p. 104).

There is always a risk that when quality is defined too narrowly quality programs become too narrow in scope. For example, the technical specification of a service or a good is frequently considered the quality of the product, or at least the most important feature of the perceived quality. The more technology oriented the firm is, the bigger this risk tends to be. In reality, customers often perceive quality as a much broader concept, and, moreover, aspects other than the technical ones may frequently dominate the quality experience. In the firm, one has to define quality in the same way customers do, otherwise, in quality programs, wrong actions may be taken and money and time may be poorly invested. It should always be remembered that *what counts is quality as it is perceived by the customers.*

Quality Dimensions: What and How

Services are basically more or less intangible and quite subjectively experienced processes where production and consumption activities take place simultaneously. Interactions including a series of moments of truth between the customer and the service provider occur. What happens in these interactions, so-called *buyer-seller interactions* (or service encounters) will obviously have a critical impact on the perceived service.

Basically, the quality of a service as it is perceived by customers has two dimensions, namely, a *technical or outcome dimension* and a *functional or process-related dimension* (Grönroos 1983a and 1984; also compare Parasuraman et al. 1985 and Lehtinen 1986). The hotel guest will be provided with a room and a bed to sleep in, the consumer of a restaurant's services will get a meal, the airline passenger will be transported from one place to another, the client of a business consultant may get a new organization scheme, a factory may get its goods transported from its warehouse to a customer, the bank customer may be granted a loan, the technical service of a machine may be taken care of by the manufacturer, a claim by a unsatisfied customer may be settled by a retail store, and so forth. All of these outcomes of the operations of the firm obviously are part of the quality experience.

What customers receive in their interactions with the firm is clearly important to them and to their quality evaluation. Internally this is very often thought of as *the quality* of the product delivered. However, this is not the whole truth. It is merely *one* quality dimension, called the *technical quality of the outcome* of the service production process. It is *what* the customer is left with, when the production process and buyer-seller interactions are over. Frequently, but by no means always, this dimension can be measured rather objectively by customers, because of its character as a technical solution to a problem.

However, as there are a number of interactions between the provider and the customer, including more or less successfully handled moments of truth, the technical quality dimension will not count for the total quality which the customer perceives has been received. The customer will obviously also be influenced by the way in which the technical quality, the outcome or end result of the process, is transferred to him or her. The accessibility of a teller machine, a restaurant, or a business consultant, the appearance and behavior of waiters, bank tellers, travel agency representatives, bus drivers, cabin attendants, plumbers, and service and maintenance technicians, and how these service employees perform their tasks, what they say, and how they do it also influence the customer's view of the service.

Furthermore, the more customers accept self-service activities or other production-related routines they are expected to perform themselves, the better they will, probably, consider the service. Moreover, other customers simultaneously consuming the same or similar services may influence the way in which a given customer will perceive a service. Other customers may cause long lines, or disturb the customer; on the other hand, they may have a positive impact on the atmosphere of the buyer-seller interactions.

In summary, the customer is also influenced by *how* he or she receives the service and how he or she experiences the simultaneous production and consumption process. This is *another* quality dimension, which is very much related to how the moments of truth of the buyer-seller interactions themselves are taken care of and how the service provider functions. Therefore, it is called the *functional quality of the process.* Hence, as illustrated in Figure 2–1, we have *two* basic quality dimensions, namely, *what* the customer receives and *how* the customer receives it; the technical result or outcome of the process (technical quality) and the functional dimension of the process (functional quality). It is easy to see that the functional quality dimension cannot be evaluated as objectively as the technical dimension; frequently it is perceived subjectively.

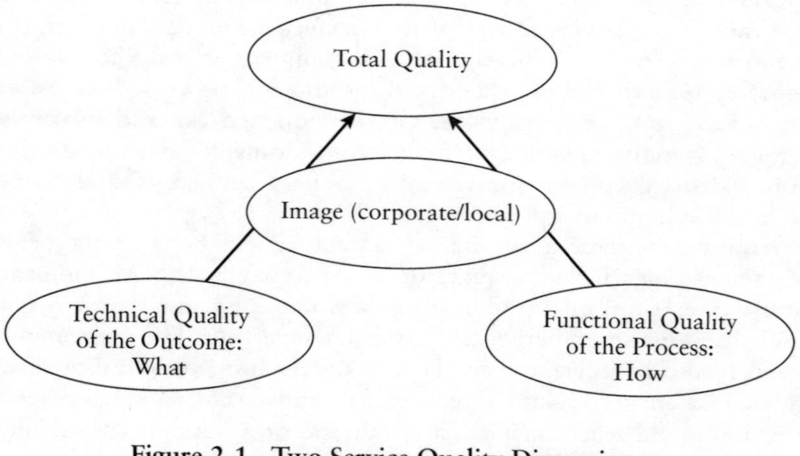

Figure 2-1. Two Service Quality Dimensions

Usually the service provider cannot hide behind brand names or distributors. In most cases the customers will be able to see the firm, its resources, and its ways of operating. *Corporate and/or local image* is therefore of utmost importance to most services. It can impact the perception of quality in various ways. If the provider is good in the minds of the customers, that is, if it has a favorable image, minor mistakes will probably be forgiven. If mistakes occur often, the image will be damaged. And if the image is negative, the impact of any mistake will often be considerably greater than it otherwise would be. As far as the quality perception is concerned, image can be viewed as a filter.

The two quality dimensions, that is, *what* and *how*, are not valid for services only. The technical solution for a customer—provided by, for example, a machine or another good—is part of the overall technical quality perceived by this customer. But attempts to tailor-make the machine according to the specific demands of a customer is an additional value of a functional nature and therefore part of the overall functional quality which this customer experiences.

Various services such as deliveries, materials administration, technical service, claims handling, and customer training provide added value, which is partly of a technical nature, that is, adds to technical quality, and partly of a functional nature, that is, adds to functional quality. For example, if a claim is settled with satisfactory results for the customer, the outcome of the claims handling process has good technical quality. The customer may nevertheless be less satisfied with the other party if it has been, for instance, complicated and time-consuming to get results. In such a case, the functional quality of the claims handling process has been low and *total perceived quality* lower than it otherwise would have been.

Quality and the Competitive Edge

Today, quality is often considered one of the keys to success. In fact, according to the most recent major publication based on the PIMS (Profit Impact of Market Strategy) data base, including information from manufacturers and service firms alike, customer perceived quality is found to be of exceedingly great importance to success (Buzzell & Gale 1987, pp. 103 ff.). The competitive advantage of a firm is said to depend on the quality of the goods and services provided. As Lee Iacocca, Chairman of Chrysler, puts it in his straightforward words: "The only job security anybody has in this company comes from quality, productivity, and satisfied customers" (Iacocca 1988, p. 249). The same goes for manufacturers and service organizations alike. However, because of the complex nature of quality in service contexts, one has to be more explicit. In service contexts, quality may certainly be the foundation of the competitive edge, but which quality dimension (*what* or *how*) is the vital part of excellent total quality? If this question is not answered correctly, wrong internal actions may be taken, and a stronger competitive position is not achieved after all.

Too often technical quality considerations are thought of as the paramount quality issues. However, this is true only in situations where firms are able to develop excellent technical solutions. A technical quality strategy is successful if a firm succeeds in achieving a technical solution that the competition cannot come up with. Today, this is more and more seldom the case; there are a number of firms that can produce more or less the same technical quality. Moreover, creating a technical advantage is difficult, because, in many industries, competitors can introduce similar solutions rather quickly. Even when an excellent solution is achieved, the firm may be unsuccessful, if the excellence in technical quality is counteracted or nullified by badly managed and handled buyer-seller interactions, that is, by an unsatisfactory functional quality of the process.

Consequently, competitive advantage cannot be achieved this way too often. On the other hand, implementing a service strategy is a possible option for most firms. This means, in principle, that improving the buyer-seller interactions becomes the basis for quality programs. Developing the functional quality dimension may add substantial value to the customers and thus create the necessary competitive edge. As William L. Pierpoint, President and CEO of Summit Health Limited, a for-profit health care organization with over 5,500 beds in five Southwestern states of the United States and abroad, observes: "Quality of care means expert, efficient delivery of health care service, not only in the technical sense, but in a personal sense. Therefore, Summit has concentrated on employee training and education programs which emphasize patient relations." He continues by stating that this investment in functional quality will pay off, not immediately, but as a competitive edge supporting long-term growth.

To state this in a somewhat more simplified way, you can beat the competition if you provide the customers with more and better services. Of course, this is not to say that technical quality issues should not be kept in mind constantly, and that technical quality improvements would not be necessary in service competition.

The Perceived Service Quality

In the previous sections we discussed the two basic quality dimensions—the what and the how—in the minds of the customer. We also noted that quality is to a large extent perceived subjectively. However, the quality perception process is more complicated than that. It is not just the experiences of the quality dimensions that determine whether the quality is considered good, neutral, or bad.

Figure 2–2 illustrates how the quality experiences are connected to the traditional marketing activities resulting in a *Perceived Service Quality*. When we consider in addition to service firms manufacturers of goods providing services as part of their offerings, it may be more appropriate to talk about *total perceived quality.* Good perceived quality is obtained when the *experienced quality* meets the expectations of the customer, that is, the *expected quality*. If the expectations are unrealistic, the total perceived quality will be low, even if the experienced quality measured in some objective way is good. As shown in Figure 2–2, the expected quality is a function of a number of factors, namely, market communication, word-of-mouth communication, corporate/local image, and customer needs. *Market communication* includes advertising, direct mail, public relations, and sales campaigns, which are directly under the control of the firm. The *image* and *word-of-mouth* factors are only indirectly controlled by the firm. External impact on these factors may also occur, but basically they are a function of the previous performance of the firm, supported by, for example, advertising. Finally, the *needs* of the customer also have, of course, an impact on his or her expectations.

When quality programs, which may even include functional quality aspects, are implemented, Perceived Service Quality may still be low, or even deteriorate, if, for example, the firm simultaneously runs advertising

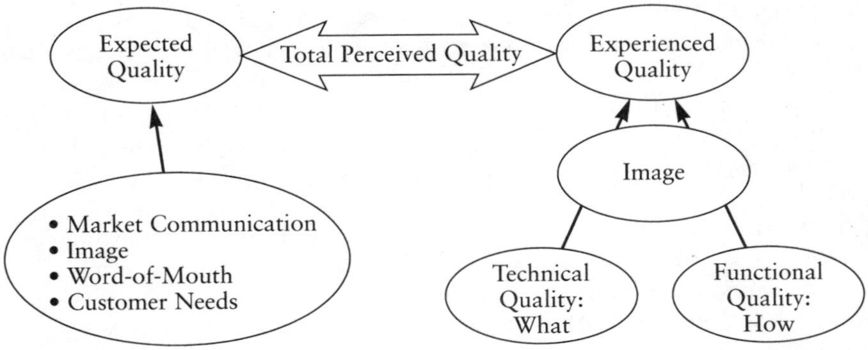

Source: Grönroos, C. (1988): Service Quality: The Six Criteria of Good Service Quality. *Review of Business* 3 (New York: St. John's University Press): p. 12.

Figure 2-2. The Total Perceived Quality

campaigns that promise too much or are inadequate in some other respect. The level of total perceived quality is not determined by the level of the technical and functional quality dimensions only, but rather by the *gap between the expected and experienced quality* (Grönroos 1983a and 1984). Consequently, every quality program should involve not only those involved in operations, but those responsible for marketing and market communication as well.

Image plays a central role in customer perception of service quality, and is as important to a service firm as to any other organization, so it is imperative that image be managed in a proper manner. The issues of how image develops and what causes image problems are not always very well understood. Therefore we are going to dwell upon these issues at some length in chapter 7.

The Moments of Truth and Quality

As noted in this chapter, the situations in which the customer meets the resources and the ways of operating of the service provider are critical to the quality experience. These buyer-seller interactions or service encounters determine the level of the functional quality dimension. Moreover, in these interactions most or all of the technical quality of the outcome is transferred to the customer. As stated earlier, in service management such situations are called the *moments of truth*. This concept was introduced into the service management literature by Normann (1984).

The moments of truth concept literally means that this is the time and place when and where the service provider has the opportunity to demonstrate to the customer the quality of its services. It is a true *moment of opportunity*. In the next moment the situation is over, the customer has gone, and there are no easy ways of adding value to the Perceived Service Quality. The moment of opportunity is gone. If a quality problem has occurred, it is too late to take corrective actions. In order to do so, a new moment of truth has to be created. The service provider can, for example, actively contact the customer to correct a mistake or to at least explain why things went wrong. This is, of course, much more troublesome and probably less effective as compared to a well-managed moment of truth.

In reality, the customer will experience a whole series of moments of truth when patronizing a service organization. When using the services of an airline company the passenger goes through a number of such moments, beginning with arrival at the airport and ending with baggage claim and transportation away from the airport.

The service production and delivery process must always be planned and executed so that no badly handled moments of truth take place. If such situations go unmanaged there is an evident risk that unexpected quality problems may occur. As Albrecht and Zemke (1985b) put it: "When the moments of truth go unmanaged, the quality of service regresses to mediocrity" (p. 62). In particular, the functional quality of the process will be hurt and cause quality deterioration.

How Is Total Service Quality Perceived? Some Research Results

During the 1980s studies of factors that influence the total perceived quality have been reported. This is a field of research that is being explored to a considerable extent right now, so more information will be available in due course. In Figure 2–3 a the results of a large study on how a number of services are perceived by customers are summarized. This study was conducted by Berry and his colleagues from Texas (Parasuraman et al. 1985).

One of the ten determinants, *competence*, is clearly related to the technical quality of the outcome, and another, *credibility*, is closely connected to the image aspect of perceived quality. However, it is interesting to observe that the rest of the ten determinants are more or less related to the process dimension of perceived quality. The importance of the functional quality dimension is very much stressed by these findings.[a]

Another extensive study, by British Airways in the 1980s, is also of interest in this context. Although this study covered airline services by British Airways only, the results seem to be more generally valid. The researchers wanted to find out what airline passengers considered most important in their flying experience. The following four factors emerged (Albrecht & Zemke 1985a):

1. *Care and concern*, that is, the customer feels that the organization, its employees, and its operational systems are devoted to solving his or her problems.

---

[a] In a more recent report (Zeithaml et al. 1988) the ten determinants of service quality have been further elaborated on. The number of quality-determining factors were decreased to five, namely, *tangibles, reliability, responsiveness, assurance,* and *empathy.* The researchers achieved this by means of a large-scale quantitative study in which they statistically analyzed the data and thus were able to condense it to these five factors.

2. *Spontaneity*, that is, the employees demonstrate a willingness and readiness to actively approach customers and take care of their problems. They show that they can think for themselves and not just go by the book.
3. *Problem solving*, that is, the contact employees are skilled to take care of their duties and perform according to standards. Moreover, the rest of the organization, including operational support employees and operational systems, are also trained and designed to give good service.
4. *Recovery*, that is, if anything goes wrong, or something unexpected happens, there is someone who is prepared to make a special effort to handle the situation.

Two of these factors, care and concern and problem solving, were explicitly recognized earlier by British Airways, as they probably would be by most service providers. However, the spontaneity and recovery issues were new. They had not been thought of in any concrete manner as characteristics of good service. This would probably be the case for other service providers as well. Here again the importance of the functional quality dimension is stressed. Only problem solving is a technical quality factor; the three other factors are process related.

Lindqvist (1988) studied the perceived quality of passenger transportation services by sea. His findings include a price dimension as well as an advertising (or market communication) dimension. However, the perception of price and advertising campaigns does not seem to be a straightforward quality determinant. Perhaps one could conclude from Lindqvist's study that the effects of price and advertising (market communication) are mainly indirect in nature. There seems to be an image effect which has an impact on the quality perception, and this effect is a function of advertising campaigns and other market communication activities, price level and price offerings, and a range of other factors as well. Garvin has studied quality factors from a manufacturing point of view, but he has simultaneously taken into account the fact that services are an integral part of the offerings of manufacturers (Garvin 1984 and 1987). He has suggested a list of eight quality dimensions.

Perceived Control

An aspect of service perception clearly interrelated with the perceived quality of a service is *perceived control.* This concept has been introduced in the service literature by Bateson to explain consumer behavior in buying and consumption situations (Bateson 1985). If customers lose control of the

1. **Reliability** involves consistency of performance and dependability:
   - the firm performs the service right the first time
   - accuracy in billing
   - keeping records correctly
   - performing the service at the designated time
2. **Responsiveness** concerns the willingness or readiness of employees to provide service:
   - timeliness of service
   - mailing transaction slips immediately
   - calling the customer back quickly
   - giving prompt service
3. **Competence** means possession of the required skills and knowledge:
   - knowledge and skills of the contact employees
   - knowledge and skills of operational support personnel
   - research capability of the organization
4. **Access** involves approachability and ease of contact:
   - the service is easily accessible by telephone
   - waiting time to receive service is not extensive
   - convenient hours of operation
   - convenient location of service facility
5. **Courtesy** involves politeness, respect, consideration, and friendliness of contact personnel:
   - consideration for the consumer's property
   - clean and neat appearance of public contact personnel
6. **Communication** means keeping customers informed in language they can understand and listening to them:
   - explaining the service itself
   - explaining how much the service will cost
   - explaining the trade-offs between service and cost
   - assuring the consumers that a problem will be handled
7. **Credibility** involves trustworthiness, believability, honesty, and having the customer's best interests at heart:
   - company name
   - company reputation
   - personal characteristics of the contact personnel
   - the degree of hard sell involved in interactions
8. **Security** is the freedom from danger, risk, or doubt:
   - physical safety
   - financial security
   - confidentiality
9. **Understanding/Knowing the Customer** involves making the effort to understand the customer's needs:
   - learning the customer's specific requirements
   - providing individualized attention
   - recognizing the regular customer
10. **Tangibles** include physical evidence of the service:
    - physical facilities
    - appearance of personnel
    - tools or equipment used to provide the service
    - physical representations of the service (cards, etc.)
    - other customers in the service facility

Source: Parasuraman, A., Zeithaml, V.A. & Berry, L.L. (1985): A Conceptual Model of Service Quality and Its Implications for Future Research. *Journal of Marketing,* (American Marketing Association, Fall): p. 47.

Figure 2–3. Determinants of Perceived Service Quality

consumption situation, they will start feeling uncomfortable. A situation, for example, crowding or waiting, which otherwise would be acceptable, becomes awkward and creates a feeling of stress if the service firm takes away the sense of control from the customer. "Consumers want to feel in control of the service encounter and anything that interferes with that sense of control will reduce consumers' satisfaction. Managers must therefore consider seriously the building of perceived control into the encounter" (Bateson & Hui 1987, p. 190).

The connection between perceived control and recovery as a quality determinant is easily observed. If an unexpected situation occurs, for example, a flight is delayed for technical reasons, customers lose control of the situation, and the negative effects of the feeling of lack of control develop quickly. If airline employees promptly and courteously, showing empathy, give the waiting passengers information about the situation, even negative pieces of information, the situation is probably recovered. If passengers know that it will take at least two hours, they perceive control of the situation, even if they perhaps do not like the situation. They at least are less unsatisfied than they would have been if there had been no information at all. Recovery, of course, means much more than informing customers of potential disaster. It should include attempts to find a new and acceptable solution, or if that is not possible, at least make life as comfortable as possible for the passengers.

In conclusion, keeping customers in control of the service purchasing and consumption situation can be an effective means of turning around a potentially dangerous situation as far as the perception of service quality is concerned, and in any case a powerful way of enhancing good perceived quality.

A Summary: The Six Criteria of Good Perceived Service Quality

There are a range of smaller studies from various countries that seem to support the findings reported above. In order to make such lists of determinants or factors of good service quality useful for managerial purposes, they have to be short enough yet still provide a comprehensive list of aspects of good quality, which have to be taken into account. In Figure 2–4 such a list is provided. These *Six Criteria of Good Perceived Service Quality* are not the result of additional empirical research, but an

1. Professionalism and Skills
The customers realize that the service provider, its employees, operational systems, and physical resources, have the knowledge and skills required to solve their problems in a professional way (outcome-related criteria).

2. Attitudes and Behavior
The customers feel that the service employees (contact persons) are concerned about them and interested in solving their problems in a friendly and spontaneous way (process–related criteria).

3. Accessibility and Flexibility
The customers feel that the service provider, its location, operating hours, employees, and operational systems, are designed and operate so that it is easy to get access to the service and so that they are prepared to adjust to the demands and wishes of the customer in a flexible way (process–related criteria).

4. Reliability and Trustworthiness
The customers know that whatever takes place or has been agreed upon, they can rely on the service provider, its employees and systems, to keep promises and perform with the best interest of the customers at heart (process–related criteria).

5. Recovery
The customers realize that whenever something goes wrong or something unpredictable unexpectedly happens the service provider will immediately and actively take actions to keep them in control of the situation and find a new, acceptable solution (process–related criteria).

6. Reputation and Credibility
The customers believe that the operations of the service provider can be trusted and gives adequate value for money, and that it stands for good performance and values which can be shared by customers and the service provider (image–related criteria)

Figure 2–4. The Six Criteria of Good Perceived Service Quality

integration of available studies. Some of these studies have been discussed in this section. One of the six, *professionalism and skills*, is outcome related and thus a technical quality dimension. Another criterion, *reputation and credibility*, is image related, thus fulfilling a filtering function. However, the other four criteria, *attitudes and behavior, accessibility and flexibility, reliability and trustworthiness,* and *recovery,* are clearly process related and thus represent the functional quality dimension.

These six criteria of good perceived service can be viewed as guidelines based on a solid body of empirical and conceptual research as well as on practical experience. Therefore, they should be useful as managerial principles. Of course, the list is not exhaustive. In various industries and for various customers certain criteria are more important than others. And of course, there may in specific situations be other determinants of good quality that are not covered by these six criteria. Moreover, the role of *price* in a quality context is not very clear. In reports on research into service quality price is not discussed very much, with the exception of the previously cited study by Lindqvist (1988). Normally, however, the price of a service can be viewed in relation to the quality expectations of customers or to their previously perceived service quality. If the price of a service is considered too high, the customers do not buy. Price also has an impact on expectations. But in some situations price seems to be a quality criterion. Especially when the service is highly intangible, a higher price level may equal a better quality in the minds of customers. In many cases professional services are examples of such services. In the next chapter we continue the quality issue by describing frameworks and models for managing service quality.

Summary

In this chapter we first discussed the nature of services and surveyed some definitions from three decades of literature on services. Characteristics of services were presented and discussed and a number of classification schemes suggested as a means of better understanding how to manage services. Then, a model of customer perceived quality, the *Perceived Service Quality* model, was put forward and discussed. The technical quality and functional quality dimensions (the what and the how) of perceived quality were discussed, as well as the filtering role of corporate and local image. Finally, studies of how customers perceive quality of services were illustrated and, as a synthesis of available studies, the Six Criteria of Good Perceived Service Quality were put forward.

3
Managing Customer-Perceived Service Quality

Introduction

In the present chapter we are going to discuss issues related to why it is profitable to pay attention to service quality, how quality and productivity interact, and how Perceived Service Quality can be managed. Two models of analyzing and managing service quality are presented and discussed: the Gap Analysis Model and the Grönroos-Gummesson Quality Model.

Why Bother about Service Quality

Recently the word "quality" has come into the everyday vocabulary of management. The need for quality goods and services and for quality improvements is mentioned so often that quality has almost become a buzzword, which easily loses its meaning. There is too much talking about quality and not enough real efforts to do something to make quality a source of competitive advantage. Nevertheless, quality is a major issue today. As Tom Peters (1988b) observes:

> Every day brings new reports of lousy American product or service quality, vis-à-vis our foremost overseas competitors. The news of buyers rejecting our products pours in from Des Moines; Miami; Santa Clara County, California; Budapest; Zurich; and even Beijing. Industry after industry are under attack—old manufacturers and new, as well as the great hope of the future, the service industry. Changing on an unimagined scale is a must, and islands of good news—those responding with alacrity—are available for our inspection. But it is becoming increasingly clear that the response is not coming fast enough. (p. 103)

Robert E. Allen, Chairman of AT&T in a paid advertisement in *Fortune* (September 26, 1988) stated that ". . . I can't think of a business problem, issue, or priority that is unaffected by the quality trust. *Quality does it all. It saves. It sells. It satisfies* [emphasis by the author]." Bradley Gale, Managing Director of the Strategic Planning Institute, adds some empirical support to this statement: "Businesses with superior quality create shareholder value by increasing market share and higher prices at competitive costs" (*Fortune,* September 26, 1988). (Also, compare the previously cited conclusions of the PIMS project concerning the vital importance to success of customer perceived quality; see Buzzell & Gale 1987.) Developing quality is clearly a means of achieving excellence and establishing a competitive edge.

In Europe in 1987 a study was carried out among executives in 128 major corporations about their views on key strategic issues in the 1990s. It showed that out of 18 key strategic marketing issues *quality of products and services was given highest priority* by the respondents.

Quality of services stands out for a number of reasons; as Gummesson (1989b) observes:

- Service organizations lag behind manufacturers in systematic quality efforts;
- Customers over a wide range of industries show a considerable dissatisfaction with service quality;
- In the public sector, where service originally was meant to be a key element, bureaucracy and other nonservice elements have taken over; and
- Firms manufacturing physical goods are in need of new means of differentiating themselves and developing a competitive edge, and services are a source of opportunity to do this.

It is easy to realize that service quality and how to manage quality in service contexts are pivotal issues in today's service economy. There are, of course, firms that have successfully worked with these issues, but as Gummesson (1989b) concludes, ". . . there has been a lack of widespread focus on services" (p. 83). However, this is changing now, as *service management* (and service quality as part of it) has established itself as a recognized field.

Why Managers Hesitate: It Costs Too Much

However, managers often feel uncomfortable with the demands for better quality. They feel that improved quality, in the final analysis, does not pay off. Two related reasons why the firm cannot improve its quality are normally offered, namely, improving quality costs too much, more than what can be achieved in additional revenues and new business, and improving quality means that productivity will go down, which the organization cannot afford. As Pickworth (1987) observes: "As managers, we recognize the need to improve quality, and we also realize that we must raise productivity. But it has long been accepted thinking that increases in productivity are likely to come at the expense of quality, and that improvement in quality will increase operating costs. Caught in this apparent dilemma, managers often concentrate on either quality or productivity, but not both" (p. 40). Far too often attention to productivity is given priority, and how to improve quality remains an unsolved problem.

Both of these reasons for why quality cannot be improved are related to cost considerations. To increase quality requires too much resources and incremental costs, and it lowers productivity, which leads to higher costs per unit. Both reasons are wrong, and are based on an insufficient understanding of the relationships between quality and productivity on the one hand and the use of resources and the sources of costs and revenues on the other. As Leonard and Sasser (1982) say, ". . . efforts to raise quality almost always result in heightened productivity . . . [and] . . . efforts to raise productivity usually pay off in better quality" (p. 168). However, they add that in order to achieve positive results, managers will have to develop a new and correct understanding of the relationship between quality and costs (Leonard & Sasser 1982). If managers are able to define this relationship, they are probably able to exploit the strengths of it as far as, among other things, production effectiveness and employee satisfaction and profitability are concerned. The strength of this quality-productivity relationship has been emphasized by Fedele Bauccio, former president of Saga Corporation's specialty foods division, when he coined the phrase "*wheel of fortune*" to describe this relationship (Pickworth 1987).

Quality Does Not Cost—A Lack of Quality Does

In this section we are going to deal with the misunderstanding related to quality improvement and costs. In the next chapter, the relationship between quality and productivity will be discussed.

The notion that high quality implies higher costs is not based on facts. Normally, it is the other way around. Frequently the more important issue is that it is a lack of quality that costs. As Philip Crosby, the American quality guru who coined the phrase "*quality is free*" (1979), explains: "If you concentrate on making quality certain, you can probably increase your profit by an amount equal of 5 to 10 percent of your sales. That is a lot of money for free." He bases his statement on a notion that American firms spend more than 20 percent of their sales dollars doing things wrong and then having to correct these mistakes. Lee Iacocca of Chrysler confirms this by stating that "if there's any doubt that lack of quality costs American industry a ton of money, get this statistics: *As many as one out of four factory workers produces nothing at all. They spend their entire workday fixing the mistakes of other workers* [emphasis by the author]" (Iacocca 1988, p. 251).

These are facts from manufacturing. However, service organizations are probably no better off. On the contrary, Gummesson (1987a) notes that as much as 35 percent of their operating costs may be caused by a lack of quality. This, of course, follows from the fact that service quality is a much more complicated phenomenon and that, consequently, it is much more difficult to monitor and assure quality in service than in manufacturing. Furthermore, manufacturing has a long history of quality control research and a whole collection of quality monitoring techniques at its service, whereas for more than a decade service quality issues have not been addressed explicitly.

Hence, improving quality by creating customer-oriented and foolproof systems and by training employees to know how to perform is a way, not to increase costs, but to get rid of unnecessary costs of a low quality level or a lack of quality. If we assume that 35 percent of the operating costs are unnecessary, because they are due to bad quality, quality improvement by removing these quality problems would save 35 percent of these costs. All of this would be visible on the bottom line. However, such an improvement would not go unnoticed by the market, and some new business and additional revenues could be expected to be achieved. This would add even more to the bottom line, that is, profits would be boosted by more than 35 percent of original operating costs. Furthermore, if the firm would spend this 35 percent on improving quality even more, the operating costs would remain on the same level as they were originally. This quality improvement process could be expected to bring in more business, and perhaps, even probably, enable the firm to get a better price for its services. The effects on the bottom line are obvious.

Why Managers Hesitate: We Are So Special

Another common reason why managers feel that developing and offering services with 100 percent quality is impossible is their feeling that "we are so special; our industry is so difficult; it is impossible to guarantee customers top quality all the time; it cannot be done." Consequently, the organization accepts that mistakes happen, and failures are allowed. Psychologically, the battle for excellent performance is over before it even started.

Tom Gillett, Director of Services of GTT, tells the following anecdote to his employees when they argue that in such a complicated business as the telecommunications business top quality just cannot be produced and thus cannot be offered to their customers: "Imagine a large international airport with hundreds of take-offs and landings each day. If they at this airport would accept a quality level of 99%, they would have a number of accidents every day. That just cannot be allowed to happen. And can you imagine a more difficult and technically complicated service and service production system in this respect than an airport?" The conclusion is, of course, that if an airport can offer and maintain a 100-percent quality level, you can do it as well, whatever your business is.

As Howard Deutsch, Senior Vice President of Nat West USA, quoted in a paid advertising in *Fortune* (September 26, 1988) says: "By setting high service standards and putting our money where our mouth is, we're doing much more than simply talking quality service—we're guaranteeing it." He is, in the same context in *Fortune*, supported by D.C. Staley, Chairman of NYNEX, the public telecommunications network which serves a customer base larger than the population of Canada. Stately launched a quality process in NYNEX by stating that "it is the policy of NYNEX to offer totally reliable products and services which always meet our customers' needs in a timely manner."

Saying and maybe believing that a particular firm is so special and its services are so complex and difficult to produce that top quality cannot be achieved is only an excuse for not trying hard enough. True enough, hard and long-term efforts may frequently be required, but it is never impossible.

Reasons Why Quality Improvement Processes May Fail

In spite of the obvious benefits of quality improvement, many firms which have implemented quality programs feel that these programs did not pay off. Normally, the problem is in the approach to quality enhancement. If it is considered a program only, if a limited time frame is given to the effort, and it is perceived by everybody in the organization, top management and all other employees alike, as only a tactical issue, the risk of failure is high. For some managers, quality improvement is, by and large, a matter of time-

and-motion studies or investment in machinery or equipment which allows the firm to reduce the labor force. Still, for others, it is mostly a training program, or introducing a new monetary reward system.

While all these elements can be parts of a quality improvement process, as isolated programs they are bound to fail in the long run. The main problem is in the approach. Quality enhancement must not be considered only a program, or even worse a campaign, it has to be an ongoing *process*. One of the key goals is to enhance what can be called "*quality behavior*" among the personnel (King 1984). A continuous appreciation of the importance of quality and an understanding of how to influence good service quality is required of every single individual in the organization. And such a "quality behavior" has to be constantly maintained by management. Pickworth (1987) says, ". . . once a quality program is begun, management should plan to stay with it, because letting a quality-improvement initiative fall by the wayside can have severe repercussions on management credibility" (p. 42). Quality and hence quality improvement and assurance processes are strategic issues, which require continuous attention by top management.

A Service Quality Management Framework

In the previous chapter we presented a basic three-dimensional conceptual model of the total perceived quality (including a *technical outcome dimension*, a *functional process dimension*, and a *filtering image dimension*) as well as some research findings concerning the perception of service quality. In this chapter we are going to present a general framework for managing service quality, as well as some more explicit models of quality management.

In Figure 3–1 a *general framework for managing service quality* is illustrated in a schematic form. There are three groups of *actors* involved: A. management, B. employees, and C. customers (letters and numbers in the text refer to letter and numbers in Figure 3–1). On the *management* level the policies to follow are set. Analyses of market demands and requirements concerning quality (1) and of internal perceptions of quality level and performance among employees (2) are initiated. This knowledge is needed so that quality specifications can be decided upon (3) and internal marketing of such specifications and of desired performance can be implemented (4). (We will return to the concept "internal marketing" in chapter 10.) Moreover, external marketing programs (5) are planned on this level, and ex post facto quality control measurements (1) are made.

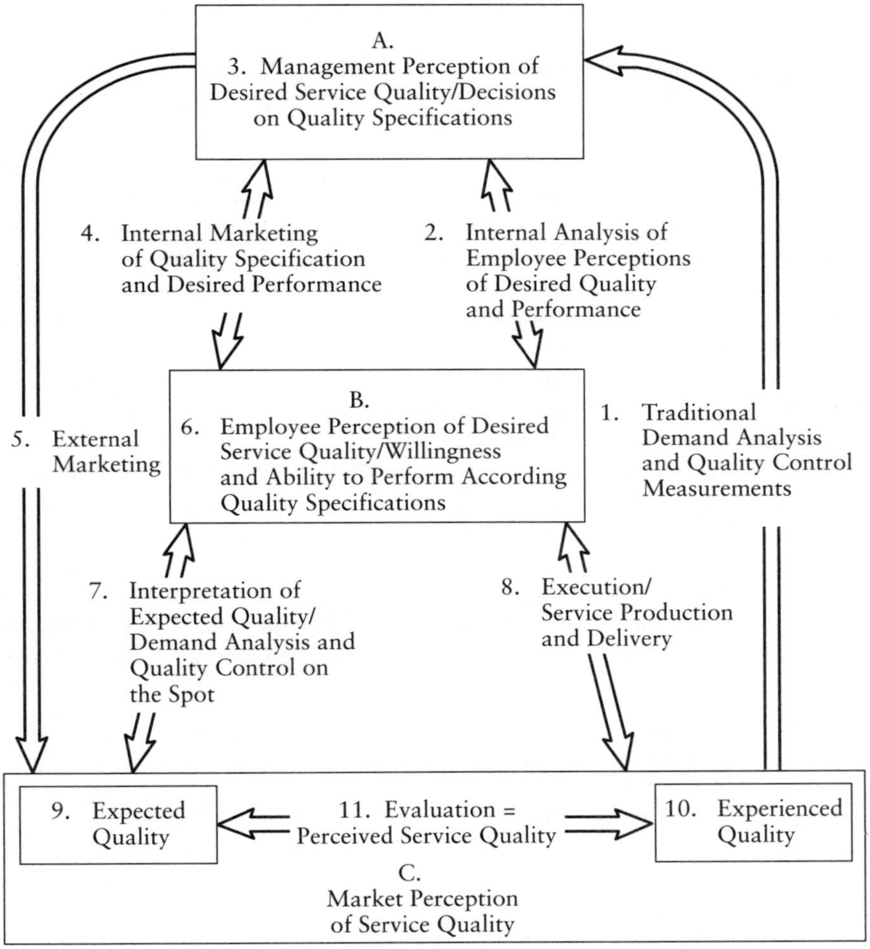

Figure 3–1. A Service Quality Management Framework

On the *employee* level the quality and performance standards are to be met by the way the organization operates. Employees in various functions perceive the quality specifications and are to a certain extent willing and able to perform according to the specifications (6). The employees interacting with customers (so-called contact persons) see and feel signals from the market and have the opportunity to immediately and in a flexible manner adjust to customer demands. They are in a position to follow up (analyze) customer demands and wishes as well as to control the quality of the service rendered in the buyer-seller interactions immediately when changes in the initial demand and quality problems occur (7). At the same time they are, of course, involved in producing and delivering the service (8).

Finally, on the *customer* level, it is decided whether the quality is "acceptable" or not. Customers expect a certain quality (9) and they also, of course, experience a certain quality (10), depending on what they receive and how they receive it in the interactions with the organization. The quality is evaluated by the customers, and the result of this evaluation is the total perceived quality, or, if we only look at service operations, the total *Perceived Service Quality* (11). As discussed in the previous chapter, this depends not only on how the organization performs. The impact of external marketing programs (such as advertising campaigns) on customer expectations must be considered as well.

In Figure 3–2 the possible outcomes of the evaluation process are schematically illustrated. In principle, there are four possible outcomes—underquality, confirmed quality, positively confirmed quality, and overquality. Good quality, of course requires that experiences at least equal expectations, or are higher than expectations. Otherwise the quality expectations of customers are not met. *Acceptable quality* is always required. However, if the firm wants to make its customers really happy

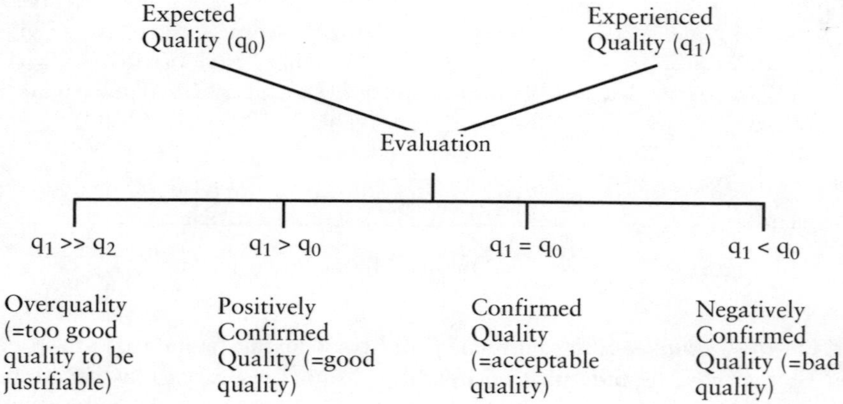

Source: Derived from a figure in Smith, R. & Huston, M. (1983): Script–Based Evaluations of Satisfaction with Services. In Berry, L.L., Shostack, G.L. & Upah, G., eds., *Emerging Perspectives on Services Marketing*. Chicago: American Marketing Association.

Figure 3–2. The Quality Evaluation Options

with its services, an acceptable quality may not be enough. *Positively confirmed quality* should, then, be the objective to aim for. This may really make customers interested in continuing the relationship with the service provider, and, moreover, it creates good word-of-mouth effects. There is a danger here, of course. If the perceived quality is too high, the costs of production are probably unnecessarily high. The cost-benefit ratio will be low or maybe even negative. Then we have an *overquality*, which cannot be justified for economic reasons. Moreover, an overquality may simply be perceived by the customer to exceed what is really needed, which in turn can create even bad word-of-mouth. Overquality may also give the impression that the service is overpriced, even if this, in fact, is not the case.

Figure 3–1 illustrated a general framework for service quality management. In the next sections we are going to present more specific models of analyzing and managing quality.

Services Have to Be Designed

Goods are the object of product development and design before they are launched onto the market. However, as Gummesson (1989b) observes, "we have yet to hear of service designers" (p. 84). Rathmell (1974) noticed over fifteen years ago that "new services happen," rather than being formally developed. Unfortunately, this seems to be the case in too many situations even today. Services are not carefully designed *before* they are produced. However, if good and consistent service quality is to be maintained, service design has to be a forethought and not just an object for corrective actions after mistakes have happened (Gummesson 1988 and 1989b; compare also Berry 1988).

One of the main reasons for the absence of service design processes is the fact that there is no tradition of service design. Or, if there is a planned design process, it is not in the hands of people who have a thorough understanding of the needs and wishes of the market and of the consumers of the services to be designed. In the private sector, operations is often responsible for design-related issues, although no formal design takes place as in manufacturing firms; and in the public sector people with training in law are given responsibility for designing services, which makes legal matters exceedingly more important than customer benefits and customer satisfaction aspects (Gummesson 1989b). In some parts of the private service sector, for example, the insurance industry, this may be the case as well. The services developed become rigid and production oriented.

If a service is not well designed, quality problems follow. The opinion of customers and of the service provider as to what services should be and how they should function easily remain totally different, or different enough so that a gap between the *expected service* and the *experienced service* emerges. Consequently, customer perceived service quality deteriorates.

However, there are some new approaches to service design today. *Service blueprinting* introduced by Shostack (1984 and 1987) is the most well known. For example, a whole session of the 1989 Services Marketing Conference arranged by the American Marketing Association in Chicago was dedicated to this approach to designing and developing new services. Other approaches are being developed as well.

Gap Analysis

Berry and his colleagues have developed a so-called *Gap Analysis Model*, which is intended to be used for analyzing sources of quality problems and for helping managers understand how service quality can be improved (Parasuraman et al. 1985 and Zeithaml et al. 1988). The model is illustrated in Figure 3–3.

First of all, the model demonstrates how service quality emerges. The upper part of the model includes phenomena related to the customer, the lower part shows phenomena related to the service provider. The *expected service* is a function of the customer's *past experience* and *personal needs* and of *word-of-mouth communication*. Moreover, it is influenced by the *market communication* activities of the firm (compare Figure 2–2 in chapter 2).

The experienced service, which in this model is called the *perceived service*, on the other hand, is the outcome of a series of internal decisions and activities. *Management perceptions of customer expectations* guide decisions about *service quality specifications* to be followed by the organization, when *service delivery* takes place. The customer, of course, experiences the service delivery and production process as a process-related quality component, and the technical solution received by the process as an outcome-related quality component. As is illustrated, *market communication* can be expected to influence the perceived service as well as the expected service (compare also the quality study by Lindqvist 1988).

This basic structure demonstrates which steps have to be considered when analyzing and planning service quality. Next, possible sources of quality problems can be detected. In Figure 3–3 *five* discrepancies between the various elements of the basic structure, so-called *quality gaps*, are illustrated as well. These quality gaps are the result of inconsistencies in the

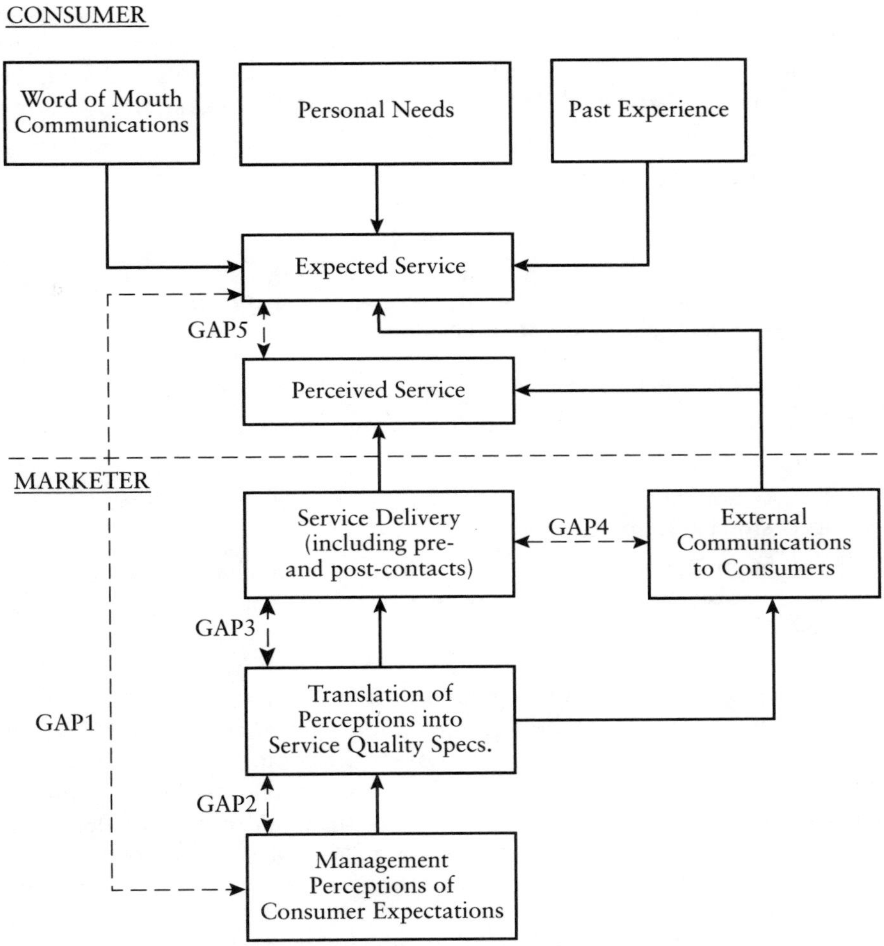

Source: Reprinted from Zeithaml, V.A., Berry, L.L. & Parasuraman, A. (1988): Communication and Control Processes in the Delivery of Service Quality. *Journal of Marketing*, American Marketing Association, April, p. 36.

Figure 3–3. Conceptual Model of Service Quality — The Gap Analysis Model

quality management process. The ultimate gap, that is, the gap between expected and perceived (experienced) service (Gap 5), is, of course, a function of the other gaps which may have occurred in the process. The five gaps, their consequences, and the reasons why they occur (Parasuraman et al. 1985 and Zeithaml et al. 1988) are discussed in the next section.

Managing the Quality Gaps

The Management Perception Gap (Gap 1)

This gap means that *management perceives the quality expectations inaccurately*. This gap is, among other things, due to:

- Inaccurate information from market research and demand analyses;
- Inaccurately interpreted information about expectations;
- Nonexistent demand analysis;
- Bad or nonexistent upward information from the firm's interface with its customers to management; and
- Too many organizational layers which stop or change the pieces of information that may flow upward from those involved in customer contacts.

The cures may be of various nature. If the problems are due to bad management, obviously either a change of management or an improvement in the knowledge of the characteristics of service competition on the part of management is required. Most often, but not always, the latter action is more appropriate, because normally the problems did not occur due to a genuine lack of competence but rather to a lack of knowledge or of appreciation of the nature and demands of service competition among managers.

Part of any cure is always better research, so that the wants and wishes of customers are better observed and appreciated. The information that is obtained through market research and from internal flows of information from the customer interface is perhaps not good enough or only partly appropriate. Necessary actions to open up or improve the various internal information channels have to be taken in such cases. This may even have implications for the organizational structure of the firm. We are going to return to this issue in chapter 8.

The Quality Specification Gap (Gap 2)

This gap means that *service quality specifications are not consistent with management perceptions of quality expectations*. This gap is a result of:

- Planning mistakes or insufficient planning procedures;
- Bad management of planning;
- Lack of clear goal setting in the organization; and
- Insufficient support for planning for service quality from top management.

Depending on the size of the first gap, the potential planning-related problems vary. However, even in a situation where there is enough and sufficiently accurate information on customer expectations, planning of quality specifications may fail. A fairly normal reason for this is a lack of true commitment to service quality among top management. Quality is not considered an issue of highest priority. An obvious cure in such a situation is to change the priorities. Quality as perceived by customers is such a vital success factor today, certainly in service competition, that it is imperative that commitment to quality rank high on the priority list of management.

Of course, the problem may be in the planning process itself. Those providing the services also have to feel a commitment to the quality specifications. This has to be taken into account in the goal-setting and planning routines. Planning at the top without any collaboration of those who actually produce the service is never a good procedure. Ideally, goals and specifications should be agreed upon by the service providers as well as by the planners and management. Also, it is good to remember that too rigid specifications hurt flexibility and decrease the willingness of employees to take flexible actions involving risks. And this, again, normally hurts service quality.

In summary, commitment to service quality among management as well as service providers is far more important to closing the Quality Specification Gap than any too-rigid goal-setting and planning procedure.

The Service Delivery Gap (Gap 3)

This gap means that *quality specifications are not met by the performance in the service production and delivery process*. This gap is due to:

- Too complicated and/or rigid specifications;
- The employees do not agree with the specifications, as, for instance, good service quality seems to require a different behavior;
- The specifications are not in line with the existing corporate culture;
- Bad management of service operations;
- Lacking or insufficient internal marketing; and
- Technology and systems do not facilitate performance according to specifications.

The possible problems here are many and varied, and normally the reasons for the existence of a Service Delivery Gap are complicated. There is seldom only one reason, and the cure is, therefore, almost always complicated. The reasons for this gap can be divided roughly into three categories, namely, management and supervision, employee perception of specifications and rules and of customer needs and wishes, and lack of support by technology and systems of operations.

Management and supervision-related problems may be many. For example, the methods of supervisors may not be encouraging to and supportive of quality behavior. Or the supervisory control systems may be in conflict with good service and even with quality specifications. In any organization where control and reward systems are decided upon separately from the planning of quality specifications, which far too often is the case, there is an inherent risk for a Service Delivery Gap to occur. And this risk is not small. Too often wrong and nonessential activities are controlled, perhaps even rewarded; and activities that contradict quality specifications are encouraged by the control system. They too may even be rewarded. Of course, this puts the employees in an extremely awkward position. Control and reward systems partly determine the corporate culture, although there are other even more important determinants as well, and goals and specifications that do not fit the existing culture are not very well executed. The cure here involves changes in the way managers and supervisors treat their subordinates, and in the way supervisory systems control and reward performance. Moreover, larger issues related to the culture of the firm and internal marketing may have to be attended to. We will return to the issues of internal marketing and corporate culture in chapters 10 and 11.

From what has been discussed above it follows, among other things, that the employees may feel that their role as service providers is ambiguous. We have already mentioned the awkward position in which the performance requirements of the specifications on the one hand and the existing control and reward systems on the other hand are in conflict with each other. Furthermore, an awkward situation for personnel occurs when a customer contact person realizes that a customer, or at least sufficiently many customers, requires a different behavior on the part of the service provider than what is expected according to the existing specifications. The service provider knows that the customer does not get what he or she expects and, moreover, may feel that the demands and wishes of the customer are justified and perhaps could be fulfilled, but the service provider is not allowed to perform accordingly. This slowly but surely kills any motivation for good quality behavior among the personnel.

The cure in situations like these is to remove all reasons for ambiguity on the part of the personnel. This may, on the one hand, require changes in the supervisory systems so that they are in line with the quality specifications. It may, on the other hand, also require better training of employees, so that they are aware of the limitations for performance due to, for example, strategic considerations or profitability reasons. Here again the issue of internal marketing is critical.

Third, the skills and attitudes of personnel may cause problems. It may be that wrong persons have been recruited in the first place. The firm may have people who cannot adjust to the specifications and systems that guide operations, however justifiable they are. The cure in this situation is, of course, to improve the recruitment routines so that wrong decisions in this respect can be avoided. Furthermore, the workload perceived by employees may be a problem. There may, for example, be too much paperwork or other administrative tasks involved, so that quality specifications cannot be fulfilled. Because of this, the service provider does not have time to attend to customers as is expected.

The cure, for instance, is to clarify the tasks of the personnel and to find a solution where necessary matters are attended to without interfering with quality performance. Finally, the technology or the systems of operating, including decision-making and other routines, may not fit the employees. The problem may be the employees, of course, but it is more probable that technology and operational and administrative systems have been introduced in the wrong way. The technology and systems are perhaps wrong. They just do not support quality behavior. Or they may be appropriate, but they have not been properly introduced to the employees who are expected to live with them. The cure is either to make proper changes in the technology and systems so that they are supportive of the execution of the quality specifications or, here again, to improve training and internal marketing.

The Market Communication Gap (Gap 4)

This gap means that *promises given by market communication activities are not consistent with the service delivered*. This gap is due to:

- Market communication planning is not integrated with service operations;
- Lacking or insufficient coordination between traditional marketing and operations;
- The organization fails to perform according to specifications, whereas market communication campaigns follow these specifications; and
- An inherent propensity to exaggerate and, thus, promise too much.

The reasons for the occurrence of a Market Communication Gap can be divided into two categories, namely, planning and executing of external market communication and operations do not go hand in hand, and an often-occurring inherent propensity to overpromise in all advertising and market communication.

In the first case, the cure is to create a system that coordinates planning and execution of external market communication campaigns with service operations and delivery. For example, at least every major campaign should be planned in collaboration with those involved in service production and delivery. Two goals can be achieved by this. First, the promises in market communication become more accurate and in conformity with reality. Second, a greater commitment to what is promised in external campaigns can be achieved, which also tends to have the side effect that more can be promised than what otherwise would be the case. The second category of problems, overpromising because of the very nature of market communication where superlatives are far too easily used, can only be coped with by improving planning of market communication. The cure may be better planning procedures, but a closer supervision from management also helps.

The Perceived Service Quality Gap (Gap 5)

This gap means that *the perceived or experienced service is not consistent with the expected service*. This gap results in:

- Negatively confirmed quality (bad quality) and a quality problem;
- Bad word-of-mouth;
- Negative impact on corporate or local image; and
- Lost business.

The fifth gap may, of course, also be positive, which leads either to a positively confirmed quality or overquality. If a Perceived Service Quality

Gap occurs, the reason for this could be any of those discussed in this section, or any combination of them. Of course, there may also be other reasons in addition to those mentioned here.

The Gap Analysis Model should guide management in finding out where the reason (or reasons) for the quality problem is and in discovering appropriate ways to close this gap. As Brown and Swartz (1989) concluded, after having studied quality gaps of professional services," . . . gap analysis is a straightforward and appropriate way to identify inconsistencies between provider and client perceptions of service performance. Addressing these gaps seems to be a logical basis for formulating strategies and tactics to ensure consistent expectations and experiences, thus increasing the likelihood of satisfaction and a positive quality evaluation" (p. 97).[a]

The Grönroos-Gummesson Quality Model

Gummesson and Grönroos have suggested a synthesis of some recent research into the quality of goods and services (Gummesson & Grönroos 1988). This model is intended to assist both manufacturers and service firms in quality management. It is based on two models with two separate approaches to describing how quality is created: the Gummesson 4Q mode, based on a notion that everybody contributes to quality and that there are a number of different sources of quality in a firm (Gummesson 1987a); and the Grönroos model of Perceived Service Quality, which revolves around the dimensions of quality perception. It is schematically illustrated in Figure 3–4.

To the left in the figure are four *sources* of quality, namely, design, production, delivery, and relations (Gummesson 1987a). The way of managing and handling these aspects of business has an impact on the *customer perceived quality*. Both the technical quality of the outcome of goods or services and the functional quality of interactive processes involving buyer and seller are influenced by these quality sources.

The *design* of goods or services has an impact on technical quality. However, this function may also be a source of functional quality. For example, the customer or potential customer may get involved in the design process. This could improve the technical quality, but it has a quality

---

[a]Berry and his colleagues have developed the Gap Analysis Model into an *extended service quality model* (SERVQUAL) (see Parasuraman et al. 1986 and Zeithaml et al. 1988). They expand the gap concept with basic theoretical constructs and specific variables or factors derived from these theoretical constructs. SERVQUAL includes a set of standard items which could be used in any given situation. Probably they can be used frequently, but one should keep in mind, however, that all situations are to some extent unique, and in some cases the items of SERVQUAL may have to be reconsidered (compare Vogels et al. 1989).

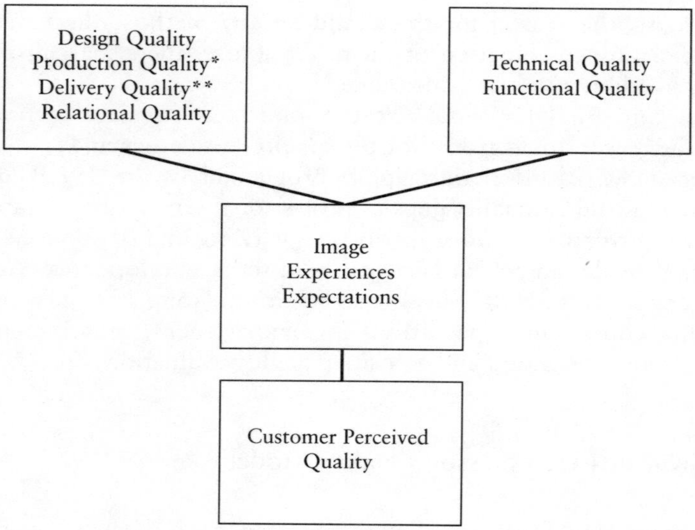

* Invisible/Visible Noninteractive/Interactive
** Own/Subcontracted

Source: Reprinted in part from Gummesson, E. & Grönroos, C. (1987): Quality of Services. Lessons from the Product Sector. In Surprenant, C., ed., *Add Value to Your Service*. Chicago: American Marketing Association, p. 38.

Figure 3–4. The Grönroos-Gummesson Quality Model

impact in itself. It may make customers realize that this particular seller takes a special interest in them and makes extra efforts to solve their problems. This is the functional quality impact of the interaction process.

As far as services are concerned, *production* is a quality source. The technical quality of the outcome is a result of the total production process. A substantial part of this process is, however, visible and seen by the customer, who participates in the process as well. Buyer-seller interactions emerge. Production has an impact on functional quality as well. This goes for manufacturing, too. Here production, of course, determines the technical quality. However, the customer may occasionally get exposed to the production process. For example, the production facilities and processes may be demonstrated to the customer. The way in which the customer perceives interactions with production, the resources and machinery of production, and the production processes has a functional quality impact.

As far as services are concerned, *delivery* is difficult to distinguish from production in many cases. It is more or less a part of the total production process. Hence, in services, what has been said about the quality aspects of production above also applies to delivery. However, for a manufacturer of goods, deliveries form a separate function. The outcome of delivery is, of course, the fact that the buyer receives the goods. This is an outcome-related technical quality aspect of delivery. In addition to this quality aspect there is also a process-related quality component. The way in which deliveries are carried out, promptness, behavior of truck drivers, and so on is a functional quality dimension. Deliveries can be taken care of by the organization itself or by subcontractors. It is, however, important to realize that subcontractors always perform on behalf of the service firm or manufacturer and that, in the eyes of the customer, the mistakes of a subcontractor are mistakes made by the service or manufacturing firm.

Finally, *relations* between the employees of the seller and the buyer are a source of quality in service firms as well as in firms manufacturing goods. The quality impact of relations is mainly functional and process related. The more customer conscious and service oriented the employees are in their relations with customers, the better the quality impact.

As implied by the Grönroos model of Perceived Service Quality in the previous chapter, customers have quality expectations prior to experiencing what the firm, in reality, offers. They also have some kind of an image of the firm, which has a quality impact in itself and functions as a filter. A good and well-known image is a shelter, whereas a negative image can easily make reality look less attractive than it in fact is. The *customer perceived quality* is the result of the evaluation of what was expected and what was experienced, taking into account the influence of the image of the organization.

Management has to observe and understand the quality impact of various functions of the firm, and that *there are several sources of quality, of which production is just one*. Technical as well as functional issues will have to be recognized when developing and implementing, for example, design, production, and delivery processes, and, of course, when planning and managing relations between people in the seller's and buyer's organizations.

Lessons of the Contemporary Service Quality and Quality Management Research

The models and frameworks of customer perceived service quality and of how to manage service quality presented in this and the previous chapter demonstrate a number of important lessons of the contemporary service quality research. Some of these issues have been focused upon in studies of goods quality management as well. However, it is nevertheless justified to say that service quality research has most explicitly pointed out the importance of these issues. The lessons are:

1. *Quality is what customers perceive.* Quality cannot be determined by management alone, it has to be based on customer needs and wishes. Moreover, quality is not what is planned in objective measures, rather it is how customers more or less subjectively perceive what has been planned.

2. *Quality cannot be separated from the production and delivery process.* The outcome of the service production process is only part of the customer perceived service quality. The production and delivery process itself is perceived by customers who also actively participate in this process. Therefore, the perception of the process and of the buyer-seller interactions of this process becomes another part of total quality. From a competitive point of view, this so-called functional quality dimension frequently is equally important as or even more important than the so-called technical quality of the outcome.

3. *Quality is produced locally in the moments of truth of the buyer-seller interactions.* Because of the existence of the important functional quality dimension of total service quality, the buyer-seller interactions, including a number of moments of truth, or moments of opportunity, become a pivotal factor in quality perception. Since buyer-seller interactions take place locally, where the customer meets the service provider, and not in centrally located quality design and planning departments, quality is also produced locally. Therefore, the planning and design of quality has to move out to the local level. Technical quality aspects and overall design of how to create quality can, of course, be planned centrally, but the interface between the organization and its customers has to be involved in quality management and design as well. Otherwise, well-designed quality may remain a desk product which does not materialize in a good customer perceived quality.

4. *Everyone contributes to customer perceived quality.* As quality is created and produced in the moments of truth of the buyer-seller interactions, a large number of employees get involved in the production of quality. Moreover, since these frontline employees who actually handle customer contacts in order to serve their customers well are dependent on the support of people beyond them in the service process, these "support" people also become responsible for the ultimate customer perceived quality. Hence, a large number of employees, not far from "everyone," contribute to quality. If someone in customer contacts or beyond the direct customer interface fail, quality suffers.

5. *Quality has to be monitored throughout the organization by the organization.* As quality is produced by a large number of people and functions throughout the organization, quality performance has to be

monitored and assured at the point where a quality contribution is produced. A centrally located quality control and management staff cannot normally do this. The task is overwhelming, and, moreover, a separate staff function or department for this has a negative effect psychologically on the people in the organization. The mere fact that such a function exists can easily draw the attention of those producing quality away from quality assurance. It is easy to stop worrying about the tricky issue of constantly producing, maintaining, and monitoring high-class quality when there is a group of specialists to turn to, and to blame when problems occur. Such a staff function may contribute to quality assurance and monitoring and quality design if it is perceived by everyone as an internal consultancy function in quality issues. However, the organization itself has to do the job of assuring quality.

6. *External marketing has to be integrated in quality management.* Customer perceived quality is a function of expectations as well as of real experiences of the quality dimensions. Therefore, improvement of the experiences of quality may be counteracted by, say, a market communication campaign that promises improvements or gives customers reason to believe that improvements will be greater than they in reality are. Customer expectations that are not met by reality are created. The perceived quality is bad, although improvements, objectively measured, may have occurred. Such negative effects of external marketing may have far-reaching consequences, for example, because bad word-of-mouth is created and the corporate image may be damaged. If market communication campaigns are planned in collaboration with those responsible for the quality improvement process, these mistakes can be avoided. Hence, external marketing, predominantly market communication, has to be integrated with quality management.

Summary

In chapter 2 the characteristics of services were discussed, and the basic nature of service quality and how service quality is perceived by customers presented. The importance of *customer perceived quality* and the *Perceived Service Quality* concept were dwelt upon to some extent. The role of market communication, word-of-mouth, and corporate and local image in the formation of perceived quality was discussed alongside the two basic quality dimensions, that is, the technical quality of the *outcome* (the what) and the functional quality of the *process* (the how). Also, some empirical findings concerning factors that describe good perceived service quality were introduced.

In this chapter we have introduced a framework and some models of managing service quality. The basic models of service quality in chapter 2 are here developed into management tools. A *Service Quality Management Framework* was introduced in Figure 3–1, which points out the actors and factors that have to be taken into consideration in quality management. Then, two models of quality management were discussed, the *Gap Analysis Model* and the *Grönroos-Gummesson Model*. Finally, six lessons of the contemporary research into service quality and quality management were presented. In subsequent chapters various aspects of managing services and coping with the emerging service competition will be covered. These two chapters on service quality are, however, a basis for the rest of the book, because customer perceived quality is of such vital importance to success.

4
Managing the Service Product: The Augmented Service Offering

Introduction

In the present chapter we will discuss the service as a product, that is, as an object that can be developed, produced, and delivered, marketed and consumed. A conceptual model called the Augmented Service Offering will be presented. This framework for describing the elements of a service as perceived by customers is geared to the characteristics of services and the concept of Perceived Service Quality. The Augmented Service Offering takes into account the impact of the outcome of the service production process (the technical quality of the service) and the impact of how customers perceive the process itself (the functional quality) as well as the additional effects on perceived quality of the corporate and local image of the organization.

The Service as a Product

One of the most essential cornerstones in developing service management models is a thorough understanding of the phenomenon to be studied. In other words, we need a good model of services as objects to be produced, marketed, and consumed. However, such a model is lacking today. The literature covers this topic only to a very limited extent, normally by using the concept of the service package (see, for example, Eiglier & Langeard 1976 and 1981, Langeard & Eiglier 1987, Sasser, Olsen, & Wyckoff 1978, Lehtinen 1983, and Normann 1984). Eigler and Langeard (1981) also use the concept "global service," consisting of various service elements.

There is very little literature on the development of new services today (see, for example, George & Marshall 1984, Bowers 1987, de Brentani 1989, and Langeard et al. 1986). However, the existing literature indicates that standard models from the product development literature can be only partially applied (e.g., Bowers 1987). One of the main reasons for this and for the general scarcity of new service development literature may be the fact that there is no adequate conceptual model today of services as products to be developed, produced, and marketed.

A Service Is a Bundle of Features and Customer Benefits

In the present chapter we are not going to discuss a total new service development process from idea generation to launching. Instead, we will concentrate on the core of such a process, that is, how to understand and manage the object of development itself, *the service as a product.*

Berry (1983) talks about augmenting the service by building extras into the basic service as a relationship marketing strategy. In this way the service is differentiated from those of the competitors. Using "extras" as part of the service product in order to differentiate the service has also been discussed by Levitt (1983): "Having been offered these extras, the customer finds them beneficial and therefore prefers doing business with the company that supplies them" (pp. 9-10). In this chapter we are going to expand the service package concept into a more comprehensive model of the service offering.

Any attempt to conceptualize the service product, or the service as a product, has to be based on a customer perspective. Far too often only internal aspects and far too little market research information, or far too limited understanding of the customers' point of view, guide the process of conceptualizing services to be offered to the market. However, well planned does not automatically mean well executed. In the following sections we are going to address, in detail, the topic of how to develop the service offering so that all aspects of it are thoroughly covered. This requires, among other things, that service production and delivery issues be incorporated as inseparable parts of the process of planning a service offering. Otherwise well-planned service offerings may remain paper products only, unless execution of plans is made an integral part of the total undertaking to create a service product or offering.

Service Package

According to the service package model, the service as a product is described as a package or bundle of different services, tangibles and intangibles, which together form the total product. The package is divided into two main categories: the *main service,* which often is called the "core service" (e.g., Grönroos 1978, Eiglier & Langeard 1981, Lehtinen 1983, and Normann 1984) or "substantive service" (Sasser, Olsen, & Wyckoff 1978); and *auxiliary services* or "extras," which often are referred to as "peripherals" or "peripheral services" (e.g., Eiglier & Langeard 1981, and Normann 1984), sometimes also as "facilitator services" (Maister & Lovelock 1982). A hotel service may include the lodging element as the main or core service, and reception service, valet service, room service, restaurant services, and the concierge as auxiliary services or peripherals in the package.

It is easily realized that this is an attractive and realistic way of illustrating at least some of the nature of any service. However, it has a few weaknesses if it is to be used for managerial purposes. First of all, a service is much more complicated than this model would suggest. There are auxiliary services which, from a managerial perspective, are used for totally different reasons. This has to be recognized. Second, the main service/auxiliary service dichotomy is not geared to the customer perception of a service and of total service quality. Only *what* is supposed to be done for customers is recognized. *How* the moments of truth are to be handled, that is, the functional quality aspects of a service, is not included.

A model of the service as a product has to be customer oriented. It has to recognize all the aspects of a service that customers perceive. *How* customers perceive the interactions with the service provider (the functional quality of the service process) as well as *what* the customers receive (the technical quality of the outcome) have to be taken into account. And in addition to this the image and communication impact on service quality perception has to be recognized as well. What has to be planned and marketed to customers is not only a package of services, but a total, more comprehensive, *service offering* (see Grönroos 1987a).

Managing the Service Offering

Based on a well-defined *customer benefit concept,* which states which benefits or bundle of benefits customers seek or would appreciate, managing the service offering requires three (or actually four) steps:

1. Developing the *service concept*
2. Developing a *basic service package*
3. Developing an *augmented service offering*

Finally, a fourth step also has to be taken into account:

4. Managing *image* and *communication*

The *service concept* or concepts determine the intentions of the organization. Based on this concept the offering can be developed.

The *basic service package* describes the bundle of services that are needed to fulfill the needs of customers or target markets. This package, then, determines *what* customers receive from the organization. A well-developed basic package guarantees that the technical quality of the outcome will be good. However, even a good package of service can be destroyed by the way in which the interactions with the customers are taken care of. Therefore, a good service package does not necessarily mean that the perceived service is acceptable. According to the quality models of services, the service production and delivery process, especially the customer perception of the buyer-seller interactions, is an integral part of the product. This is the reason why the basic service package has to be expanded into an augmented service offering before we have a description of the service as a product.

In the *Augmented Service Offering* are included the service process and the interactions between the organization and its customers, that is, the service production (including delivery) process. In this way the model of the service product is geared to the total customer perceived quality of services.

Finally, image has a filtering effect on quality perception. Therefore, the firm has to manage its corporate and/or local *image* and its *market communication* so that they enhance the perception of the Augmented Service Offering.

The Basic Service Package

As noted previously, in the literature a distinction between core services and peripheral services is often made. However, for managerial reasons, it is necessary to make a distinction among *three* groups of services:

- core service;
- facilitating services (and goods); and
- supporting services (and goods).

The *core service* is the reason for being on the market. For a hotel it is lodging and for an airline, transportation. A firm may also have many core services. For example, an airline may offer shuttle service as well as long-distance transportation.

In order to make it possible for customers to use the core service some additional services are often required. Reception services are needed in a hotel, and check-in services are required for air transportation. Such additional services are called *facilitating services*, because they facilitate the use of the core service. If facilitating services are lacking, the core service cannot be consumed. Sometimes *facilitating goods* are also required. For example, in order to be able to operate an automatic teller machine, a customer needs a bank card. However, it is often difficult to say whether the physical things involved in the service offering are goods given to the customer as part of the service production process or are physical production resources. For instance, the bank card can be considered a physical thing (a facilitating physical good), but it can equally be considered a production resource. The ATM equipment, on the other hand, is definitely a physical production resource and not a facilitating good.

The third type of services are called *supporting services*. These, like facilitating services, are also auxiliary services, but they fulfill another mission. Supporting services do not facilitate the consumption or use of the core service, but are used to increase the value and/or to differentiate the service from the services of competitors. Hotel restaurants and a range of in-flight services related to air transportation are examples of supporting services. In some cases physical things that can be considered *supporting goods* are used to enhance the service offering. Shampoo and shoeshine in hotel rooms are such goods. However, the same difficulty in distinguishing between real supporting goods and physical production resources required to use a supporting service exists here. A bottle of shampoo can just as well be considered such a resource.

The distinction between facilitating services and supporting services is not always clear. A service which in one situation is facilitating the core service, for example, an in-flight meal on a long-distance route, may become a supporting service in another context, for example, on a short flight.

From a managerial point of view it is important to make a distinction between facilitating and supporting services. Facilitating services are mandatory. If they are left out, the service package collapses. This does not mean that such services could not be designed in such a way that they differ from the facilitating services of the competitors. The facilitating services can and should be designed so that they also become means of competition and thus help to differentiate the service. The supporting services, however, are used as a means of competition only. If they are lacking, the core service can be used nevertheless. However, the total service package may be less attractive and perhaps less competitive.

The basic service package is, however, not equivalent to the service product customers perceive. This package corresponds mainly to the technical outcome dimension of the total perceived quality. The elements of this package determine *what* customers receive. They do not say anything about *how* the process is perceived, which in the final analysis is an integral part of the total service product or offering customers experience and evaluate.

As the perception of the service process cannot be separated from the perception of the elements of the basic service package, the process has to be integrated into the service product. Otherwise the product concept used by management will not equal the one perceived by customers. Therefore, the basic service package has to be expanded into a more comprehensive model, called the *Augmented Service Offering*.

The Augmented Service Offering

The service process, the buyer-seller interactions, are perceived in a number of ways, which naturally differ from situation to situation. Due to the characteristics of most services, there are, however, three basic elements, which from a managerial point of view constitute the process (Grönroos 1978 and 1987a):

- Accessibility of the service;
- Interaction with the service organization; and
- Consumer participation.

These elements are combined with the concepts of the basic package, thus forming an *Augmented Service Offering* (see Figure 4-1). It is, of course, essential that these three elements of the service offering are geared to the *customer benefits* which have initially been identified to be sought by customers in the selected target segments.

Accessibility of the service depends, among other things, on:

- The number and skills of the personnel;
- Office hours, time tables, and the time used to perform various tasks;
- Location of offices, workshops, service outlets, etc.;
- Exterior and interior of offices, workshops, and other service outlets, etc.;
- Tools, equipment, documents, etc.; and
- The number and knowledge of consumers simultaneously involved in the process.

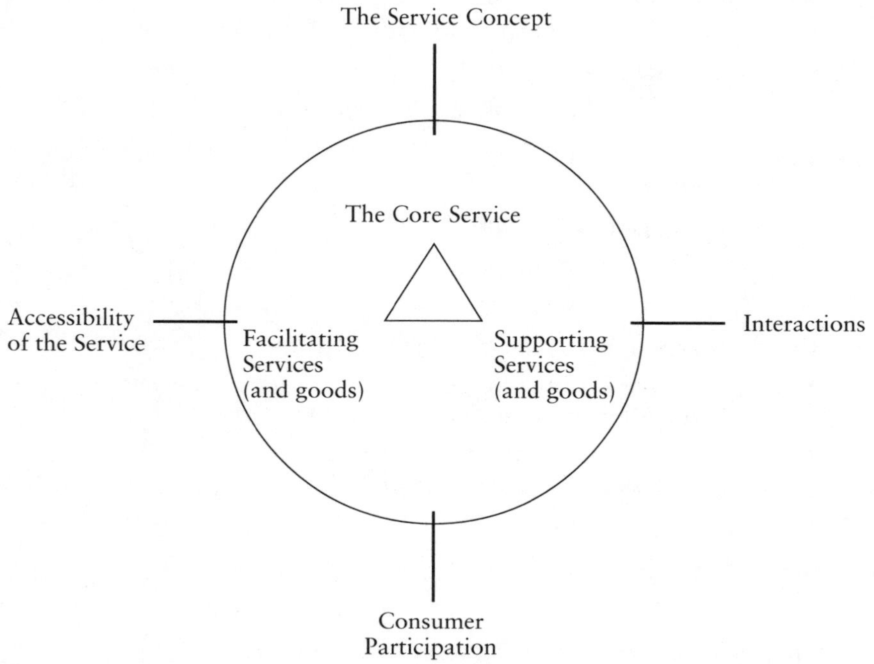

Source: Adapted from Grönroos, C. (1987): Developing the Service Offering — A Source of Competitive Advantage. In Surprenant, C., ed., *Add Value to Your Service.* Chicago: American Marketing Association, p. 83.

Figure 4–1. The Augmented Service Offering

Depending on these and other factors customers will feel that it is easy, or difficult, to get access to the services and to purchase and use them. If the telephone receptionist of a repair firm lets the customer wait before answering the telephone, or if he or she cannot find a service technician for the customer to talk to, there is no accessibility to the service. Even an excellent service package is destroyed in this way. And even if the service package does not deteriorate totally, the perception of the service product may be severely damaged.

For example, for Sonora Laboratory Sciences, Inc., a rapidly growing for-profit laboratory in Arizona, the accessibility issue could be broken down into four parts (Flocken et al. 1988): site accessibility, customer ease of use of the physical resources of the laboratory, frontline personnel's contribution to accessibility, and ease of customer participation. The following variables were identified for each of the four aspects of accessibility:

1. *Site accessibility*
   - The convenience and ease of access from a major street
   - The amount of parking available adjacent to the facility
   - The number of medical facilities located nearby
   - The relative ease of locating the laboratory inside the building
   - Office hours
   - The ease of getting an appointment
   - The size of the waiting room

2. *Customer ease of use of the physical resources*
   - The attractiveness and condition of the exterior and interior of the medical building where the laboratory is located
   - The exterior of the laboratory facility
   - The waiting room
   - The patient rooms
   - The bathrooms

3. *Frontline personnel's contribution to accessibility*
   - The response time to phone calls
   - The number of employees
   - The skills of employees
   - The response time to people walking in the front door
   - The response time to patients in the back room
   - The professionalism of the employees
   - The care taken to reduce unpleasantness of drawing blood
   - The billing procedures
   - The types of payment accepted
   - The insurance arrangements available

4. *Ease of customer participation*
   - The number and difficulty of forms to fill out
   - The instructions given to patients concerning procedures the patient must participate in or do alone
   - The difficulty of these procedures

Interaction with the service organization can be divided into the following categories:

- Interactive communication between employees and customers, which in turn depends on the behavior of the employees, on what they say and do, and how they say and do it
- Interactions with various physical and technical resources of the organization, such as vending machines, documents, waiting room facilities, tools and equipment needed in the service production process, etc.
- Interactions with systems, such as waiting systems, seating systems, billing systems, systems for deliveries, maintenance and repair work, making appointments, handling claims, etc.
- Interactions with other customers simultaneously involved in the process

Customers have to get in touch with employees, they have to adjust to operative and administrative systems and routines of the organization, and they sometimes have to use technical resources like teller machines, vending machines, and documents. Moreover, they may get in contact with other customers. All these interactions with human as well as physical resources and systems are part of the service perception. Again, if these interactions are considered unnecessarily complicated and troublesome or unfriendly, the perceived quality of an excellent basic service package may be low.

For Sonora Laboratory Sciences, interaction between the organization and its customers was broken down into the following parts (Flocken et al. 1988):

- Interactions with medical personnel (their attitudes, attention to the customer, skills in drawing blood)
- Interactions with customer service department (attitudes, phone answering promptness, prompt and accurate answers to questions)
- Interactions with waiting room environment (space, cleanliness, crowdedness)
- Interactions with other customers (communication between patients)
- Interactions with payment or billing system (means of payment available to choose from, readability, understandability of invoices and receipts)
- Interactions with scheduling systems (waiting time for service)

- Interactions between physicians (referring patients to the laboratory) and customer service department (attitudes, phone answering promptness, prompt and accurate answers to questions, calling results, follow-up)
- Interactions between physicians and courier (attitudes, promptness, helpfulness)

Customer participation is a concept used, for example, by Lehtinen (1983 and 1986). It means that the customer has an impact on the service he or she perceives. Often the customer is expected to fill in documents, give information, operate vending machines, and so forth. Depending on how well the customer is prepared and willing to do this, he or she will improve the service or vice versa. For example, if a patient is not able to give correct information about his or her problems, the physician will not be able to make a correct diagnosis. The cure may, therefore, be wrong or less effective than otherwise. The service rendered by the physician is damaged.

For Sonora Laboratory Sciences, the following aspects of customer participation could be identified:

- Are patients knowledgeable enough to identify their need or problem
- Do patients have a reasonable understanding of the time constraints involved
- Is the patient willing to cooperate in the process
- Can additional information be obtained quickly enough from physicians

Thus, in buyer-seller interactions the core service, facilitating services, and supporting services of the basic service package are perceived in various ways, depending on how accessible the services are, how easily and attractively the interactions are perceived, and how well customers understand their role and tasks in the service production process.

Finally, in Figure 4-1, the *service concept* is seen as an umbrella concept, to guide development of the components of the Augmented Service Offering. Thus, the service concept should state which core service, facilitating, and supporting services are to be used, how the basic package could be made accessible, how the interactions are to be developed, and how customers should be prepared to participate in the process.

The service concept should also be used as a guideline when, in the next phase of the planning process, adequate production resources are identified. In a going concern, there are, of course, a set of human and physical resources as well as functioning systems already existing. They naturally to some extent determine which resources are going to be used. However, the development of an Augmented Service Offering requires a fresh analysis of which types of resources and how much of them are needed. Otherwise, existing resources may restrict the implementation of a new service offering unnecessarily. Existing resources must never become a hindrance for successful implementation of new ideas.

In summary, developing the service offering is a highly integrated process. A new supporting service cannot be added without explicitly taking into account accessibility, interaction, and customer participation aspects of that service. On the other hand, a proper introduction of an additional supporting service, or an improved facilitating service, may become a powerful source of competitive advantage.

Managing Image and Communication and the Service Offering

As illustrated by the model of Perceived Service Quality, *image* has an impact as a filter on the experienced service. A favorable image enhances the experience; a bad one may destroy it. Therefore, managing image and communication becomes an integral part of developing the service product. Because of the intangible nature of services, market communication activities have not only a communicative impact on customer expectations, but a direct effect on experiences as well. This latter effect is sometimes minor, sometimes of more importance.

In the long run, *market communication* such as advertising, sales, and public relations enhances, and to some extent forms, image. On the other hand, even an advertisement or a brochure—which a given customer notices and perceives at the point and time of consumption, or slightly in advance—may influence his or her quality perception, at least to some extent. Moreover, *word-of-mouth* is essential in this context. It has a long-run impact on image, but word-of-mouth communication at the point and time of purchasing and consumption may have a substantial immediate effect as well. A negative comment from a fellow customer may easily change a given person's perception of the service he or she receives. The way in which image and communication affects the perception of the *Augmented Service Offering* is illustrated in Figure 4–2.

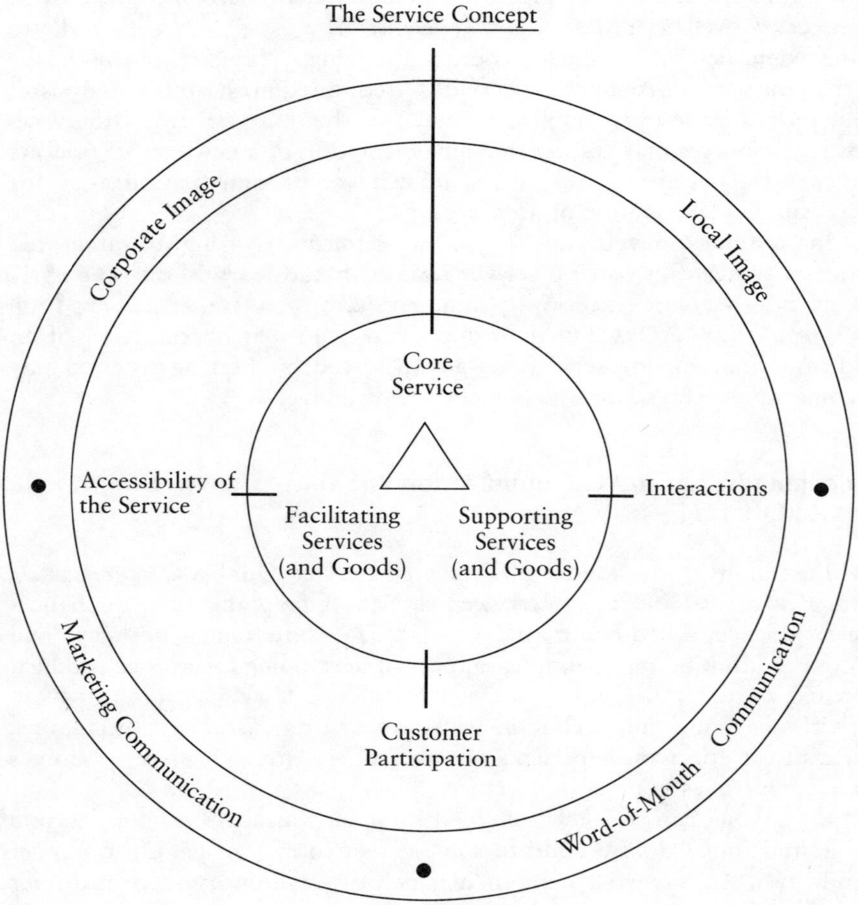

This way of describing how communication affects the perception of the Augmented Service Offering was suggested by Mr. Kalevi Etelä, Deputy Managing Director, AMC Advisor, Management Consulting Partners, Finland.

Figure 4–2. Image, Communication, and the Augmented Service Offering

Developing the Service Offering: A Dynamic Model

The composition of the Augmented Service Offering in Figures 4–1 and 4–2 is static. The model merely lays out the phenomena that have to be taken into account and introduce appropriate concepts. In this section the model of the Augmented Service Offering will be placed in a dynamic framework, which more realistically illustrates how the service as a product emerges. Because services are activities or processes in which consumption is partly inseparable from production (and delivery), the service product by definition is a dynamic phenomenon. The service exists as long as the production process goes on. Hence, any model of services as products, such as the Augmented Service Offering, and of the creation of such products, has to include a dynamic aspect.

First of all, an assessment of the *customer benefits* is needed, so that the development process is geared to customer experiences of total service quality. Next, the desired *features of a competitive Augmented Service Offering* have to be defined as a basis for further planning. These features, following the model of Figures 4–1 and 4–2, should be related to the service concept, the elements of the basic service package, and the various aspects of the service production and delivery process, as well as to corporate and local image and market communication.

The next step is to plan the *basic package,* including core service, facilitating services and goods, and supporting services and goods, according to the service concept. Then, the *Augmented Service Offering* which materializes through the *service production and delivery process* has to be developed, so that the service is made accessible in a way that reflects the service concept, and interactions and customer participation meeting the same criterion emerge.

The next step is to plan *supportive market communication*, which not only informs customers about the service and persuades them to try it but also has a positive impact on the very consumption of the service and, moreover, enhances a desired image.

If all steps so far are properly taken care of, the result should be a concrete offering, a service product, which—in the elements of the basic package as well as in the accessibility, interaction, and customer participation aspects of service production and delivery—includes the desired features, which in turn create the benefits customers seek. However, still another step is required, that is, *preparing the organization* for producing the desired customer benefits through production and delivery of the Augmented Service Offering.

One of the fatal mistakes one can make is to believe that the service, once it has been planned, is automatically produced as planned. The discussion of customer perceived quality, and especially of the Gap Analysis Model, in chapters 2 and 3 demonstrated what problems and pitfalls there are in producing excellent perceived service quality and how complicated a process it is. Hence, the preparation of the organization has to be made an inseparable part of any development of service products or service offerings. Otherwise, as such, even sound and customer-oriented plans can easily fail.

The preparation of organizations for a desired performance involves the *creation of sufficient resources* and *internal marketing* of the new offering to the employees, so that they first understand it, then accept it and feel committed to producing it. In subsequent chapters we cover service development, as well as the concept and phenomenon of internal marketing, at some length.

To sum up this discussion of the dynamic model of the Augmented Service Offering, the first stage is always an assessment of what benefits customers in target segments are looking for and would appreciate. Proper market research and use of internal information, for example, from the interface between customers and the organization, should provide management with the necessary knowledge of what quality customers expect, so that corresponding features can be built into the service.

The first two steps of the process, assessing a customer benefit concept and determining desired features of the service offering to be produced, are separable processes. However, the next two phases, developing the basic package and planning the additional elements of the augmented service offering in the service production and delivery process, as well as the last phase, preparing the organization, are definitely inseparable processes. They have to go together, otherwise the risk is far too great that a good plan will not materialize in anything more than a mediocre service. The basic package may include the correct features. However, the crucial importance to total customer perceived quality of the accessibility, interaction, and customer participation aspects of service production and delivery will not be fully understood or appreciated. Moreover, the need to actively market the new service internally will be neglected, or not taken care of with sufficient determination.

Next, a case describing a successful development and launching of a new, or rather renewed, service will be described. The case includes most of the features of the models of the Augmented Service Offering described in this chapter.

Developing an Augmented Service Offering: The Interrent Case

The Company and Its Service Concept

Interrent operates nationwide in Sweden in the car rental market. It belongs to the Volkswagen/Audi-dominated Interrent Group based in West Germany, but is managed as an independent Swedish firm. It is the top car rental firm in Sweden according to size, and possibly also profitability. Here, the available information is somewhat inaccurate, so a definite statement cannot be made.

Interrent has for more than a decade operated as a distinctly service-producing firm. Says Hans Åke Sand, CEO for twenty years:

> Over ten years ago, when this industry was starting to grow here, we realized that we should not just provide our customers with a car, if they ask for one, which our competitors were doing, and still to some extent seem to be doing. Instead we wanted to position us as a provider of transportation services. We developed a service concept, according to which we *provide immediately accessible transportation solutions to temporarily occurring transportation problems.*

This service concept still holds and guides new service development and marketing strategies of Interrent.

Although Interrent was doing well, by 1986 the competition had increased substantially, and continued to do so. Therefore, it was decided that the car rental service of Interrent should be developed into an even more service-oriented direction. Says Hans Åke Sand: "The objective was to create a unique position for Interrent, where the most important key words were Trustworthiness and Reliability." According to Sand, they wanted to be able to offer something more real and tangible as customer benefits than just "we do it with a smile" or "we try harder."

The Elements of the Basic Service Package

The *core service* was a *transportation solution.* The basic ingredients of the service package were broken down into elements that needed to be designed and planned, so that an "immediately accessible solution to temporarily occurring transportation problems" would emerge as required by the guiding service concept. Both purely *facilitating services* and *supporting services* were needed, and most of the necessary facilitating services were designed so that they simultaneously served as supporting services as well.

The elements considered were (F denotes facilitating service, S denotes supporting service):

- Information about terms (S)
- Reservation (F, also S)
- Delivery of car to customer (F, also S)
- Customer use of car (F, also S)
- Return of car (F, also S)
- Pricing (S)
- Billing (F, also S)
- Payment/directly or billed (F, also S)
- Handling complaints (S)

These are the major elements included in the service development process. Three important observations can be made at this point. First, it is interesting to note how elements such as billing and complaints handling, which normally are not considered services, just administrative routines, can be turned into services in a basic service package. Second, most or all facilitating services, even payment and the actual use of the car, can be thought of as supporting services as well. And lastly, some traditional marketing mix variables, such as pricing in this case, can be transformed into supporting service elements.

When all the elements of the basic package are there, the service will produce an outcome, that is, the *technical quality dimension* of the total customer perceived quality has been planned. However, the way in which the basic package functions, that is, *how* the buyer-seller interactions or the service process functions and is perceived by the customers, is yet to be planned.

Augmenting the Offering: The Goals to Be Achieved

At this point, the elements of the *basic service package* had been defined. The next step was to design these elements so that the basic package really functions in a service-oriented way, that is, so that the service concept is transformed into a working service product or a successful *Augmented Service Offering*. When this has been done, the *functional quality* dimension of total perceived quality is accounted for as well. In the next phase, *accessibility* issues, *interactions* between customers and Interrent, and the *customers' role during the service process* were looked into. Three general goals to achieve, expressed as service guarantees, are general *features* the company decided to build into the new service. They were: (1) A *"Get to the Destination"* guarantee which addresses the operational security of the service; (2) A *"Lowest Price"* guarantee which addresses the issue of cost efficiency *for the customer;* and (3) An *"Trouble-Free Service"* guarantee which addresses any problems related to convenience and accessibility of the service.

"Get to the Destination." To achieve this goal the cars must, of course, be in as good a condition as possible; but as there is always a chance of breakdown a system for taking the customer to the destination if that were to happen had to be designed. It was decided that customers have to be on their way toward their final destination not later than 45 minutes after they inform Interrent of the breakdown. Interrent made an agreement with a security firm which had a 24-hour telephone answering service. If the customer could not continue the trip without assistance, he or she was advised to call the security firm's number. The customer was guaranteed that *within 45 minutes he or she would be on the road.* If no other solution could be found, a taxi was sent to pick up and transport the customer to his or her final destination at Interrent's expense, even if the costs could be expected to be high. This, of course, led to substantial internal discussions, but as it turned out, this "rescue service" has not become very expensive. It has, however, created a lot of good will and positive word-of-mouth. Says Hans Åke Sand: "We wanted to create reliability in our booking and delivery commitment. Our customers have to be absolutely sure that there will be a service available. And we wanted to give our booking center and locations and our subcontractor a strong signal saying that a customer who has a reservation number is entitled to the service, either by car or taxi."

"Lowest Price." To achieve this goal a nationwide computer system was required, so that the lowest possible fee, taking into account the various ways of calculating the final price, could always be given to the customer—and immediately. The nationwide system also enabled Interrent to do this when the car was returned to a location other than where it had been initially picked up. No other firm had this capability. Because of this system, customers did not have to figure out whether they should rent a car on a daily basis or for a weekend, or whether they should choose a no-mileage fee or not. Before, or definitely after, the customer has used the service he or she will be quoted the lowest possible fee.

"Trouble-Free Service." To achieve this goal, it was decided that picking up the car and returning it must be as convenient as possible for the customer.

First of all, Interrent decided that a car could be picked up at any Interrent location, or it could be delivered to company addresses, railway stations, or hotels. Moreover, Interrent decided to promise that the car would be delivered *not later than five minutes* after the time agreed upon. If a customer has to wait any longer for a car, he or she would not be billed by Interrent. Says Hans Åke Sand: "The signal to the organization and to the market is clear: It is not acceptable to deliver a car ten minutes late and offer explanations about unexpected traffic jams." Second, customers are not required to return the car to the same place they got it, but to any Interrent location. And they would be guaranteed the "Lowest Price" quotation at any location, and immediately.

Developing the Augmented Service Offering

Once these goals were explicitly determined and decided upon, the next phase was to develop the resources necessary for implementation. Most of the resources existed already, but some had to be created. For example, the current computer system was nationwide, but it could not fulfill the "Lowest Price" goal, so it had to be further developed. The telecommunication system and the "rescue center" did not exist and had to be developed. As mentioned earlier, a subcontractor was engaged here.

The *accessibility* of the service was enhanced by the actions taken to fulfill the "Get to the Destination," "Lowest Price," and "Trouble-Free Service" goals. The customers had to be well informed about how to react in case of a flat tire, motor breakdown, or accident in order to be able to activate the "rescue activities." The *participation of the customers* was ensured by written information on how the three "guarantees" function both in the cars and on the accompanying documents, as well as verbally by the employees. Information about these guarantees and the benefits they offer was also included in Interrent's market communication when the new service was launched. In this way Interrent wanted to prepare the customers to be co-producers of the service as much as possible.

In order to make sure that the *interactions* with the systems and physical resources would be favorable, the new car rental service required some specific resources. As far as technology, systems, and physical resources are concerned, Interrent already had its nationwide network, where the locations operated in isolation from each other and headquarters and therefore were used to making decisions on their own, to some extent. Also, Interrent had a nationwide computer system, but its pricing system had to be developed. Furthermore, the German Volkswagen and Audi cars were of good quality and dependable. However, the cars had to be maintained and kept as dependable as possible to avoid unnecessary extra costs due to breakdowns. Support by the garage and the mechanics had to be secured. This was achieved by internal information, oral as well as written, to the mechanics, during the weeks before the new service was launched. The "security alarm system" involving the subcontracted 24-hour telephone reception and rescue system had to be developed and the staff of the subcontractor had to be trained and motivated to accept the commitments.

The frontline contact persons in the reservation center and at the locations, also, of course, had to be trained and motivated to fulfill the goals of the new car rental service, so that the customers would experience favorable and positive *interactions* with the employees. The "five-minute maximum delay" commitment and the "within 45 minutes on the road again" commitment caused some internal controversy, but the *internal marketing* approach, headed by the CEO in person, convinced the organization at least to a sufficient degree of the rationale of the new service. And eventually, as the service turned out to function well and without significant extra costs, a total commitment seemed to have been achieved. This internal marketing process had to be squeezed into a ten-day period before the service was launched, so that no information would leak outside the organization ahead of time. Meetings, called "service seminars," were arranged, including oral and written information, and where discussion and communication was encouraged. Hans Åke Sand himself, as CEO, took an active part in this process. The new service, the goals, and the rationale behind the very concrete and demanding promises to the market were explained and discussed. Hans Åke Sand concludes that "the people in the organization perceived the total program we were to offer our customers as a challenge, but they also realized that the firm trusted them, and we achieved a commitment for the new service."

The new service was launched in September 1986. The external marketing campaign was directed toward travel agencies, although there was also a short but well-observed advertising campaign involving the leading daily newspapers (there is no commercial TV in Sweden) which focused on the three guarantees. Building upon its previous good image, Interrent wanted to create a *communicated image* of trustworthiness, and real value and comfort for its customers.

The Results

In August 1986, sales through travel agencies had gone down by 10 percent. Immediately after the service was launched sales developed favorably, improving 15 percent in September, 9 percent in October, and 17 percent in November. Up until mid-1987 sales was 23 percent higher than during the same period a year earlier.

The costs of operating the new service have not gone up to any significant extent. The fear of enormous extra costs following the three warranties turned out to be unnecessary. Also, positive and service-oriented standards have been set for the organization: promises must be kept 100 percent, no unnecessary (more than five minutes) delays can be accepted, no customer must be left without help if a breakdown occurs (on the road not later than 45 minutes after a phone call to the alarm center), the lowest price must always and immediately be calculated and quoted. The effects of these and other standards are even greater because of the trust in the organization that management showed. The goals cannot be fulfilled without decentralized decision-making authority. Top management supports this, and provides the car rental clerks with sufficient information, guidance, and managerial support. The new technology, which includes, for example, the nationwide computerized pricing system, also produces such support.

As Hans Åke Sand says: "We wanted to get rid of general promises to our customers, such as 'We do it with a smile' or 'We try our best,' and demonstrate real excellence and trustworthiness."

Summary

In the present chapter we have discussed the nature of service as products, that is, objects offered to and consumed by customers. As services are complicated phenomena, the offering is also complicated. The Augmented Service Offering was introduced as a conceptual model of the total service product customers perceive when consuming a service. Because of the nature of services, for example, the inseparability of consumption and production, aspects of service production and delivery become integral parts of the service offering.

The service as a product consists, first of all, of a basic service package, which includes elements—core service, facilitating and supporting services, and goods—needed to build in features that correspond to the technical quality of a service. Second, it includes an augmentation of the basic package to an Augmented Service Offering, where accessibility, interaction, and customer participation aspects of service production and delivery are added. Third, as image is part of the customer perceived service quality, image enhancement through market communication is part of the total offering.

Finally, a dynamic model of the Augmented Service Offering was presented. This dynamic aspect of the service product is inevitable, because services are activities or processes that are produced, in part simultaneously, as they are consumed.

5
Service Strategy and Principles of Service Management

Introduction

In this chapter we are go
which is geared to the ch
competition, based on th
customer perceived qual
service organizations of t
the development of a se
profit equation. Thus,
forward, including a disc
contexts. Finally, Servi
defined and some principles of this approach to management are discussed.

Some Traditional Strategy Lessons from Manufacturing

For a manufacturer of goods conventional managerial thinking includes, generally speaking, three rules of thumb to follow in order to strengthen the competitive edge of the firm:

1. Decrease the costs of production and administration, to decrease the unit cost of the products;
2. Increase the budget for traditional marketing efforts such as advertising, sales, and sales promotion in order to make the market buy the goods produced; and
3. Strengthen product development efforts.

Strategic management includes, of course, a range of other elements as well. However, in this context we are going to concentrate on these aspects, because understanding them correctly seems to be crucial to managing services.

For manufacturing these rules of thumb usually make sense, because they are geared to the world of goods. If the costs of production can be decreased, lowered prices can be offered, or higher margins can be obtained. The quality of the goods is the same, because the output of the production process does not change, although different, more cost efficient technology or processes are used. Economies of scale normally pay off.[a] Moreover, more marketing efforts usually will have a positive effect on demand. Continuous product development is of vital importance to manufacturing as well as to services, of course, but the two other rules of thumb may misguide management and even cause serious problems.

An improved profit orientation is needed in services, too. However, if lessons from the manufacturing sector are followed unchallenged, the profit achievements may fail. This is due to the characteristics of services and service production. There is a *strategic management trap*, which management has to observe and avoid.

The Strategic Management Trap

When the traditional rules of thumb outlined in the previous section are followed, the consequences for a service firm or service operation may be those illustrated in Figure 5-1. We may assume as an example, that the service firm or service operation has either financial problems or is facing increasing competition or both. Irrespective of the impact of technology, labor costs are high in most service operations. In order to control costs, strategic decisions concerning personnel are often made: personnel reductions, increased volumes are not met with an increase in the number of employees, more self-service is introduced, people are replaced by machines, and so forth.

In manufacturing, such decisions should improve the efficiency of production, lower the cost level, and have no effect on the output. They may even improve the quality of the goods produced. In a service context some of this may sometimes happen. However, far too often none of these effects will occur, at least not in the long run.

Efficiency is a complicated phenomenon with at least two dimensions, *internal efficiency* and *external efficiency*.[b] The former kind of efficiency is

---

[a]However, the discussion of niching strategies and of the development of tailor-made solutions to customers as a strategic approach, which has occurred in the literature, shows that looking for scale economies is not always necessarily a virtue, not even for manufacturers of goods.

[b]These two aspects of efficiency were in this respect introduced by the Finnish researcher Bo-Göran Ekholm, who also added a third dimension, *product/market efficiency*, which refers to the capability of a firm to combine a given product or set of products with a given market segment (see Ekholm 1984).

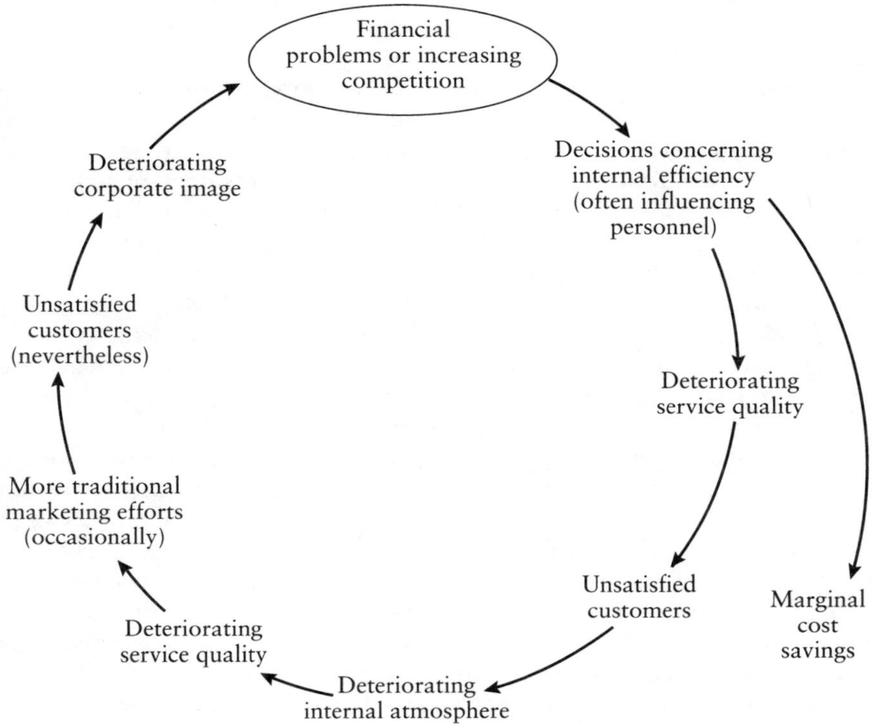

Source: Grönroos, C. (1983): *Strategic Management and Marketing in the Service Sector*. Cambridge, Mass.: Marketing Science Institute, p. 41. Reprinted with permission.

Figure 5–1. The Strategic Management Trap

related to the way the firm operates and the productivity of labor and capital. It can, for example, be measured by the unit costs of the production output. External efficiency, on the other hand, is the way the customers perceive the operations and the output of the firm.

In manufacturing, the interrelationship between internal and external efficiency is of less importance. The customers only perceive the physical output of the production process. In a service operation the situation is often altogether different. According to the basic characteristics of services, the customer gets involved in the production process and perceives not only the output of the process but parts of the process itself. As Tansik (1988) points out: "In service systems a purely efficient manufacturing orientation may well alienate customers and deprive the organization of repeat business, or it may deprive the organization of the ability to sell more services during the existing service encounter. . . . As customer-server interactions increase so do additional sales opportunities, but production efficiency will fall" (p. 8–9).

Management decisions concerning the production process in a service context are, however, too often thought of as having impact on internal efficiency only. This often leads to operations and reward systems that support wrong actions. Said Roger Dow, Vice President of Sales and Marketing Services, from Marriott: "We used to reward restaurant managers for things that were important to us, e.g., food costs. —When have you heard a customer ask for the restaurant's food costs? You have to reward what the customers are looking for in your business."

In reality, as illustrated by Dow, the external efficiency issue is highly relevant as well. If only internal efficiency goals are pursued, the perceived service quality changes. Too often it deteriorates. Thus, an improved internal efficiency may in service operations lead to a negative shift in external quality. The personnel has less time for a single customer, or for paying attention to the customer, and the customer's problems are not rewarded. This may increase waiting times, decrease the employee's possibility to penetrate the problems of a given customer, and leave less time for flexibility on the part of the employee. Self-service procedures and technology, which may be introduced as a substitute for personal service, may help the customer. However, often they change the perceived quality in a unfavorable direction, because the customer either does not accept the new industrialized system or is not prepared or trained to operate it.

Far too often decisions concerning improvements in internal efficiency lead to a deterioration in quality as perceived by the customers. Usually the technical quality of the outcome of the service process is not the critical one, but the functional quality dimension of the process itself. Customers may feel that they get the same technical quality as before, but the manner in which the service is provided has deteriorated.

If customers are unsatisfied, they normally show it to the employees and to fellow customers. Employees in contact with such customers are easily affected by such feedback from the market. The result may be a deteriorating internal atmosphere, in which the employees no longer feel satisfied with their jobs nor as motivated as they may have been initially. Moreover, the direction of decisions taken in the organization, where people are treated mainly as a cost-generating burden, also has a demotivating impact on performance. The decision making of the employer has in itself a negative effect on the internal atmosphere.

This process may be fatal to the service operation. As the internal atmosphere is hurt, the functional quality of the service easily continues to deteriorate. The employees may have less time to perform well, but what is worse, they may also be less motivated to do so. Normann (1984) calls such negative sequences of management decisions *vicious circles*. He also argues that once a firm has got into such a circle, its growth potential is seriously affected.

The destructive process illustrated here and in Figure 5-1 seems to be caused by a lack of understanding of the interrelations of the internal and external efficiency in service competition. Decisions guided primarily by cost-saving intentions have an unexpected external effect. The output of the service operation, the service with a technical and a functional quality dimension, is not the same as it was, as it is supposed to be according to traditional management thinking from manufacturing.

At this point the firm sometimes turns to traditional marketing in order to keep its customers. A temporary boom may be achieved by, for example, heavy advertising, but in the long run the new customers as well as the old ones will observe the decrease in quality and become unsatisfied with what they get. Especially if marketing campaigns make promises which are far above reality, the disappointment will be severe among the newcomers who wanted to give the firm's services a try.

Consequently, in spite of the traditional marketing efforts, in the long run one often ends up with unsatisfied customers. At the same time the corporate image of the firm will change. A decreasing perceived quality and unrealistic promises by marketing efforts have a negative impact on image. Moreover, a growing number of unsatisfied customers and ex-customers creates a substantial negative word-of-mouth effect on image, as well as on purchase decisions directly.

In the end one will probably find that the decisions taken may have caused more or less severe damages. In the worst case, service quality, especially functional quality, has decreased, the internal atmosphere deteriorated, word-of-mouth has become a problem instead of a support, the corporate image has been hurt, and finally, no financial problems or problems caused by increased competition have been solved.

A Vicious Circle: An Example

What is going on in many hospitals seems to be an example of such a development, caused, maybe not predominantly but to a great extent, by a wrong management approach and a lack of understanding of the characteristics of service. When financial problems have occurred, doctors are urged to concentrate on professional and technical issues, which they gladly do, as any professional would, and nurses are requested not to interact too much with patients and maybe not at all with family members. The intention here is, of course, to achieve a more effective use of time and as a consequence of that to cut costs.

The consequences of these actions are a lower level of service quality as perceived by the customers, the patients and their relatives and friends. But this approach from management has a much more severe internal effect, which eventually is perceived by the customers as well. The employees, probably the nurses and staff personnel first, start to feel a role conflict. Patients and relatives would demand more, but management says no. They are not encouraged and authorized to give good service. This rather quickly hurts the internal atmosphere, which, in turn, almost immediately leads to a deterioration of the customer perceived quality of the service. At this point, TV commercials featuring nurses who tell us that "We Care" have no significant positive effect on customers or potential customers. They know better, or will soon find out what the truth is, and not return. Moreover, they will create a substantial amount of bad word-of-mouth.

However, in one respect, such promotional campaigns as TV commercials clearly have an effect. This effect is normally not recognized by managers, nor by advertising people. It is an *internal effect*, and it is *negative*. The employees realize that management deliberately attempts to fool the customers and potential customers. It may, in reality, not be deliberate, it may just be a result of bad and less-insightful management, but it is easily perceived as deliberate. For example, nurses know that they cannot fulfill the promise "to care." They just do not have the time, and they are encouraged not to do that. This, of course, by itself hurts the morale and damages the internal atmosphere even more. Second, nobody wants to deliberately take part in lies and cheating, which such promotional campaigns, in connection with the management actions mentioned, are. It goes against the ethics of most people, and increasingly damages the internal atmosphere. Consequently, good employees quit, they have no interest in saving the face of the employer, and quality continues to deteriorate. And if the financial problems initially were minor, they grow as the internal crisis deepens and the service quality, the reason for the external crisis, decreases. A few wrong management decisions easily lead to a downward spiral, a negative trend which gains momentum once it has started.

Cost Efficiency and the Risk of Falling into the Trap

Any initial cost savings often turn out to be marginal in the long run. Employee absence due to illness or other reasons tends to increase. Extra personnel, without proper training, has to be hired. The work surroundings and the technology used are perhaps not handled with proper care.

The process illustrated in Figure 5–1, and in a sketchy way by the hospital example, can be called the *Strategic Management Trap* of services (compare Grönroos 1983a). By making wrong decisions based on manufacturing know-how only, the organization may be thrown into a *vicious circle* (Normann 1984), or negative downward spiral, which weakens the competitiveness of its operations and causes or intensifies the financial problems that were often the reason for making the inappropriate decisions in the first place.

Why did it go wrong? Why does conventional wisdom and guidelines from manufacturing not help? The main reason is the fact that a service organization is not a traditional manufacturing firm, but an organization with certain characteristics of its own. The nature of services and service competition requires a different approach to strategic thinking and management.

In traditional management thinking the productivity of capital and labor, internal efficiency considerations, are the factors that predominantly drive profit. However, a service firm, or any service operation, is different in some vital aspects. As noted earlier in this chapter, external efficiency, how the organization performs and the output of its operations—in short, the perceived service quality—is what customers experience and evaluate. Actions to improve internal efficiency and productivity as traditionally measured easily have a negative impact on external efficiency and perceived quality. For service organizations, *customer perceived service quality drives profit* (see Grönroos 1983a; see also Normann 1984, Carlzon 1987, and Albrecht 1988). From this follows, among other things, that productivity conceptually and operationally has to be treated differently than in manufacturing. We shall return to this issue in subsequent sections of this chapter.

However, we do not argue that decisions that are only or predominantly related to internal efficiency always lead to negative consequences. Moreover, we by no means mean that cost savings and more effective use of resources should not be attempted. Improved productivity of resources—labor as well as capital—and better internal efficiency should always be an objective, and new technology and production processes that save costs should be used. The main point here is that such internal developments have to be based on the characteristics of services, *so that the interrelationships between the internal and external effects are taken into account.* We want to emphasize that all costs are not equal. On the contrary, there is a pivotal difference between various types of costs, which has to be taken into account when strategic and operational decisions about efficiency, productivity, and cost savings are considered.

Good Costs and Evil Costs

In the turn-around process of Scandinavian Airlines System, the interrelationship between internal and external efficiency, and thus the different impact of various types of cost on these two kinds of efficiency, were recognized. A psychologically very powerful pair of concepts were used by Jan Carlzon and one of his key advisors, Leon Nordin of Brindfors Advertising Agency, the concepts of *good costs* and *evil costs*.

Good costs are costs that are directly productive costs, because they improve the capabilities of the organization to produce high-quality services and thus enhance revenue. Costs of maintaining frontline and back-office operations are mostly good costs. Also, costs of training personnel, goods and service development, and so on are examples of other types of costs which most often are good costs. The connection between such costs and the enhancement of external efficiency is obvious. Evil costs are costs that follow from unnecessary bureaucracy, too-heavy middle and top management layers, big staff functions, and, of course, unnecessarily complicated and time-consuming operational and administrative routines.

For example, if management wants to improve productivity, achieve better results, or just cut costs as a means of enhancing the competitiveness of the firm, what is normally done? Far too often the main actions are to save costs of frontline operations or back-office operations. Staffs and the management layers are left untouched. It is much easier to cut costs in operations than in other parts of the organization. If the firm is facing hard times with low or negative results, training of personnel, product development efforts, and external marketing activities are also often affected by cost-cutting programs. What management does is to *cut good costs without touching evil costs to any considerable extent*. From this follows, of course, that productivity and internal efficiency may or may not improve, but external efficiency and customer perceived quality is damaged, and the net effect is all too often negative. The result is not improved, on the contrary, and the competitive position of the firm is worse than it was.

A clear distinction between *good costs* and *evil costs* has to be made, before any cost-saving actions are even considered. Even if the firm suffers from hardships, good costs may have to be increased so that the competitive capabilities are improved or at least not damaged. Good costs should not be touched. Instead, the existence of evil costs has to be the focus of management. Evil costs destroy profits, not good costs. First, evil costs and sources of such costs have to be identified. Second, actions to eliminate or at least decrease evil costs can and should be taken.

Of course, evil costs may also occur in operations, in the customer contact activities of the frontline, or in the back office, and these should be fought as much as evil costs creating unnecessary bureaucracy. The point is, however, that all costs are not equal wherever they occur. And not until a particular cost is identified as good or evil must actions to eliminate or decrease it be taken. Moreover, even if the total cost level has to be decreased, good costs may have to be increased so that the firm stays competitive and can produce good customer perceived quality.

Scale Economies or Market Economies?

Internal efficiency and productivity of capital and labor must not, however, remain the predominant goals for managerial actions. Decisions concerning customer perceived quality and external efficiency and decisions concerning internal efficiency have to go hand in hand. This is a major shift in management focus. Heskett (1987) has introduced the concept of "*market economies,*" as opposed to "scale economies," to demonstrate this shift in management focus. Whereas economies of scale mean that competitive advantage and profit are achieved by large-scale production of more or less standardized products to keep costs down and productivity up, market economies mean that a competitive edge and profits are accomplished by a closer market orientation. A focus on customer perceived quality and smaller-scale production of solutions that better satisfy customer needs and expectations creates a better competitive position and higher profits than does an orientation toward scale economies.

This approach fits the characteristics of services and the nature of service competition very well. The large and strategically critical interrelationship between external and internal efficiency in service production emphasizes the importance of an exploitation of market economies. However, there are situations in which large-scale production is profitable. The concept of many fast-food restaurants is an example. But even in large-scale operations where the organization is built up in a network fashion, every local outlet is a smaller unit which at least to some extent may face unique market conditions and customer needs. Then, a local orientation toward market economies within the large-scale operation may be a good solution.

There is evidence enough to support the potential dangers of wrong decision making, where internal efficiency is treated entirely separately from external efficiency (see, for example, Grönroos 1983a and Normann 1984). This tendency is especially obvious in larger firms. On the other hand, as long as the market potential is constantly growing, the negative effects of a manufacturer-oriented approach may not occur. When the situation changes and competition gets tougher, the problems occur; and they may develop very quickly.

Productivity, Costs, and Quality

It is, of course, imperative for most service organizations to be able to raise productivity. It is, however, too often said that improving service quality is likely to impact adversely on productivity, and vice versa (Haywood & Pickworth 1988). This notion is based on a lack of understanding of the characteristics of services and the nature of service operations. As was shown previously, it is probably not too much quality that costs, but rather too low quality, which results in a need for corrective action and unnecessary work.

It was said that in service contexts, as much as 35 percent of operating costs may be caused by corrections of others' mistakes, that is, by a lack of quality. This, of course, implies that the productivity of the firm's operation is low. Removing such unnecessary tasks by creating a system that minimizes mistakes is a major improvement of productivity. Probably the new system, with customer-oriented and foolproof technology and well-trained employees, will not cost much more, if at all, to operate than the initial one. However, the quality has improved, and hence, increasing quality (external efficiency) and improving productivity (internal efficiency) have gone hand in hand.

As observed by Steedle (1988), most service firms' measures of productivity are unsophisticated. One of the main reasons, perhaps the single most important reason, why productivity assurance and improvement are considered tricky issues, and contradictory to developing better quality in service contexts, is the manufacturing orientation of the ways of measuring productivity used in many service organizations. Traditionally, in manufacturing, productivity is measured using *internal measurements*. Such devices, when used in service firms, have nothing or very little to do with quality. Typical ways of measuring the productivity are, for example, the amount of meals served per hour or the costs per meal in a restaurant. However, because of the service organization's dependence on its personnel, productivity measurements are most often related to internal efficiency measures of the performance of employees; for example, the number of phone calls dispatched per day by a telephone receptionist handling, say, information issues or complaints. As Armitage and Atkinson (1988) found in a study of large service firms in Canada, the output or activity per employee-hour was the major focus of productivity measurement systems.

Internal efficiency considerations determine what is considered high productivity; "increased efficiency in the transformation of production inputs into consumable outputs," as observed by Mahoney (1988, p. 14). The productivity of the whole operation is seldom considered. Instead, detailed activities such as the one mentioned are measured separately.

In manufacturing this approach to productivity often makes sense, because one unit of produced goods can be separated from another and scale economies are not necessarily a threat to customer perceived quality. However, in service operations it does not make sense, of course, because services are much more complex in this respect. Hence, a more *holistic approach* to productivity is required. Customers do not evaluate the outcome of the production process only; moreover, they do not evaluate single activities, but the whole operation they perceive and get involved in.

For example, if customers are discontented with a restaurant's services, the reason may be related to something other than what is measured as productivity by internal efficiency devices. Customers' perception of low-quality service may be due to the general approach of the waiters, not the amount of time they spend with each customer. If only the latter variable is measured as a criterion of productivity, then neither improved nor lowered productivity,—that is, waiters are supposed to spend more or less time with customers—has any significant impact, positive or negative, on perceived quality. As noted by Pickworth (1987), using restaurant operations as an example," . . . the issue is whether food-service managers should think of their outputs *as meals produced or customer satisfied*. If customer satisfaction is the measure, a quality dimension is also needed in productivity measurement [emphasis by the author]" (p. 43). What is needed in a holistic approach to productivity, in addition to the traditional internally oriented measurement devices, is an *external measurement* of productivity, which reflects customer satisfaction and perceived quality.

Many manufacturers have realized that quality pays and that productivity requires a holistic approach. Ford's "the best of the rest" approach to designing cars is an example of this. The best features and qualities of cars in the world as defined by customers are taken and analyzed and used in the design of new cars.

The use of external measurements of productivity is geared to the notion that external efficiency is more important, or at least equally important, to success than internal efficiency, as long as the internal efficiency aspect is controlled. External measurement of productivity links productivity to perceived service quality. High productivity is of low value if it leads to low perceived quality and lost business. On the other hand, high perceived quality is of little value if it demands low productivity and such a cost level that no profits are generated, at least over the long run. Hence, *productivity has to be monitored both by external and by internal measurement*. External measurements are geared to customer satisfaction with quality (external efficiency), whereas internal measurements are linked to the costs of using resources to achieve a certain perceived service quality (internal efficiency).

Long-Term Productivity Counts

One other aspect of productivity improvement has to be taken into account as well. The above-mentioned analyses may imply that the firm, in order to produce an acceptable quality, has to make investments in new technology and in training its personnel in order to be more customer oriented. In the short run, say, for the first 18 to 36 months, this may increase costs more than it can be expected to generate sufficient revenues. However, this short-term perspective must never guide management decisions. In American as well as most other Western companies there is an established inclination to demand quick results and to reject actions that only pay off in the long run if there are no short-term benefits. This is a devastating approach, and one of the major reasons why American and many Western European firms have problems with Japanese and other Asian competition.

By such an approach long-term profitability may be sacrificed in the pursuit of quick revenues, often without management even realizing this. However, a short-sighted scope easily leads to deteriorating customer perceived quality, which in turn leads to dissatisfied customers and lost business. If the market share is to be maintained, huge increases in the budget for traditional marketing is then required. And in the long run even this may not help. A longer time perspective should, therefore, always guide management decisions. As Jim Unruh, Executive Vice President of Unisys, requires of his organization: "If there ever is a conflict between revenue and quality, quality comes first." This perspective may mean lost revenues in the short run, but by maintaining the quality level, this pays well off in the long run.

An investment program as the one illustrated in this section will probably pay off in more internally efficient operations and in more externally efficient and higher quality services after 18 to 36 months. If the firm in its strive for quick profits instead take actions justified by internal efficiency aspects only to cut costs and that way increase productivity, the perceived quality will suffer, the firm will lose business, and it may eventually be forced out of business.

Improving Productivity and Quality at the Same Time

As has been shown here, it is a mistake to believe that improving productivity and increasing service quality are contradictory. Current research results indicate that modern quality assessment and monitoring approaches, on the contrary, can improve productivity and at the same time increase customer satisfaction (Groocock 1987). In services, this is certainly the case as well as in manufacturing. All steps taken to improve productivity should be based on (1) *a thorough understanding of what constitutes good service quality,* as perceived by the customers in the selected target markets, and (2) *an equally thorough analysis of how the firm operates today* to produce that quality, which resources, human and physical, are needed and which are inadequate or unnecessary, and how effective or ineffective are the systems and routines that are used. Good costs and evil costs have to be identified and kept apart. When these two pieces of research (the external and internal ones) are compared, a powerful basis has been established for improving productivity and quality simultaneously. Next, we are going to discuss ways of simultaneously improving service quality and productivity.

Improving the Technical Skills of the Employees. High-quality service means, among other things, that the employees know how to do things correctly and at the first time. If they have inadequate skills, the technical quality of the outcome of the service process is damaged. However, at the same time, customers will probably have to wait longer, and be more active themselves, to get an acceptable technical quality. Moreover, they will perceive the lack of skills and the corresponding fumbling on the part of the employees. All these aspects of interactions with the firm lower the perception of the functional quality of the interaction process. At the same time, this lack of skills and the need for corrective actions and repetitions of activities hurt productivity as well. Consequently, improving the technical skills of the personnel may be a means of simultaneous improvement of quality and productivity.

Service Orientation of Attitudes and Behavior of Employees. A lack of interest in good service and unfriendly and negative attitudes and behavior on the part of the personnel have a significant negative impact on the functional aspect of perceived service quality. Moreover, this has backlash effect on productivity. Angry customers, by their reactions, tend to create problems for employees on the spot, which slows down the service process. Moreover, angry and unsatisfied customers may complain either on the spot or later on, which creates extra work and hurts productivity. Service-oriented employees, on the other hand, enhance the quality perception and cause customers to support productivity by their actions as well. Of course, if, for example, the employees spend an unnecessarily long time with each customer which does not pay off even in the long run, a productivity problem may occur.

Making Systems and the Technology More Supportive to Employees and/or to Customer Participation. If the operational systems and routines used are considered complicated, difficult to handle or even to understand, this may create problems for either employees or customers or both. Hensel (1988) reports an example from AAA Florida/Georgia, which illustrates how improved systems based on better technology enhanced the possibility and motivation for both employees and customers to handle their part in the service production process. At one time as much as 40 percent of the telephone calls received by the ERS (emergency road service) operated by AAA Florida/Georgia were non-ERS calls. Customers used the ERS number listed on their membership card to get access to other AAA services. For the employees, this created barriers to meeting customer service specifications and made them unnecessarily busy and thus unable to care enough for the customers. For the customers, it often meant busy signals and long waiting times for help. Productivity as well as service quality was damaged. In this situation, a front-end automated device to respond to calls on ERS exclusive lines was installed. A recorded voice directs customers to call a number if they want access to the emergency service, whereas all other calls are directed immediately to the appropriate station. This improvement in the system decreased waiting times and frustration for customers and increased the effectiveness of the AAA services, especially the ERS service. Thus, both service quality and productivity were influenced favorably.

Industrializing the Service Operation. Applying manufacturing-like methods of operations as a means of improving services was suggested in the 1970s by Levitt (1972 and 1976). Generally speaking, industrializing a service means to substitute technology and automation for people. ATM's and insurance vending machines are examples of such an industrialization approach. In some cases industrialization is an appropriate way of improving both service quality and productivity. Today, when retail banks offer ATM's to customers who, for example, want to withdraw cash from their accounts with the convenience offered by such an automated system, but offer personal service when they want to deposit money or discuss financial problems, this way of industrializing the service works well. However, problems easily arise if industrialization is offered for all types of services to all segments of customers in all situations, which often is the case. Productivity measured by internal measurements may increase, but service quality is hurt, and this may have a negative effect on the bottom line, both in the short run and/or at least in the long run. Hence, industrialization as a means of improving productivity and quality always demands extremely careful internal as well as external quality impact-oriented analyses. Mistakes are so easily made.

Increasing Customer Cooperation in the Service Production Process. Another way of improving productivity and quality is to turn to the customer impact on the production process. There are, in principle, two ways of doing this. First, more *self-service elements* can be introduced. However, it is extremely important that this is not done for internal efficiency reasons only. The customers have to see big enough benefits from participating in self-service processes. If they do not find those benefits, perceived quality suffers. The customers have to be rewarded for taking part in self-service, and they have to be motivated to do so. The other aspect of improving productivity and quality by paying attention to customer participation is to *improve the participation skills* of customers. Sometimes customers do not know exactly what they are supposed to do or say, or how documents are to be filled out, and so on. This has a negative impact on the functional quality aspect; it may also affect the technical quality of the outcome. In addition to this, more of the employee's time is required to make customers fulfill their role in the production process. Thus, productivity is hurt as well. Better-informed customers feel more secure, make fewer mistakes, and need less unnecessary attention from employees. Consequently, they are more satisfied with the service. At the same time, there is a twofold effect on productivity. The customers speed up the production process and thus themselves improve productivity, and the employees can serve more customers, which enhances productivity as well.

Reducing the Mismatch between Supply and Demand. Goods can be kept in stock, if demand is low; services cannot. The consequences of this characteristic of services were addressed by Sasser (1976) in the mid-1970s. If the demand curve has high peaks and corresponding lows, service quality will probably be good in the latter situations, whereas at peak times too many customers present at the same time will lead to long lines, longer waiting times, less personal attention, and so forth. At the same time, productivity is low, because too often the firm will have idle resources. Hence, reducing the mismatch between supply and demand is a way of making quality more consistent and better and of improving productivity simultaneously. Using part-time employees may be one way of doing this, but it is not always successful. For example, when retailers replace professional sales clerks with part-time personnel without sufficient training and motivation, service quality suffers permanently, at slow times as well as at peak times. Another way of matching supply and demand is to attempt to manage the flow of customers. Offering better prices during slow periods and making customers change their consumption habits by means of communication are ways of doing this using traditional marketing activities.

In addition to these means of simultaneously improving service quality and productivity, there are others that sometimes can be used (e.g., Cowell

1984). Reducing the service level (quantity or quality), introducing totally new services (credit cards instead of short-term loans), and substituting goods for services (new data transfer equipment replacing cable and mail services) are examples.

Services and the Profit Equation

The rules of thumb from manufacturing described earlier are, of course, intended to improve profitability. It is axiomatic to state that profit equals revenues minus costs. What is not, however, is to state how and by what means revenues and costs are influenced. Figure 5-2 illustrates, in a simplified way, what the profit equation traditionally is expected to look like.

In manufacturing, production, including the production resources used as well as the production processes, and administration, including general administration, personnel, research and development, training, planning and budgeting procedures, and so on, are thought of as mainly *cost-generating* functions. Their immediate impacts on revenues are considered minimal.

Traditional marketing activities, such as product design and packaging, personal selling, advertising and sales promotion, distribution, and pricing, are thought of as the function that *generates revenues*. Production and administration, on the other hand, are considered to be cost generating, thus cost implications are the key issue in decision making. But since traditional marketing efforts are considered revenue generating, marketing is given responsibility for successful external impact on the marketplace. Often marketing is thought of as *the* revenue-generating function.

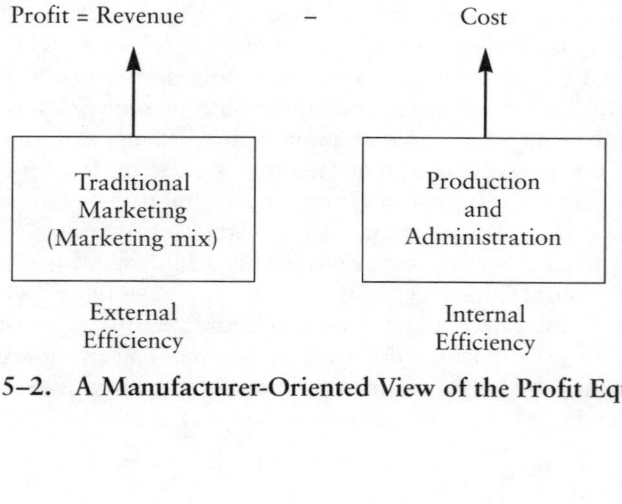

Figure 5–2. A Manufacturer-Oriented View of the Profit Equation

In this way of thinking no interrelationship between internal efficiency and external efficiency is included, nor is a distinction between good costs and evil costs made. As noted previously, in manufacturing of goods this assumption often holds true. There, high productivity of labor and capital keeps costs down and thus drives profit as well.

In order to avoid the strategic management trap one should realize that in a service context the customer relationships are not influenced according to the requirements of Figure 5–2. According to the characteristics of services and the service quality models, resources and activities that have an impact on future buying and consumption behavior can be found in most functions of the service firm. Production as well as administration, including their various subareas, do affect the customers' behavior. As Lovelock and others (Lovelock et al. 1981) observed, operations management and personnel management at least are interrelated with marketing management in a service context. Drucker's (1973, p. 62) view that marketing, from the customers' point of view, is too important to the result of the firm's performance to be treated as a separate function is very valid, indeed.

We demonstrate in Figure 5–3, that decisions concerning production and administration not only affect internal efficiency and costs, they also have an impact on external efficiency and revenues. Thus, the formation of the profit equation changes altogether. The revenue-generating effects of

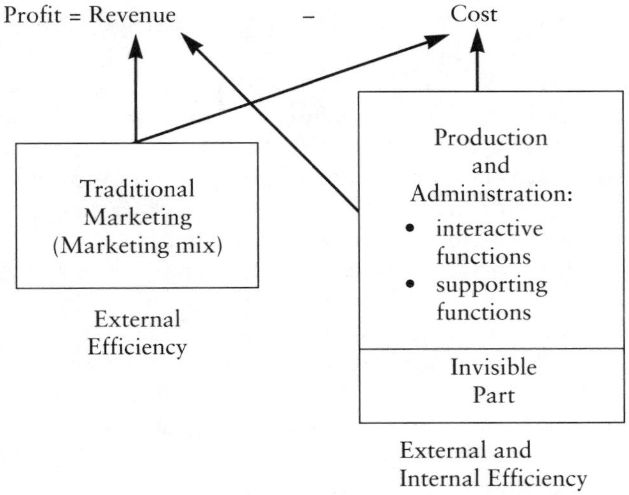

Figure 5-3. A Profit-Oriented View of Revenues and Costs in a Service Context

such resources must not be forgotten in the philosophy that guides the strategic planning process and decision making.

As further shown in Figure 5–3, decisions that simultaneously influence internal and external efficiency should not be made before both the revenue-generating effects *and* the cost-generating effects of such decisions have been taken into consideration and analyzed. Good costs, which are revenue generating, and evil costs, which predominantly enhance bureaucracy, should be kept apart and treated in different ways. The simultaneous occurrence of perceived quality (external efficiency) and productivity consideration (internal efficiency) is clearly demonstrated in Figure 5–3. Moreover, because the customer relationships should be the starting point for planning, according to the marketing concept, the effects of planning on external efficiency may be considered the more important ones. So, in the final analysis, customer perceived quality drives profit.

In other words, strategic planning and management should, of course, begin with the revenue-generating implications of a given decision, but as an integrated process, cost implications should be considered. This is *not* to say that costs are of minor importance. Saving costs, especially evil costs, is needed in most firms, and monitoring costs is always of crucial importance. However, if, for example, a cost-saving decision can be expected to have a negative impact on quality and revenues that is bigger than the cost reduction, it should probably not be made.

Not all production and administration resources and processes can be expected to have effects on revenue. As shown in Figure 5–3, there are interactive functions, with which customers have direct contact, and supporting function such as warehousing, information processing, and other back-office activities, which indirectly influence the perceived service quality. Such functions are critical, because they have an impact on both revenues and costs. However, there are functions that from the customers' point of view are totally invisible, such as some production processes and internal bookkeeping. These functions are only cost generating. Here, the occurrence of evil costs should constantly be monitored.

Industrialization of service production in a manufacturer-like manner can be done in the truly invisible part of the organization. However, when the gains to be achieved by industrialization are discussed, this circumstance is usually not taken into account (see, for example, Levitt 1972 and 1976 and Bonoma & Mills 1979). In the other parts of the organization industrialization has to be implemented much more carefully if one wants to gain cost savings without hurting service quality and revenue generation (compare the previous discussion of good costs and productivity, respectively).

Traditionally, marketing activities (marketing mix) are considered to be more or less solely responsible for revenues. However, this is not true as far as services are concerned, and manufacturers of goods face a new reality as well. As Donald Myles, Vice President of Information and Services from IBM Canada, observed: "Over 60% of our customer contacts are with non-marketing persons, and the percentage is growing." If the organization produces bad service quality, advertising and selling cannot satisfy customers and make them buy again. As a matter of fact, the scope of marketing has to be broadened. We will return to this in a later chapter.

A Service-Oriented Strategy

Figure 5–4 illustrates schematically a favorable process which may occur if *a service strategy* is followed (Grönroos 1983a, p. 128; compare also Normann 1984). Figure 5–4 can be compared to Figure 5–1, which demonstrated the strategic management trap. To give an example, if financial problems or problems with increased competition, or perhaps some other reason, makes it necessary to change the strategies of, say, an airline company, cost considerations and internal efficiency only should not govern the strategic thinking in the firm. Instead, management ought to focus upon the interactions with customers and the customer relationships. Effects on external efficiency and customer relationships primarily should guide the decisions to be made. Of course, cost considerations and the implications for productivity and internal efficiency must not be overlooked. Especially in the totally invisible part of the organization concern for internal efficiency should be given priority. And a distinction between good costs and evil costs should always be made.

Especially in the interactive functions, but also in the supporting functions, external efficiency and service quality concerns should be given top priority. In our example improving buyer-seller interactions, for instance, by increasing the space between seats in the planes, upgrading meals and other in-flight services, and offering the employees appropriate customer contact training, just to mention a few possibilities, would probably lead to improved perceived quality from the customers' point of view.

Such decisions may or may not necessitate more personnel, or advanced technology, but if the effects on revenues overrun the additional costs, such good cost increases should obviously be allowed. Here the difficulties in calculating the effects on revenues are no excuse for ignoring the external efficiency effects. It should be noticed that improved service quality often does not require additional costs. The only thing that is needed, in many

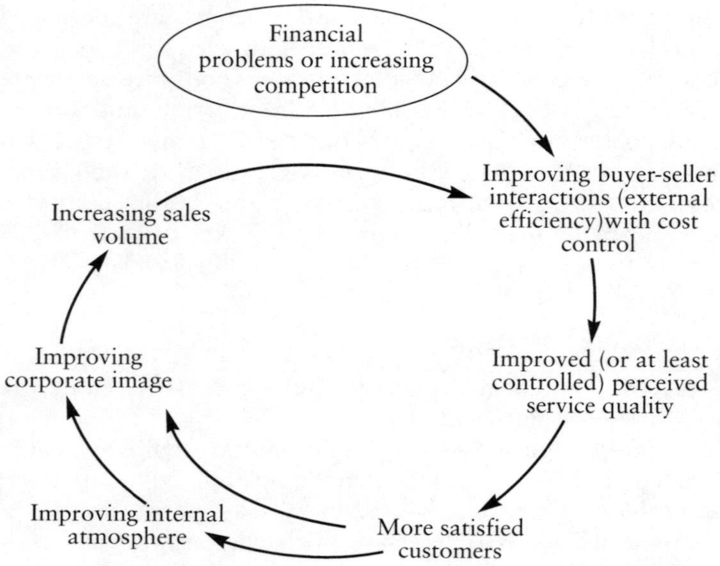

Source: Grönroos, C. (1983): *Strategic Management and Marketing in the Service Sector*. Cambridge, Mass.: Marketing Science Institute, p. 58. Reprinted with permission.

Figure 5–4. A Service–Oriented Approach

cases, is a better understanding of the customer relationships, of how quality is perceived, and finally, of the importance of the functional quality dimension. Once these points are made clear, internal arrangements for using existing resources in a more systematic and market-oriented way can in many cases be made.

To return to Figure 5–4, improved quality usually means greater customer satisfaction, which in turn has a twofold effect. Internally, the atmosphere will probably improve. The increased customer satisfaction is noticed by the employees. The positive effects are often very obvious. Moreover, this favorable trend is supported by the service-oriented strategic direction that management has chosen. Decisions directed toward improving the buyer-seller interactions and service quality imply that management is prepared to accept the revenue-generating power of the employees and to support it. Such a strategic attitude has a considerably positive effect on the internal environment of the firm and on employee motivation (compare, for example, Schneider 1980). Again, this results in increased productivity.

Improved customer satisfaction also has external effects. Favorable word-of-mouth is created. Existing customers may increase their business with the service provider and new customers are attracted to the organization. The corporate image and/or local image is enhanced by positive customer experiences and by favorable word-of-mouth.

Finally, sales volume will probably increase. If internal efficiency and external efficiency and service quality, are controlled simultaneously, larger sales volume can be expected to have a sound financial effect and to improve the firm's competitive position. Such a positive trend may easily continue. The improved atmosphere in the company makes the buyer-seller interactions even better, and the firm will generate more financial resources to be used to back up this trend.

Customer Benefits of a Service Strategy

Good service means certain benefits for the customer. Industrial customers especially may be able to calculate these benefits and see the results on the bottom line. Consumers may sense these benefits more than see them in their purses.

The better the total customer relationship is taken care of, the better the functional quality is, and the less complicated it is for the customer to maintain the relationship with the service provider. Cooperation between the two parties becomes much easier. For example, the buyer can rely on the seller that deliveries will always be made on time, technical service will be good and nontechnical service will be accessible when needed, claims will be handled promptly and with the interest of the buyer in mind, and social contacts will be satisfactory. Not only is it more convenient for the buyer to do business with a seller who can be trusted in all respects, in many situations *such a relationship equals a cost reduction for the buyer as well.*

If the level of functional quality is high and the cooperation between the two parties is smooth, three sources of cost reduction can be distinguished:

1. *less resources* (persons) are needed to maintain the contacts with the seller;
2. the person (persons) involved in contacts with the seller will *need less of their time* for handling these contacts; and
3. it is psychologically less demanding to maintain the contacts with the seller, which in turn *increases the mental capacity* to be used for other tasks.

In many cases the cost reductions that can thus be achieved are easy to calculate (compare Hirsch 1985). The psychological effects of good service may be less so, but the other effects can easily be transformed into dollars—dollars that, for the buyer/customer, can be used productively elsewhere. The seller, in turn, can transfer some of this cost reduction to the price. The benefits of improved customer relationships by a service strategy can thus be shared between the buyer and the seller. This should have a favorable impact on profitability.

The Service Concept

Every service provider needs some guidelines for performance. Overall, the concept of *business mission* is used to determine which markets the firm should operate in and what kinds of problems it should try to solve. Heskett (1986 and 1987) uses the term *service vision* to indicate a service-oriented business mission. Within the framework of the business mission concrete guidelines have to be developed. These can be called *service concepts.*

The service concept is a way of expressing the notion that the organization intends to solve certain types of problems in a certain manner. This means that the service concept has to include information about *what* the firm intends to do for *a certain customer segment, how* this should be achieved, and with *what* kinds of *resources.* If there is no service concept which has been agreed upon and generally accepted, the risk of inconsistent behavior is evident. Supervisors do not know what it is that should be achieved and what priorities to set. The same goes for the rest of the personnel. What we have is a situation in which an organization consists of a range of suborganizations all of which perform inconsistently. This, of course, adds to the confusion.

The service concept should be as concrete as possible so that it can be understood by everybody. To give an example, a Scandinavian car rental company stated their service concept as follows: "To offer immediately accessible solutions to temporary transportation problems." This service concept states that the problems are immediate and temporary, therefore the solutions to them must be quick and easy to obtain. This firm has been very successful.

Depending on how differentiated the operations are and how many different customer segments there are, there can be one or several service concepts. It is, however, important that they all fit the overall business mission. Before a service concept can be determined, careful market research must be done. Otherwise there is always a risk that there will be an insufficient market for the services produced according to the service concept.

Implementing a Service Strategy

Implementing a service strategy requires appropriate actions on the operational level. Here one should notice that a service strategy can be pursued by actions of many kinds. What often is needed is a new kind of thinking, a service know-how. Old rules and ways of thinking may misguide management and leave many opportunities unexploited.

The service impact on customer relationships can in principle be increased in three ways:

1. Developing *new services* to be offered to the customer;
2. Activating *existing services or service elements* in a business relation; and
3. Turning the *goods component into a service element* in the customer relation.

Too often only the first possibility is taken into account, but there are many additional opportunities for strengthening the customer relationships through a better service impact.

The first category of activities literally means that new services are added to the offering. *New services* are typically various consultancy services, repair and maintenance services, software development, materials administration services, customer training, and joint R&D activities. Clearly, this may be a powerful means of differentiating the offering from that of the competition and of adding value to the offering. Such efforts should be used whenever appropriate.

The second type of activities seems much less dramatic and is therefore frequently not thought of as a strategic issue which should initiate major changes in the customer relationship. It may, nevertheless, have a dramatic impact on the offering, perhaps even more of an impact than the first type. Basically, it is a matter of *actively using existing service elements in the relation between the buyer and the seller* in order to differentiate the offering and add value to it and thus make use of them as a means of competition.

Such service elements in customer relations are, for instance, casual advice, order taking, deliveries, claims handling, invoicing, demonstration of manufacturing processes, technical quality control, and telephone reception services. *Customers do pay for these services, too,* although one seldom thinks about it. However, such service elements are far too often perceived more as nuisances than as services. The reason for this is, of course, that they are frequently *handled as mere administrative routines and not as actively rendered services.* If these service elements are thought of as services and the value added that can be created by them is recognized, the firm may improve its position in the new competition and strengthen its competitive edge (Grönroos & Gummesson 1985c).

The impact of these elements of a business relation is normally considered marginal, if thought of at all as anything other than administrative routines, which are only internal and thus of no concern to the customers. However, the service impact of, for example, customer-oriented improved invoicing procedures, telephone reception, and claims handling can be substantial. Moreover, developing such service elements often does not demand big investments or extra costs. Rearranging existing resources and routines may frequently be all that is needed. In fact, more service-oriented invoicing and claims handling may cause these activities to be more effectively handled internally as well, and operating costs can be saved. The customer benefits that can be achieved frequently exceed the additional efforts.

Third, if the goods component is offered in a flexible manner and tailor-made to fit the needs and wishes of the customer, it is in fact used as a service to the customer. Consequently, it is turned into a service element in the customer relation. A good salesperson uses such a sales strategy. However, turning the goods component into a service goes far beyond sales. In production, materials administration, installation, and so forth the same approach is required (compare Harvey-Jones 1989).

A manufacturer of industrial equipment may try to fit its goods as much as possible to the specific needs of its customers. A restaurant may cook the steak and even add spices according to the specific wishes of a customer. In both cases, *the goods component is transformed from merely a physical thing to a customized service.*

Service Management: A Service-Oriented Approach to Management

Having demonstrated the nature and characteristics of a service strategy, we can now turn to the principles of management which guide decision making and managerial behavior in service competition when a service strategy is pursued. This approach to management has been labeled *Service Management* in the Scandinavian literature on service since the early 1980s (see, for example, Arndt & Friman 1981, Lund & Knudsen 1982, Normann 1984, Lehtinen & Storbacka 1986, Clement 1985, and Carlzon 1987). The concept is also being adopted in the American literature (e.g., Albrecht & Zemke 1985a, Albrecht 1988, Zemke & Schaaf 1989, and

Albrecht & Bradford 1990). Hence, service management is a management approach in which management procedures are geared to the characteristics of services and the nature of service competition. Service management is also very much a market-oriented approach. Service management as phenomenon includes the marketing aspect of business or of any organization's customer relationships. In fact, in Denmark for example, the term "service management" has almost altogether replaced the term "services marketing" in the service literature. In the following chapter we shall turn to the marketing in service competition and the relationship between marketing and management.

We define service management as follows (Grönroos 1988b):

Service management is:

1. *To understand the utility customers receive by consuming or using the offerings of the organization and how services alone or together with physical goods or other kinds of tangibles contribute to this utility,* that is, to understand how total quality is perceived in customer relationships *and how it changes over time;*
2. *To understand how the organization (personnel, technology and physical resources, systems, and customers) will be able to produce and deliver this utility or quality;*
3. *To understand how the organization should be developed and managed so that the intended utility or quality is achieved; and*
4. *To make the organization function so that this utility or quality is achieved and the objectives of the parties involved (the organization, the customers, other parties, the society, etc.) are met.*

This is a fairly exhaustive way of describing what service management is. Shorter definitions lose some of the information content, but may still be clear to readers, and they are easier to remember. Hence, we present two alternative but substantially shorter definitions from the service literature. Albrecht (1988) states that "*service management is a total organizational approach that makes quality of service, as perceived by the customer, the number one driving force for the operation of the business*" [emphasis by the author]. Schneider and Rentsch (1987) conclude that firms that apply service management principles consider "service as *the* organizational imperative."

Organization in this context, of course, refers to the bundle of quality-generating resources involved in producing the service, that is, people—personnel and customers alike—as well as technology and physical resources and systems of operations and administration. It is also important to observe that the definition of service management requires a dynamic approach to management. It is not enough to understand which utility or benefits customers are seeking. One must understand also that the benefits customers are looking for change over time, and that the utility or customer perceived quality which is produced has to change accordingly.

A service management perspective changes the general focus of management in service firms as well as in manufacturing firms (Grönroos 1988b, p. 30):

1. From the product-based utility *to total utility* in the customer relationship;
2. From short-term transactions *to long-term relationships;*
3. From core product (goods or services) quality (the technical quality of the outcome) *to total customer perceived quality* in enduring customer relationships; and
4. From production of the technical solution (or technical quality of a good or a service) as the key process in the organization *to developing total utility and total quality as the key process.*

Service Management—A Shift of Focus of Management Principles

Two major basic shifts in focus are implicit in the Service Management principles as compared to a traditional management approach from manufacturing. These are: (1) a shift from an interest in internal consequences of performance to an interest in the *external* consequences, and (2) a shift from a focus on structure to a focus on *process.* These two shifts are of paramount importance. A service strategy, to be successfully implemented, requires both.

As a management philosophy service management is predominantly related to managing processes in which the underlying structures are of less importance. If the structures take over, flexibility of operations and handling of customer contacts suffer. Moreover, the encouragement and support of managers and supervisors decreases and thus motivation among personnel suffers as well. In the following phase, the perceived service quality goes down and customers are probably lost. The new emphasis on process and external consequences changes the focus on (1) the profit equation and the business logic, (2) decision-making authority, (3) organizational structure, (4) supervisory control, and (5) reward systems;

and when there is a shift in the focus on reward systems, other than traditional tasks and types of achievements have to be (6) monitored and measured (compare Lund & Knudsen 1982, Normann 1984, Lehtinen & Storbacka 1986, Albrecht 1988, and Grönroos 1983a and 1988b). These *Six Principles of Service Management* are summarized in Table 5–1.

The Profit Equation and the Business Logic. As has been discussed in some detail in the present chapter, the *general economic focus* or the *business logic* is shifted from managing internal efficiency and the productivity of capital and labor to *managing total efficiency* where customer perceived

Table 5–1
Principles of Service Management: A Summary

Principle		*Remarks*
1. The profit equation and the business logic	Customer-perceived service quality drives profit	Decisions on external efficiency and internal efficiency (customer satisfaction and productivity of capital and labor) have to be totally integrated
2. Decision-making authority	Decision-making has to be decentralized as close as possible to the organization-customer interface	Some strategically important decisions have to made centrally
3. Organizational focus	The organization has to be structured and functioning so that its main goal is the mobilization of resources to support the frontline operations	This may often require a flat organization without unnecessary layers
4. Supervisory focus	Managers and supervisors have to focus on the encouragement and support of employees	As little legislative control procedures as possible, although some may be required
5. Reward systems	Producing customer-perceived quality has to be the focus of reward systems	All relevant facets of service quality should be considered, although all cannot always be built into a reward system
6. Measurement focus	Customer satisfaction with service quality has to be the focus of measurements of achievements	To monitor productivity and internal efficiency, internal measurement criteria may have to be used as well; the focus on customer satisfaction is,

quality drives profit. Scale economies may or may not be a strategically reasonable objective, but it is never sound, and it is always dangerous to automatically consider economies of scale as a source of profitability. Rather, an uncritical pursuit of large-scale production and the potential benefits of scale economies easily turns an operation into disaster. Frequently, the opportunities of developing market economies can be used to create a solid competitive advantage and a basis for profitable operations. And because of the nature of services and service competition, some sort of a pursuit of market economies should probably always be incorporated in the strategic approach.

Service management appreciates the critical importance to success of managing external efficiency and the customer relationships. Internal efficiency needed to function profitably is an inevitable issue, but it is not top priority. It must be totally integrated with external efficiency issues and geared to managing customer perceived quality. As soon as the internal perspective begins to dominate, an interest in costs and managing productivity will take over, but without a simultaneous consideration of the quality implications. Issues related to creating and maintaining excellence and revenue generation will then become secondary and get less or no management attention.

Decision-Making Authority. Because of the characteristics of services (e.g., the inseparability of critical parts of production and consumption) and the facets of customer perceived service quality (e.g., the demand for flexibility and recovery capabilities), decisions concerning how a service operation is supposed to function have to be made *as close as possible to the interface between the organization and its customers.* Ideally, the frontline employees who are involved in the moments of truth of the interactions of this interface should have authority to make prompt decisions. Otherwise sales opportunities and opportunities to correct quality mistakes and avoid quality problems in these moments of truth are not used intelligently. If these moments go totally unmanaged, service quality deteriorates quickly. Of course, a frontline contact employee, for example, a bank clerk, cannot always have the professional knowledge required if a customer wants, for example, a sophisticated financial solution for his or her international business. However, the customer should nevertheless keep the decision-making authority to, for example, ask for assistance of back-office or staff professionals.

If the employees in customer contacts are not given authority to think and make decisions for themselves, they become victims of a rigid system. As Gummesson (1989b) says in a straightforward manner: "You can *stupify* your frontline service personnel by making them robots with discretion to handle only a limited number of standard operations. Or you can *empower* them to handle also deviations . . . thus being more efficient" (p. 85). "Empowering" the personnel is a powerful way of mobilizing the energy human beings have. It means that the employees are encouraged, and trained, to recognize the diversity of customer contact situations and to use their judgment to take care of the situations and solve problems following from deviations from standard procedures so that customer satisfaction is created.

Thus, *operational decision making needs to be decentralized as much as possible;* normally more than one would first consider possible. However, some strategically important decisions have to be kept centralized; for example, decisions concerning overall strategies, business missions, and service concepts. The unique knowledge among frontline personnel of important aspects of the business that are vital to making such strategic decisions should, however, always be used in centrally occurring decision making. First of all, this improves the decisions, and second, it creates a stronger commitment to these decisions among those who in the final analysis will have to live with them and execute them.

The "local" manager, be it the head of a branch in a network organization, such as a bank or hotel chain, or the head of a department in a manufacturer of goods which produces services, such as technical service, deliveries, claims handling, or customer training, has, of course, the overall responsibility for his or her subordinates. The manager is also responsible for the total operation of his or her "local" organization. Hence, the manager has dual responsibilities, one toward the customers, one toward the corporation: *The "local" manager is responsible for perceived service quality toward the customers and for profitability toward the corporation.*

Organizational Focus. Traditionally, the *organizational focus* is to build up and maintain a structure in which management is executed through processes involving legislative control. This often creates a lack of flexibility, fuels centralization tendencies throughout, and is easily a hindrance to the vertical flow of information in the organization. Organizationally, service management shifts the focus away from structure and control procedures to how improved external efficiency with acceptable internal efficiency is to be achieved. This, in turn, requires a more flexible organizational solution, where *mobilization of resources*—management, staff, back-office—*to support customer contact activities* is imperative. The organizational structure that suits this requirement may differ from situation to situation, but some common principles can be identified. How to organize for service will be discussed in more detail in chapter 6.

Supervisory Control. In traditional management approaches, *supervisory systems* are very much related to monitoring the capability of the organization and its various parts in performing their tasks according to predetermined standards. If such standards are met, the employee, or a group of employees, has performed satisfactorily, and is perhaps rewarded.

However, such a supervisory control system does not fit the nature of services and service production very well. By their very nature, services most often cannot be completely standardized. Moreover, for employees to deliver quality services, some degree of flexibility to meet the special wishes of customers or to successfully recover negative situations in the buyer-seller interactions is needed. Here, guidelines and visions are better suited than rigidly defined standards. Only the technical quality aspects of services can be well monitored by standards; whereas, from a competitive standpoint, the highly important functional quality aspects are not very well suited for the development of traditional standards. And functional quality-creating performance cannot easily, if at all, be monitored by comparing it to predetermined standards. Instead, service management requires that the supervisory focus be on encouragement of employees and support. This may require new management methods. In subsequent chapters on "service culture" and "internal marketing" we are going to touch upon this issue to some extent.

Reward Systems. Normally, *reward systems* are geared to the focus of supervisory control. What is monitored can be measured, and what is measured can most easily be controlled and rewarded. Of course, not all, if any, of the tasks and factors that are controlled are geared to reward systems. However, a shift in supervisory focus requires a corresponding shift of focus on rewarding. Generally speaking, service management requires that *producing perceived service quality at some level*—excellent or otherwise acceptable—should be rewarded, rather than a mere compliance with predetermined standards.

Measurement Focus. What is controlled and perhaps rewarded has first to be measured, one way or the other. The focus here must, of course also be shifted, or at least expanded. The ultimate signs of success are customer satisfaction with total perceived quality and the bottom line. Thus, according to service management principles, for service-oriented supervisory approaches and reward systems, *customer satisfaction with service quality* as well as tasks that boost satisfaction have to be measured. Measuring how standards are met and the bottom line are not enough. Internal efficiency criteria may have to be used as well, so that productivity of capital and labor is kept under control. The external efficiency criteria always dominate, however, and monitoring customer satisfaction must never be surpassed, only supported by other measures.

Summary

There are clear and well-defined customer benefits in pursuing a service strategy. However, doing so requires different knowledge to a considerable degree, a "service know-how" on the part of management as well as those implementing a service strategy. The issues of quality, productivity, and profitability have to be addressed differently than in a traditional manufacturing context. This, of course, is due to the characteristics of services and the nature of the customer relationships in service contexts. What is common wisdom in managing a traditional manufacturing company may turn out to be a trap for a service business or for a manufacturer pursuing a service strategy. A "service imperative" and managing customer perceived quality is at the heart of service management.

6
Marketing Management or Market-Oriented Management

Introduction

In this chapter we shall discuss the nature and contents of the marketing function in a service organization. As the chapter title indicates, the traditional view of marketing as a function for specialists planning and executing a marketing mix may not apply where services are concerned. A relationship approach to marketing is suggested and the scope and content of the total marketing function discussed in detail. The concepts of interactive marketing and customer relationship life cycle are put forward. Finally, two types of marketing strategies on a *marketing strategy continuum* and their consequences, namely, relationship marketing and transaction marketing, are explored. Finally, we conclude that for services, marketing can better be characterized as market-oriented management than marketing in the traditional functionalistic sense.

The Role and Scope of Marketing

The marketing function includes four main parts:

1. To *understand the market* by means of market research and segmentation analysis;
2. so that *market niches and segments can be chosen;*
3. for which *marketing programs are planned, executed, and controlled*; and, finally,
4. to *prepare the organization* so that marketing programs and activities are successfully executed (*internal marketing*: see chapter 10).

This approach is based on the so-called *marketing concept*, which states what marketing as a philosophy is. This concept holds that the firm should base all its activities on the needs and wants of customers in selected target markets (see, for example, Kotler 1988). At the same time, of course, restrictions due to the surrounding society (laws, industry agreements, norms, etc.) have to be recognized. This is also called a *market-oriented* view, in contrast to a *production orientation*, where the firm's activities are geared to existing technology, products, or production processes.[a]

The fourth part of the marketing function is new. Normally, it is taken for granted that once marketing decisions are made they are properly executed. However, this may be a dangerous assumption. Especially in services, marketing programs and activities have to be marketed *internally* to those who are expected to actively execute them *externally* or just to act in a marketing-like manner (see chapter 10 on internal marketing).

Traditionally, marketing as a business activity is thought of as a separate function, which is taken care of by a group of specialists organized in a marketing or a marketing and sales department. The rest of the organization, with the exception of a few persons in top management, has no responsibility for the customers and for marketing. Employees in other departments are not recruited or trained to think marketing; nor are they supervised in a way that would make them feel any marketing responsibilities, or responsibilities for the customers. Such an approach demands that the specialists in the marketing department are the only persons who have an impact on the customers' views of the firm and on their buying behavior. In many consumer packaged goods situations this is the case. If the product is a preproduced item with no need for service or other contacts between the firm and its customers, marketing specialists are clearly capable of taking care of the customer relationships. Good market research, packaging, advertising campaigns, and pricing and distribution decisions by the marketing specialists lead to good results.

Figure 6–1 demonstrates the traditional place of marketing according to most textbooks on marketing and marketing management. The arrow pointing up indicates that the marketing specialists acquire information about the market, for example, demand analyses and buying behavior analyses, through market research. The downward arrow, on the other hand, illustrates the planning and executing of marketing mix activities. However, as soon as we get out of the area of consumer packaged goods, the situation changes. Already, as far as consumer durables are concerned, new elements appear in the relationship between buyer and seller. Many

[a]It should be notices, however, that a "production orientation" is not always negative. For example, many high-technology solutions would have been substantially delayed if the entrepreneurs and manufacturers had waited for specific signals from the market.

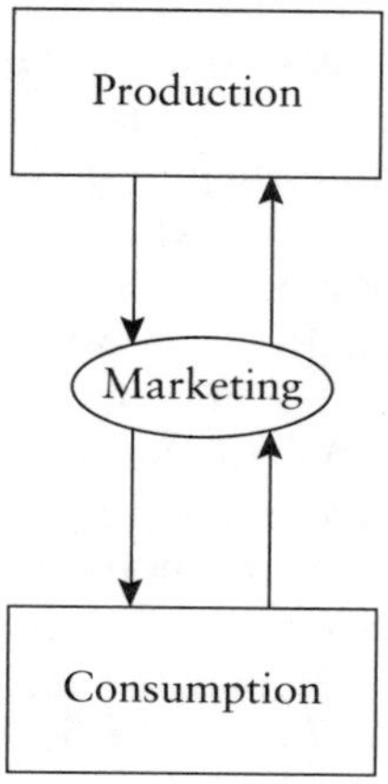

Figure 6–1. The Traditional Role of Marketing

durables need deliveries, installing, claims handling, and service. As soon as this happens, the prerequisites of Figure 6–1 are not totally valid anymore.

When services are concerned, the interface between the firm and the customer grows. This was first observed in a major services marketing context by Rathmell in 1974 (see Rathmell 1974). Moreover, the customer no longer acts passively, but takes an active part in the service production process. Also, in industrial marketing, this is often the case (Håkansson 1982).

What Is Marketing?

Marketing as a phenomenon can be approached in many ways. Far too often marketing is considered a set of tools and techniques only. This, however, is a dangerous way of introducing marketing into any organization, and especially into an organization producing services. If marketing is considered a set of tools only, marketing remains the responsibility of a group of marketing specialists only, who are familiar with these tools and know how to handle them. The rest of the organization, for example, the people involved in operations, personnel, and design and development of technology and systems, are not concerned with marketing, which in reality means that they are not interested in the customers and their desires and wishes.

Kotler (1973) distinguishes, among other things, between marketing as a *philosophy* and a *craft*. Focusing on the tools and techniques of marketing is to concentrate on marketing as a craft. However, we have to view marketing in a much larger context. The marketing activities where these tools and techniques are used do not lead to good results if the heart is not involved. For example, a per se well designed and executed advertising campaign will not lead to good results if campaign promises are not fulfilled by, for instance, the operations people, or the delivery function, which are supposed to provide the customers with the service promised. If this happens, the tool, advertising, may have been used successfully, viewed in isolation from other activities of the organization, but marketing still fails. The heart was not involved in the process.

Marketing as a *philosophy,* the marketing concept, has to guide all people, functions, and departments of an organization. It has to be understood and accepted by everyone, top management and the errand boy alike. Marketing should, first of all, be an *attitude of mind.* This is the foundation of successful marketing.

Second, successful marketing requires an appropriate *way of organizing* the firm. Various departments involved in giving and fulfilling promises have to be able to compare notes and coordinate plans and their execution, and they have to be willing to do this. The traditional disputes and lack of willingness to collaborate or even talk to each other between sales and marketing people on the one hand and design and production people on the other, and even between design and production people, are classic examples of situations in which firms are not organized the marketing way (compare, for example, Lee Iacocca's description of the situation at Chrysler; Iacocca 1984).

In today's competition, firms cannot afford to maintain barriers between functions and departments anymore. The marketing philosophy has to spread throughout the organization, and the organizational solutions will have to support the acceptance of this philosophy. As Benson Shapiro from Harvard Business School says: "The old interfunctional barriers which existed between, for example, the sales force, manufacturing, and operations executives, and the engineering/product development function, cannot be allowed to continue. People from different functional areas must work together as a well coordinated team" (Salmond 1988, p. 20; see also Peters 1988b). Hence, *marketing is a set of ideas which must be integrated throughout the entire organization and overseen by top management.*

Only finally is marketing a *set of tools, techniques and activities.* This is, of course, an important aspect of marketing because it is the one that shows and that customers are exposed to. But this is also the reason for much of the misunderstanding in many practical situations, where marketing as a phenomenon is predominantly or only thought of as these tools, techniques, and activities: for example, as packaging, promotion, distribution activities, and pricing. However, if marketing is viewed in this limited way, it will most probably fail or lead to limited results only.

To sum up, *marketing is*, in this order of importance (compare Cowell 1984):

1. an *attitude of mind* or a *philosophy* guiding the overall thinking in the organization, in decision making as well as in execution of plans decided upon;
2. a *way of organizing* various functions and activities of the firm (or any organization); and
3. a *set of tools, techniques, and activities*, which is what customers and other publics of the organization are exposed to.

The Customer Relationship Life Cycle

Far too often people in the organization view customers as an abstract phenomenon or a mass which always is present somewhere. Customers are seen in terms of numbers. When someone stops being a customer, there are always new potential customers to take their place. Customers, individuals and organizations alike, are numbers only. In reality this is, of course, not true. Every single customer forms a customer relationship with the seller, which the firm has to develop and maintain. *Customer relationships are not just there; they have to be earned.* And the same goes for relationships with distributors, suppliers, and other publics.

It may be useful to view the progress of a customer relationship as a life cycle (Grönroos 1983a). The concept of the *Customer Relationship Life Cycle* is illustrated in Figure 6–2. A potential customer, who may be unaware of a firm and its services, is in the *initial stage* of the life cycle. If this individual, or an industrial customer, has a need which he or she feels that the firm may be able to satisfy, the customer may become aware of the firm's services and get into the second stage of the life cycle, the *purchasing process.*

During the purchasing process the potential customer evaluates the service in relation to what he or she is looking for and prepared to pay for. If the outcome of this process is positive, the customer decides to try the service, that is, make a *first purchase.* This takes the customer into the third stage of the life cycle, the *consumption process* (or *usage stage*, which may be a more adequate term in a business-to-business context). During this process the customer may observe the firm's ability to take care of his or her problems and provide services, which the customer perceives have an acceptable technical and functional quality. If the customer is satisfied, the

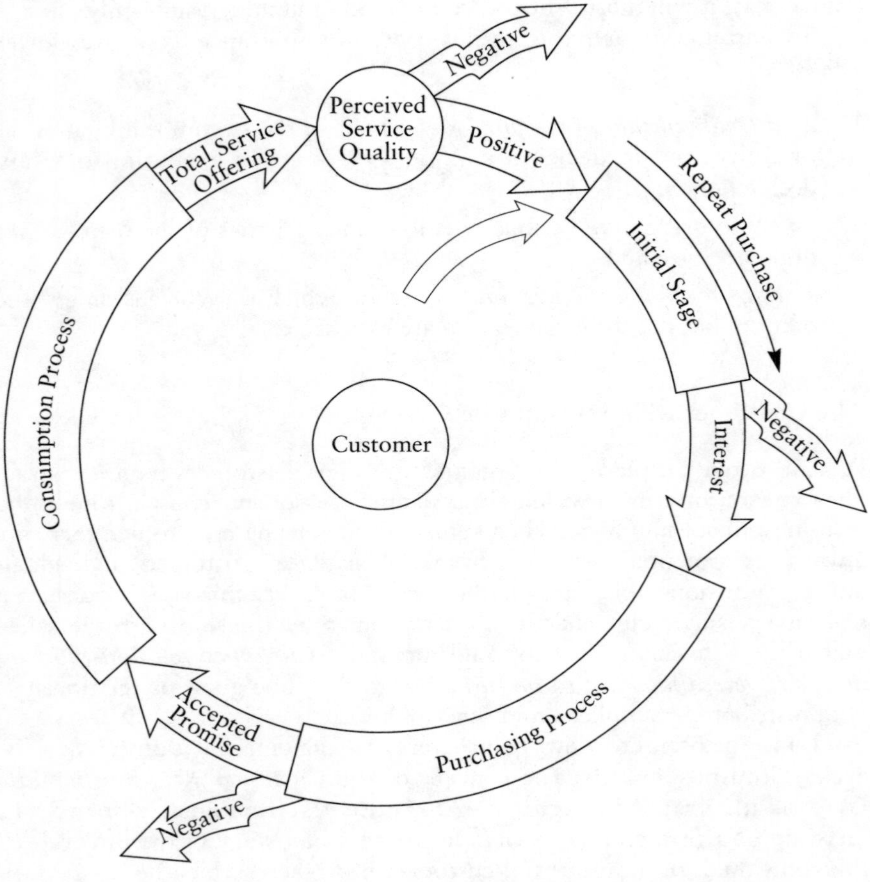

Source: Grönroos, C. (1983): *Strategic Management and Marketing in the Service Sector*. Cambridge, Mass.: Marketing Science Institute, p. 70. Reprinted with permission.

Figure 6–2. The Customer Relationship Life Cycle

probability that the customer relationship will continue and a new or prolonged consumption or usage process will follow is greater than it would be if the customer becomes unhappy with the service.

The customer may leave the circle at any stage, or may stay within the circle and go on to the following stage. After the consumption or usage process the customer may either leave or decide to buy from the same firm the next time he or she needs a similar service, or may decide to continue using the service provider. Obviously, the marketing efforts of the firm will have an impact on the decision of the customer. The objectives of the firm's marketing program and the marketing activities to be used depend on which phase of the customer relationship life cycle is at hand. The firm should therefore recognize (1) where in the customer relationship life cycle its various groups of target customers are, and (2) which marketing resources and activities are effective at the different stages of the life cycle.

The firm will have to recognize that the position of a customer in the life cycle has substantial marketing consequences. At each stage the *objective* of marketing and the *nature* of marketing—the marketing resources and activities that are effective—will be different (see Figure 6–3). At the *initial stage* the objective of marketing is to *create interest* in the firm and its services. At the second stage, the *purchasing process,* the *general interest should be turned to sales.* The potential customer (or an industrial buyer) should realize that *accepting the promises* concerning the future problem solving offering of the firm is a good option. During the *consumption process* (usage process) the customer should get *positive experiences* of the firm's ability to take care of his or her problems. Thus, *resales, cross sales, and enduring customer relationships should be achieved.*

Managing the Customer Relationship Life Cycle: An Example

As an illustration of a long-range management of customer relationships, we may consider the activities of a transportation company offering transportation services by sea. The firm operates in a consumer market as well as in an industrial market, offering both transportation services and conference arrangements to business and other organizations. This example describes how the customer relationships are managed for conference services. It is schematically illustrated in Figure 6–3.

Through advertising efforts and various kinds of public relations activities the company attempts to make potential customers interested in it as a possible conference operator. Occasionally, personal selling efforts are also resorted to. In addition, it relies heavily on word-of-mouth to influence potential customers and on references promoting the idea of using its ships as conference sites. The marketing activities applied at this stage are mostly very traditional ones, supported by indirect promotion drawing on the firm's reputation and word-of-mouth communication.

When a potential customer contacts the transportation company the activities become more specifically directed toward the unique needs of that

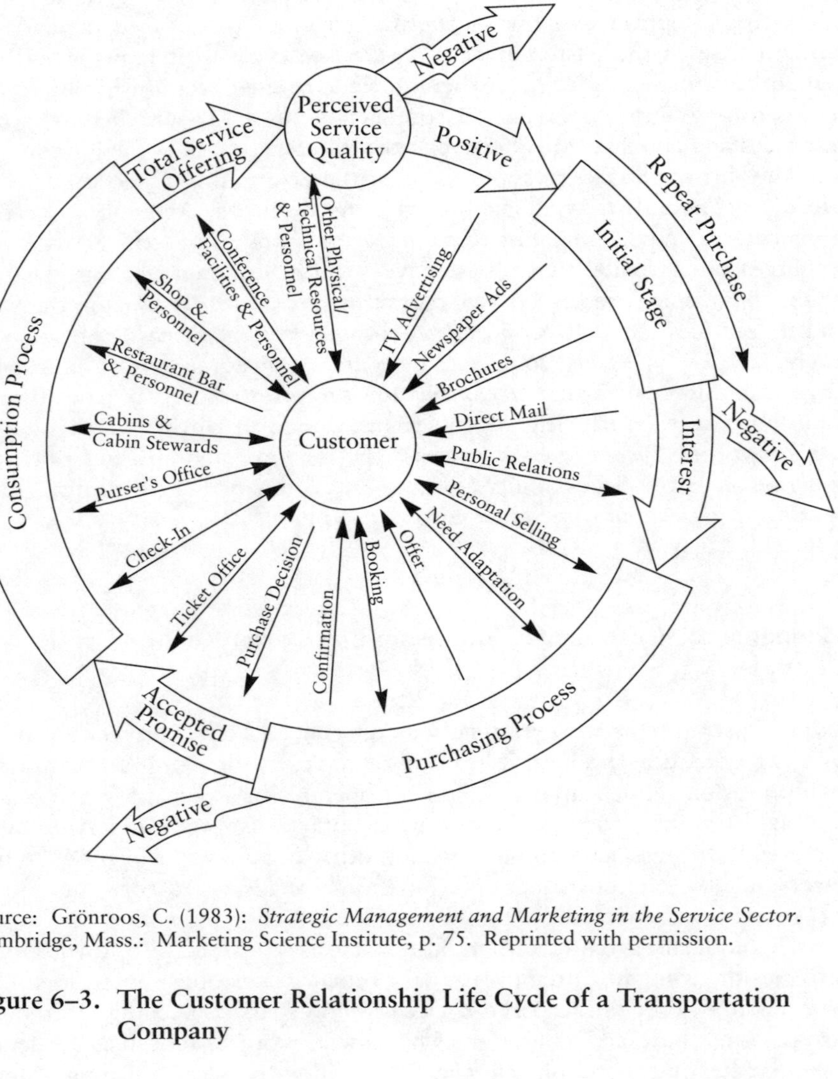

Source: Grönroos, C. (1983): *Strategic Management and Marketing in the Service Sector*. Cambridge, Mass.: Marketing Science Institute, p. 75. Reprinted with permission.

Figure 6–3. The Customer Relationship Life Cycle of a Transportation Company

customer. The purchasing process starts. At this stage a conference service that corresponds to the wishes of the customer and to the customer's conference budget must be designed. Here the output of the process, accepted promises and a first purchase, is to a great extent the result of personal selling efforts. The salesperson will have to find out what the customer really desires. His or her ability to negotiate is considered critical to success at this point. The customer should be offered a conference design, which will satisfy him or her both during and after the conference, rather than merely a minimum budget design which may seem to correspond to the customer's initially expressed needs but which in the long run will turn out to be a disappointment. The salesperson is, therefore, encouraged to think of himself or herself as a consultant more than anything else.

If the purchasing process comes to a successful end, the potential customer will accept the promises by the transportation firm and buy a conference service. The firm cannot, however, stop considering the customer as soon as the purchase decision is made. The customer relationship has to be managed with equal care throughout the consumption or usage process. During the consumption process, when the conference service is consumed and experienced and at the same time produced, a number of *moments of truth*, or *moments of opportunity* occur. As stated earlier, if the moments of truth go unmanaged, the quality of the service probably deteriorates and the customer may be lost. Moreover, opportunities to create more business are badly exploited.

The company attempts to produce a service that corresponds to the expectations of the customer. The conference facilities, arrangements for meals and accommodation, and the appearance and performance of the personnel onboard are considered to be of utmost importance to the success or failure of the company as a conference operator in the mind of the customer.

By appropriately designing the conference facilities as well as other physical surroundings—for example, cabin design, access to telex and telephone communication and computer equipment—and by conducting internal training programs to improve the customer-oriented performance and service-mindedness of its employees, the firm tries to guarantee that the customer, the conference participants, and, of course, other passengers, too, leave the ship in a state of satisfaction and with a favorable image of the transportation company and its services in mind. Eventually, the customer and the conference participants will probably return to the company when a need for conference services or other transportation services occurs. Furthermore, it is expected that they will have a considerable impact on potential customers, through word-of-mouth, resulting in increased interest in the firm and its services.

Defining Marketing: The Marketing Mix Approach

In this and subsequent sections we are going to discuss how marketing in practice can be managed. The marketing concept, which was described in the first section of this chapter, is transformed into marketing in practice in the standard literature on *marketing management* (for example, Kotler 1988). There are dozens of textbooks covering the topic in more or less the same manner. In this approach to marketing the core of marketing is the *marketing mix*. The marketer is viewed as a "mixer of ingredients" (an expression originally used by James Culliton in a study on marketing costs in 1948; see Borden 1964) who plans various means of competition and blends them into a "marketing mix" (this concept was introduced by Neil Borden; see, for example, Borden 1964), so that a profit function is optimized, or rather satisfied. Pedagogically, the marketing mix of different means of competition has been labeled the 4 P's (McCarthy 1960).

Traditionally, the 4 P's are *product, place, price*, and *promotion*. In a renewed definition from 1985 marketing, according to the marketing mix approach, is described as follows: "Marketing is the process of planning and executing the *conception, pricing, promotion* and *distribution* of ideas, goods and services to create exchange and satisfy individual and organizational objectives [emphasis by the author]" (Marketing News 1985).

Recently the P's of the marketing mix have been found to be too limited. Judd (1987) argues for *people* as a fifth P. A voice from the practice of services marketing, that of Roger Dow, Vice President of Sales and Marketing Services from Marriott Hotels and Resorts, puts it even more bluntly: "I think the 4 P's of services marketing are People, People, People, and People." In the context of *megamarketing* Kotler (1986), adding *public relations* and *politics* has expanded them to 6 P's. In services marketing researchers have found as many as 7 P's (Booms & Bitner 1982).

There are research approaches to marketing in which this way of defining the function is not considered very valid. Such approaches are the *Interaction/Network approach* to industrial marketing (see Håkansson 1982) and the *Nordic School approach* to services marketing (see Grönroos 1983a and 1987c, Grönroos & Gummesson 1985a, and Gummesson 1987c and 1987d).

The marketing mix approach is considered too limited, although it includes activities that are important and often even central components of marketing. Dixon and Blois (1983) have gone further in their criticism of the 4 P's. They state that the marketing mix approach is badly fit to fulfill the requirements of the marketing concept. And they conclude that ". . . indeed it would not be unfair to suggest that far from being concerned with customer's interests (ie: somebody for whom something is done) the views implicit in the 4 P's approach is that the customer is somebody to whom something is done!" (p. 4).[b] In line with this argument we have suggested in a recently published article that the marketing mix and its 4 P's constitute a production-oriented definition of marketing, and not a market-oriented one (Grönroos 1989a).

Defining marketing according to the marketing mix approach is like using a list of objects as a definition. Such a way of defining a phenomenon can never be considered the most valid one. A list never includes all relevant elements, it does not fit all situations, and it becomes obsolete. The extensions of the number of P's do not offer a fundamental improvement to the definition. As a matter of fact, the need during the 1980's to add new categories of marketing variables or P's is a symptom of the weakness of the marketing mix approach, and demonstrates as well as anything that, as a general marketing model, the marketing mix approach has failed. Still, it may very well be valid and helpful in some contexts, such as for consumer packaged goods.

It is interesting to note that Borden's original marketing mix was a list of twelve elements, and that it was not intended to be a definition at all. Also, Borden considered these twelve elements of the marketing mix as guidelines only, which probably would need to be reconsidered in any given situation. This is a fact that advocators of the 4 P's and of today's marketing mix approach seem to have totally forgotten. The 4 P's represent a significant oversimplification of Borden's original concept (compare Cowell 1984).

Unfortunately, the 4 P's of the marketing mix have become an undisputable paradigm, the validity of which is taken for granted (Kent 1986 and Grönroos 1989a). Kent (1986), referring to them as the "holy quadruple . . . of the marketing faith . . . written in tablets of stone" (p. 146), states that the "mnemonic of the four P's, by offering a seductive sense of simplicity to students, teachers and practitioners of marketing, has become an article of faith. Among the consequences of this have been a lack of empirical study into what are the key marketing variables and how they

---

[b]It is interesting to notice the observation by Dixon and Blois (1983) that the 4 P's ". . . fundamentally represent little more than micro-economic theory as developed 50 years ago. Thus Joan Robinson's (1933) writing discusses the subdivision of market and the firm's response through the use of the price elements of the 4 P's. At the same time Chamberlain (1933) recognizes that all aspects of the product, location, communication, as well as price may be altered with subsequent effects on demand," (p. 5). Chamberlain's basic decision variables were price, product, and promotion. Even before the introduction of the 4 P's, the microeconomic-oriented so-called Copenhagen School introduced an expanded view along the same lines, the *parameter theory*, which, in fact, was more developed than the 4 P's of today's marketing literature (see Kjaer-Hansen 1945, Rasmussen 1955, and Mickwitz 1959).

are perceived and used by marketing managers, a neglect of process in favour of structure and a neglect of product range considerations" (p. 145).

Particularly in services marketing and industrial marketing, the marketing mix approach frequently does not cover all resources and activities and the processes that appear in the customer relationships at various stages of the customer relationship life cycle. As can be seen from Figure 6–3, there are especially during the consumption process a range of contacts between the service firm and its customer which are outside the traditional marketing function as defined by the 4 P's of the marketing mix. Managing and operating these contacts (for example, the conference facilities, the cabins, and the restaurants, and managing the employees onboard) are the responsibility of operations and other nonmarketing departments only. Nevertheless, these contacts—buyer-seller interactions—have an immense impact on the future buying behavior of the customers as well as on word-of-mouth; *that is, they have marketing implications*, and should therefore be considered marketing resources and activities and managed as such.

In conclusion, the marketing mix and its 4 P's as descrided in today's textbooks represent a significant oversimplification of Borden's original notion of the marketing mix. In fact, it is almost unbelievable how the 4P model, which represents a never thoroughly tested belief from the world of consumer packaged goods of the 1950's and 1960's, is still today widely considered *the* marketing model for the 1990's.

Defining Marketing: A Relationship Approach

According to the alternative approach to defining what marketing is as mentioned in the previous section, marketing is considered to revolve around *customer relationships*, where the objectives of the parties involved are met through various kinds of exchanges. Customer relationships is the key concept here. As Donald Myles, Vice President of Information and Services from IBM Canada, observed: "Building customer relationships is our most important task. And everyone is involved in this process." Exchanges take place in order to establish and maintain such relationships.

The relationship approach to marketing is based on a systems approach, introduced in the marketing literature by Alderson in 1950 and developed by, for example, Bertalanffy (1950) and Boulding (1956). A systems-oriented approach to marketing can be found in many marketing textbooks from the 1950's and 1960's (e.g., Alderson 1957 and 1965, Fisk 1967, and Fisk & Dixon 1967). Eventually, however, the marketing mix overran the systems-based texts, apparently because of the pedagogical virtues of the 4 P's and the ease with which the marketing mix can be used in classrooms *and* practical marketing planning. However, these advantages do not make the marketing mix theoretically more sound.

Based on the systems approach, Alderson (1957) defined marketing as "the matching of segments of supply and demand" (p. 199). Implicit in this definition is a mutual relationship between parties. *Long-term relationships* with customers are especially important (Gummesson 1987d). In the long run, short-term relationships, where the customers come and go, are normally more expensive to develop. The marketing budget needed to create an interest in the firm's offerings and make potential customers accept the firm's promises is often very high. As Berry (1983) observes, "clearly, marketing to *protect the customer base* is becoming exceedingly important to a variety of service industries" (p. 25). Jackson (1985a) adds that, in very many situations, long-term relationships are profitable in industrial marketing as well (also compare the perspective of the IMP Group: see, for example, Håkansson 1982.) Of course, new customers, even those who perhaps make one purchase only, are still desirable, however, in most situations the emphasis should be on developing and maintaining enduring, long-term customer relationships. As Tom Peters puts it: "Most firms have long engaged in warlike relationships with customers—the ultimate user of the product (good) or service (witness the auto industry's approach to warranty claim adjudication). . . . *Yet in today's more competitive setting, developing lifelong customer relationships is paramount* [emphasis by the author]" (Peters 1988a, p. 10).

This long-term perspective has become more and more recognized in services marketing (e.g., Grönroos 1980 and Berry 1983) as well as in industrial marketing (e.g., Håkansson 1982 and Jackson 1985a). If close and long-term relationships can be achieved, the possibility that this will lead to continued exchanges at a profit is high. The same goes for both consumer markets and industrial markets. Furthermore, one should observe that in many situations there are several parties involved in a relation. The buyer and seller act in a *network*, consisting of, for example, suppliers, subcontractors, other customers, the customers' customers, financial organizations, and political decision makers. Especially in a business-to-business relationship context the whole network may become part of the customer relationship and may have an impact on the development of the relation (Håkansson 1982).

The Exchange of Promises

The concept of *promises* as an integral part of marketing vocabulary has been stressed by the Finnish researcher Calonius (1986 and 1988). This concept is by no means new, not even in the marketing literature, but his way of emphasizing it and including it in a buying behavior and marketing framework is unique. In establishing and maintaining customer relationships the seller gives a set of promises concerning, for example, goods, services or systems of goods and services, financial solutions, materials administration, transfer of information, social contacts, and a range of future commitments. On the other hand, the buyer gives another set of promises concerning his or her commitments in the relationship. Then, the promises have to be kept on both sides if the relationship is to be maintained and further developed for the mutual benefit of the parties involved.

The promise concept and the exchange concept are equally important elements of the customer relationships. In fact, *promises about the exchanges that are to take place are mutually given* in the relationship, and *these promises are fulfilled by the various kinds of exchanges that take place.*

A Relationship Definition of Marketing

The *marketing concept* as the basic philosophy guiding marketing in practice still holds. However, in practice, the marketing mix approach to transferring this concept to marketing is considered too narrow in scope to be more than only partly useful in most service situations.

As a conclusion to this discussion we formulate *a Relationship Definition of Marketing* (compare Berry 1983, Grönroos 1989a, and Gummesson 1987c and d):

> *Marketing is to establish, maintain, and enhance* [usually but not necessarily always long term] *relationships with customers and other partners, at a profit, so that the objectives of the parties involved are met. This is achieved by a mutual exchange and fulfillment of promises.*

This definition can, furthermore, be accompanied by the following supplement: The resources of the seller—*personnel, technology, and systems*—have to be used in such a manner that the customer's *trust* in the resources involved, and thus in the organization itself, is maintained and strengthened.

The exchange of promises indicated in the definition may be of any kind and concern any kind of activities. The same goes for the various resources the customer (representatives of a household or an industrial customer) meets in the relation. However, *these resources and activities cannot be predetermined and explicitly categorized in a general definition.*

Long-term customer relationships means that the main objective of marketing is to seek enduring relationships with the customers. Of course, in some situations short-term sales, sometimes called *transaction marketing*, may be profitable (see, for example, Jackson 1985a). Generally speaking, however, the long-term time span is vital to profitable marketing. In a relationship billable transactions concerning goods, services, know-how, information, or any other asset of value to the customer must of course, take place. Profitability cannot always be measured immediately as a result of the first transaction. Profitability is a long-run measurement, which should follow from an ongoing and enduring relationship. In addition to customer relationships, successful marketing performance often requires that long-term relationships with other parties be established and maintained. Such other relationship partners are, for instance, suppliers, retailers and distributors, and financial institutions that may be needed to offer a competitive financing arrangement to customers.

Establishing, maintaining, and *enhancing* customer relationships (if we here concentrate on customers as relationship partners), imply, respectively, that the process of marketing includes (1) the first contact with a customer so that a relationship emerges; (2) maintenance of an existing relationship so that the customer is willing to continue to do business with the other party of the relationship; and (3) enhancement of an ongoing relationship so that the customer decides to expand the content of the relationship by, for example, purchasing larger quantities or new types of products from the same seller.

These three situations are totally different from a marketing point of view. In short, establishing the first contact demands good communication skills. Favorable word-of-mouth and a good and well-known image helps. Maintaining and enhancing customer relationships mainly require other types of tools and activities, respectively. To use Berry's (1983) words: "Good service is necessary to retain the relationship. Good selling is necessary to enhance it" (p. 25). Good selling does not only, or even mainly, mean good sales performance by professional salespersons, but rather good sales and communication skills by service employees. From the service provider's point of view, (1) establishing a relationship involves *giving promises*, (2) maintaining a relationship is based on *fulfillment of promises*, and, finally, (3) developing or enhancing a relationship means that *a new set of promises are given with the fulfillment of earlier promises as a prerequisite.*

This relationship definition of marketing *does not* say that the traditional means of competition of the marketing mix, such as advertising, personal selling, pricing, and conceptualizing of the product, are any less important than earlier. However, it does demonstrate that there is *so much more* to marketing. What is important is that it represents a fundamental shift in the way of looking at marketing as a phenomenon as compared to the marketing mix. The relationship definition, based on the systems approach to the network of actors in the marketplace, is geared to the notion of the *marketing concept* as central to business behavior (or the behavior of most organizations). Hence, it is a truly *market-oriented definition* (see Grönroos 1989a).

However, this way of looking at what marketing is is certainly not the only market-oriented way of honoring the marketing concept. It is, though, a definition well suited for understanding, as well as planning and executing, marketing in service organizations and in service competition.

In practical situations, for teaching is classroom settings as well as for marketing planning in organizations, the relationship definition is not pedagogically as easy to use as the marketing mix. This is only natural, because the main virtue of the marketing mix is its pedagogical simplicity, not its proven capability to capture certain marketing situations. The relationship definition does not provide users with an easy-to-implement list of groups of marketing variables or means of competition. Instead, it forces users to think for themselves and to analyze the marketing situations at hand, as well as to develop an understanding of what resources and activities are required to establish, maintain, or enhance a relationship with a specific customer or segment of customers.

The Marketing Functions

As demonstrated by, for example, the *Customer Relationship Life Cycle Model,* marketing is by no means only an intermediate function between production and consumption or usage in a service context. Especially during the *consumption* (usage) *process*, marketing is an integral part of producing and delivering services. In other words, managing the moments of truth of the *buyer-seller interactions* (the service encounter) is a marketing task as well as a responsibility for operations and personnel and human resources management. To use the words of Tansik (1988): "While this separation (of marketing and production) may well be logical for manufacturing firms where customers order and take delivery of the product (good) at points well removed from the place of production, it does not seem appropriate for service systems where there is a simultaneity between production, delivery, and consumption" (p. 8).

There is, however, a distinct difference between handling the interactions of the moments of truth as a marketing task and executing traditional marketing activities such as advertising, personal selling, and sales promotion. Normally the latter are planned *and* implemented by marketing and sales specialists. On the other hand, the former tasks are implemented by persons who are specialists in other areas. Moreover, they frequently are planned and managed by nonmarketing managers and supervisors. To put it bluntly, they are frequently both managed and executed by people who are neither aware of their marketing responsibilities nor interested in customers and marketing.

The employees involved in marketing as nonspecialists have been called "*part-time marketers*" by Gummesson (1981 and 1987c). They are, of course, specialists in their own areas, and will certainly remain so. At the same time, they must learn to perform their tasks in such a way that the customers will want to return, thus strengthening the customer relationship. Hence, they will have to learn to act in a marketinglike manner, and their bosses as well will have to learn to think in terms of marketing and customer impact.

To sum up, the marketing function can be divided into two separate subfunctions: a specialist function, taking care of much of the traditional marketing mix activities and market research; and a marketing function, related to the buyer-seller interactions where the marketing tasks are performed by "part-time marketers."

In Figure 6–4 the two marketing functions of service organizations are schematically illustrated. The shaded areas represent the marketing functions. The *Traditional Marketing Function* is separate from other functions. It involves market research, personal selling by a separate sales force, advertising, pricing, sales promotion, public relations, and other activities traditionally considered to be part of marketing. For consumer services, the traditional marketing function is mainly a *Mass Marketing Function*. However, in business-to-business relationships personal contacts by salespersons are involved as well.

The interface between production and consumption represents the buyer-seller interactions, where the moments of truth, or, as they have also been called, moments of opportunity, occur. Because the marketing impact of these interactions occurs in interactive processes, this part of marketing is called the *Interactive Marketing Function* (see, for example, Grönroos 1980, 1983a, and 1983b). Interactive marketing, or marketing outside the marketing mix, occurs at the very moment when the buyer and seller interact. The service is actually delivered and resales guaranteed through activities in the buyer-seller interactions. Traditional marketing efforts may sometimes support the interactive marketing activities performed during these interactions.

The customer's opinion of a service is influenced both by the means of production (i.e., the production facilities, and human and nonhuman

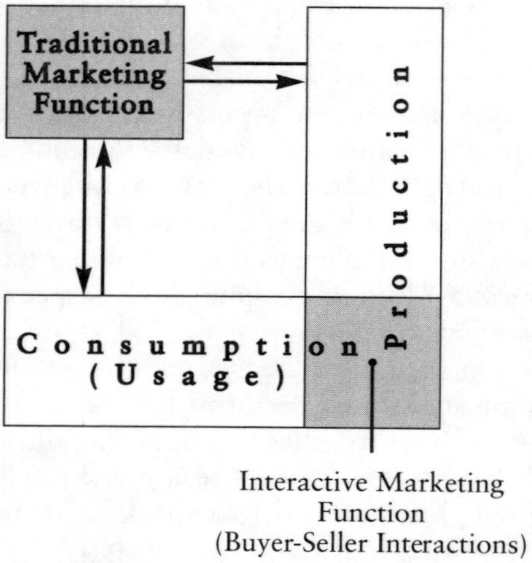

Source: Grönroos, C. (1983): *Strategic Management and Marketing in the Service Sector*. Cambridge, Mass.: Marketing Science Institute, p. 62. Reprinted with permission.

Figure 6–4. The Two Marketing Functions of Service Organizations

production resources) and by the production process (i.e., the behavior of the employees and the manner in which the production facilities are used). The interactive marketing function recognizes that every component—human and nonhuman—in producing a service, every production resource used, and every stage in the service production and delivery process should be the concern of marketing, and not considered merely operations or personnel problems. The marketing consequences of every resource and activity involved in interactive marketing situations have to be acknowledged in the planning process, so that the production resources and operations support and enhance the organization's attempts to develop and maintain long-term relationships with its customers.

The Three-Stage Model

Marketing is a dynamic process, where traditional marketing activities and interactive marketing resources and activities will have to cooperate so that profitable long-term customer relationships are developed and maintained. The *Customer Relationship Life Cycle Model* (Figure 6–2) illustrated how enduring customer relationships are created through a three-stage process. The *Three-Stage Model* demonstrates this long-term marketing approach.

Stage	Objective of marketing	Marketing function
Initial stage	To create interest in the firm and in its services	The traditional marketing function
Purchasing process	To turn the general interest into sales* (first purchase)	The traditional and the interactive marketing functions
Consumption process	To create re-sales, cross-sales, and enduring customer relations**	The interactive marketing function

* Giving promises.
** Fulfilling promises.

Figure 6–5. The Three–Stage Model

The model, illustrated in Figure 6–5, holds that, in order to satisfy the needs of its target markets, the service organization will have to consider the three stages of the Customer Relationship Life Cycle, and that recognition of the three stages in the life cycle has substantial marketing consequences. At each stage the *objective* of marketing and the *nature* of marketing—the marketing function to be used—will be different.

At the *initial stage,* when potential customers have no clear view, or perhaps old-fashioned or obsolete views, of the service, the objective of marketing is to *create interest* in the organization and its services. This is best achieved by the *Traditional Marketing Function.* Advertising, sales promotion, and public relations are appropriate means of competition. Sometimes field selling is also needed, especially in industrial markets. Moreover, one should not overlook the potential power of favorable word-of-mouth communication.

At the second stage, the *purchasing process, general interest should be turned into sales.* More specifically, *promises* about future commitments on the part of the seller *are given* and should, one hopes, be accepted. Here again the *traditional marketing* activities can be used. However, *interactive marketing* activities can also be applied whenever the customer gets in contact with the firm's production resources before he or she has made a final purchase decision.

During the *consumption (usage) process, resales, cross sales, and enduring customer relationships should be achieved.* At this stage, *promises have to be fulfilled,* so that customers realize that the firm can satisfy their needs and that it can be trusted. At this final stage in the life cycle the traditional marketing activities have only a slight chance, if any, of influencing the preferences of the customers toward the service. Here the *Interactive Marketing Function* is responsible for success or failure. The marketing orientation and service-mindedness of the production facilities and the production process are of vital importance if customers are not to be lost at this stage. Traditional marketing activities, such as contacts by salespersons and advertising, have only minor effects, if any, at this point.

Far too often marketing is viewed too narrowly. Only the traditional marketing activities are managed in a marketing context. The firm may be excellent at giving promises, but these promises are kept in a much less marketing-oriented way, and low perceived quality follows. Marketing may be managed successfully during the two first phases of the Customer Relationship Life Cycle, but in the third phase, the consumption or usage process, nobody seems to be responsible for marketing and customers anymore.

Marketing has to be planned and implemented throughout the life cycle as a continuous process. Otherwise too many customer relationships are broken, which leads to bad word-of-mouth. Moreover, lost customers have to be replaced by new potential customers to a larger extent than would otherwise be the case. This again requires an increased budget for traditional marketing.

Relationship Marketing, Transaction Marketing, and the Marketing Strategy Continuum

A long-term marketing strategy which aims at developing and enhancing continuous and enduring customer relationships has been called *relationship marketing* by Berry (1983; see also, for example, Levitt 1983, Rosenberg & Czepiel 1984, Jackson 1985a and b, Gummesson 1987c and d, Crosby, Evans & Cowles 1988, and Grönroos 1988b and 1989b). Thus, relationship marketing means that the firm uses a marketing strategy which aims at maintaining and enhancing ongoing customer relationships. Although getting new customers is still important, the main strategic interest is to market to existing customers. In a relationship marketing strategy, interactive marketing becomes essential. If the moments of truth of the buyer-seller interactions are taken care of badly, thus literally wasting moments of opportunity, no traditional marketing efforts can ensure that the customers will stay with the firm. *When implementing a service strategy a relationship marketing approach and excellent interactive marketing capabilities are essential.* Without these elements a service strategy collapses.

The reasons that drive a relationship marketing strategy are essentially the same as the forces that drive firms to adopt a service strategy, which is an interesting observation. Shapiro (in Salmond 1988) concludes that the driving forces are technological change, increasing customer sophistication, and competitive forces, which make the firm differentiate itself and its offerings through relationship excellence. Of course, relationship marketing is not the only marketing strategy, although, today, the importance of such a strategy increases all the time. As a strategy, relationship marketing can be considered one end of a *marketing strategy continuum*. At the other end of this continuum, the strategy would be to concentrate on making one transaction at a time with any given customer, without deliberately trying to develop any enduring relationship with that customer. This type of marketing strategy has sometimes been called *transaction marketing* (see Jackson 1985a and b), or order-taking marketing.

As marketing strategies can be placed on a continuum, where these two types of strategies are the extremes, there are, clearly, situations where firms combine elements of the two strategies. A relationship type of strategy may dominate, or a transaction type of strategy will do so (compare Jackson 1985a). Typically, however, a manufacturer of consumer packaged goods would find it useful to place itself toward the transaction marketing side of the continuum, whereas a service organization, offering consumer services, industrial services (services to organizational buyers), not-for-profit services, and public services, would attempt to pursue a relationship marketing–oriented strategy. This is, of course, not a law but a well-founded rule of thumb.

In Figure 6–6 strategies on the marketing strategy continuum are examined in some detail. The analysis focuses on the ends of the continuum, but the reader should, of course, be aware of the fact that it is a continuum and that therefore there are a range of in-between possibilities. Also, a firm could perhaps use different types of strategies for different types of products, market segments, or situations. In the figure we consider four types of consequences of a relationship marketing strategy and a transaction marketing strategy and point out where on the marketing strategy continuum various types of marketing situations typically fall. The four aspects of marketing strategy are: (1) *the dominating marketing function*, (2) *the dimensions of total perceived quality*, (3) *the price sensitivity of customers*, and (4) *the interface between marketing and other business functions*.

Marketing strategy continuum	Transaction Marketing			Relationship Marketing
Dominating marketing function	Traditional marketing mix dominated			Interactive marketing dominated*
Quality dimension most important for a competitive advantage	Outcome–related technical quality dominating			Process–related functional quality dominating**
Price sensitivity	Customers very price sensitive			Customers much less price sensitive
Interface between marketing and other functions, e.g., operations and personnel	Limited or nonexistent: interface of no significant strategic importance			Substantial; interface of strategic importance
Typical marketing situations continuum	Comsumer Packaged Goods Marketing	Comsumer Durables Marketing	Industrial Goods Marketing	Services Marketing

* But supported by traditional marketing mix elements
** Provided that the technical quality is at an acceptable level

Figure 6–6. The Marketing Strategy Continuum

In the bottom part of the figure, the positions on the continuum that different marketing situations, on the average, could be expected to take are indicated. A transaction marketing–oriented approach seems to fit *consumer packaged goods* the best, whereas *consumer durables* typically need to be blended somewhat more toward a relationship marketing strategy. Business or industrial marketing, where *industrial goods and equipment* are the core of the offerings to customers, is more toward the relationship-oriented end of the strategy continuum. For complicated machines and equipment this is fairly clear, but as far as mass-produced components with low unit value are concerned, one could easily argue that aggressive selling and price offerings, that is, a transaction type of strategic approach, would be more efficient and effective. This may be true in many situations, especially if the market is not too mature yet and if the seller in the long run, due, for instance, to lasting scale advantages, can maintain a lower price level than the competition. However, one should remember a remark by Philip Kotler: "There is nothing such as a commodity; there are only undifferential products that wait to be differentiated." Broadening the customer relationship by a more relationship-oriented strategic approach to marketing may be a successful way of profitably differentiating even a commodity.

Consumer services such as hospitality, transportation, health care, financial, insurance, and many more, as well as industrial services such as professional services, financial services, insurance, maintenance, transportation, and forwarding services offered to organizational buyers and users, are toward the far relationship marketing strategy end of the continuum. Although this is a solid rule of thumb, even here one should remember that in some situations a more transaction type of strategy may be more successful for services (see, for example, Jackson 1985a).

The relative importance of the four different marketing functions can be seen in Figure 6–6. The *dominating marketing function* differs in importance depending on where on the continuum we place ourselves. In a transaction-oriented strategy, marketing is dominated by resources and activities of the *traditional marketing mix* function. Mass marketing such as advertising campaigns are normal and, if well executed, create transactions. In some situations personal selling is an important tool. Price offers are almost always used. On the other side of the continuum, in a relationship-oriented strategy, the resources and activities of the *interactive marketing* function dominate. The performance of the "part-time marketers," the customer orientation of the systems of operations and of industrialized routines, such as vending machines and ATM's, and the skills and willingness of customers to perform as co-producers are critical ingredients of such a marketing strategy. Of course, some traditional marketing mix activities are also needed; for example, advertising and direct mail to create an interest among potential customers, in some situations personal selling to close a deal, and continuous attention of salespersons during the consumption (usage) phase of the Customer Relationship Life Cycle in industrial markets.

Next, the *dimensions of total customer perceived quality* which are predominantly important to customers differ depending on where on the continuum we are. In a transaction-type of strategy, the product itself, typically a consumer good, is most important. Therefore, the *outcome-related technical quality* dimension counts for most or all of the quality perception of customers. But again, as we move toward the other end of the strategy continuum, the situation changes. In a relationship-oriented strategy, where the customer relationships are much broader in scope, aspects other than the mere technical quality of the solution (a service, a good, or a system of goods and services) become pivotal. However, in most cases, an acceptable level of the technical quality is a prerequisite for good total quality as this is perceived by customers. Provided that this requirement is fulfilled, the *process-related functional quality* dimension dominates customer perception of total quality.

Third, the *price sensitivity* of customers tends to differ depending on the strategic marketing approach of the firm. In a transaction marketing situation where the customer relationship is limited to the product itself and possibly the customer perception of the image of the seller, there is normally nothing that keeps the customer relationship together. A solid image may help, but if a competitor can offer a similar technical solution to a problem, a good or a service, at a lower price, the relationship breaks down. Hence, customers are, by and large, *very price sensitive* in a transaction marketing strategy situation. On the other hand, if the seller has developed and maintains a broad and close relationship with its customers, much more than price keeps the two parties together. If, say, a financial service arrangement is fairly complicated, or if an industrial seller provides its customer with a complex solution, including, for example, design, equipment, installation, and maintenance, the buyer and seller grow together due to the technological ties and flows of information that have been established over time (compare Håkansson 1982). Such a situation demands in itself a relationship type of strategic approach, but even if there are no other major relational elements than these in the relationship, these ties are normally difficult for a competitor to break; consequently, price becomes a less central means of competition. Hence, customers tend to be much *less price sensitive* in relationship marketing situations.

Finally, in a transaction approach to marketing, such as the one normally applied by a marketer of consumer packaged goods, the marketers can take care of most or all of the marketing function. There is no interface between marketing and other business functions that would be of strategic importance. However, the more we move toward the relationship marketing end of the continuum, the more the interface between, for example, marketing and operations and personnel grows, and *the interface between marketing and other business functions becomes of strategic significance*. This, of course, follows from the paramount importance of the interactive marketing function and the "part-time marketers."

It is important for the organization to position itself along the continuum at an appropriate place, one that fits the prevailing market requirements. Otherwise wrong marketing decisions are easily made, and the limited amount of resources that normally are available are used in a unnecessarily unproductive way. In the worst case, the marketing strategy fails altogether. Also, if the wrong strategic approach to marketing is taken, marketing costs may easily become unnecessarily high, often without being noticed by management. In the following section we are going to discuss this issue in some detail.

Managing the Customer Base or Just Market Share

When a transaction marketing strategy is used, exchanges or transactions with a customer are viewed in isolation from other contacts or relations with that customer over time. The customers are numbers that come and go and, hopefully, come back again. The customers add up to a number of the total amount of exchanges or transactions, measured in volume or sales, called *market share*.

The composition of the market share is unknown, except for a breakdown of any market segments that may exist. Hence, we usually do not know whether a given, and maybe even stable, market share is accounted for by a stable customer base offering repeat business or by a large proportion of customers coming and going. In the latter case, new potential customers have to be made interested in the firm and its offerings and persuaded to purchase. In the former case, today's customers have to be convinced that it is worthwhile to continue purchasing or doing business with the firm.

If we bear in mind that it is always much more expensive to take a new customer through the Customer Relationship Life Cycle to the end of the purchase stage, compared to what it takes to make a satisfied customer purchase again, one easily understands that it is more profitable to have as many long-term customer relationships as possible. A highly unscientific rule of thumb suggests that it costs at least six times more to get a new customer than to achieve resales to an existing one. It also suggests that if a firm has to win over an unsatisfied ex-customer, it will cost at least 25 times as much.

In some situations, for example, for consumer packaged goods, some consumer durables, and maybe some industrial goods, a transaction marketing strategy is the only possible one. Close relationships with the customers cannot for one reason or the other be developed. In such situations, effectively used traditional marketing mix activities, and thorough market research, are the only means of trying to get as much repeat purchases as possible. However, when the size of the business is measured in terms of market share, we really do not know how much of the market share is stable and how much is made up for by new customers replacing lost customers. And the more lost customers that have to be replaced by new ones in order to maintain market share, the more marketing costs.

In services, and in most business marketing situations, firms have closer contacts with their customers. If, however, a firm pursues a transaction marketing strategy and does not aim at developing long-term and lasting customer relationships, probably a large proportion of its customer base will be new at any given period. This also means that the firm has a number of ex-customers who for one reason or the other have decided to quit the relationship. When customers come and go, the cost of maintaining a given market share is unnecessarily high, because marketing to new customers is always much more expensive. If the firm just measures market share, it may be very satisfied with its marketing achievements. However, management may fail to see that a substantial proportion of its customer base during a given period has been lost, having been replaced by potential customers. Management thus feels secure, believing that the firm is doing well. But, in such a situation, the firm *is not* doing well. Because of the number of lost and probably unsatisfied customers, a substantial amount of bad word-of-mouth is created; moreover, the economic result is that the firm constantly suffers from unnecessarily high marketing costs.

In the situation described above, what the firm is doing is *managing market share only*. This is, however, not enough. Management has to *manage the firm's customer base,* so that both the nature of the resulting market share and the true economic implications of a certain market share are kept under control. Otherwise there is no real understanding of how productive the marketing efforts are. Managing the *customer base* means that management is focused on the customer relationships and their enhancement, not on the market share statistics only. Failure to manage the customer base and just concentrate on market share can be fatal, especially in large corporations. Such firms often have such big pockets that the slowly but steadily advancing financial drain caused by a mismanaged or even unmanaged customer base is not recognized before a lot of bad word-of-mouth has been created, the corporate image damaged, and negative economic consequences reached substantial proportions. All of a sudden management is shaken by the fact that the operation is economically unsound, although there have been no problems with the level of market share. But it's only the market share figures that look good; the customer relationship have suffered over time and the customer base is unhealthy.

The Marketing Circle

Marketing viewed as a continuous process throughout the Customer Relationship Life Cycle can be illustrated as a circle. This *marketing circle* is seen in Figure 6–7. A continuous *need adaptation,* accompanied by marketing activities geared to the stage of the life cycle where the customer is, is required to keep the customer in the circle. A customer may, however, leave at any stage of the process if the firm is not capable of giving the customer what it has promised. For example, a customer may be lost because the company in an advertising campaign makes promises that cannot be kept by the interactive marketing function of the buyer-seller interactions. Even if the promises are realistic the customer may be lost if the firm cannot successfully manage the buyer-seller interactions of the purchasing and/or consumption processes. Furthermore, external influence by colleagues or friends (word-of-mouth) may have an impact on the customer's behavior. Finally, competitors may take away customers by promising more, for example, better functional quality or substantially lower price, than the customers are presently getting.

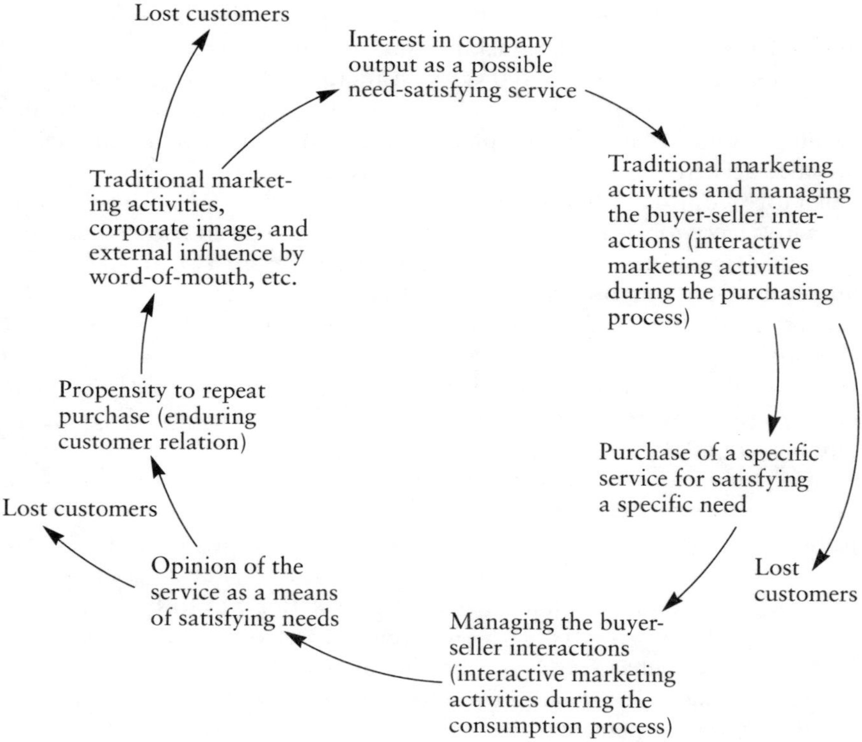

Figure 6–7. The Marketing Cycle

Marketing Management or Market-Oriented Management?

In the traditional literature on marketing, which is mainly based on consumer packaged goods experience, the concept *marketing management* is used to describe the practical applications of the marketing concept. In a consumer goods context this is perfectly appropriate. However, in situations where the typical customer relationship is extended far beyond the straightforward and impersonal relationship between a marketer and a buyer of consumer breakfast cereals, toothpaste, or soap, this straightforward view of how to manage marketing does not hold anymore.

In industrial marketing contexts the marketing management approach becomes awkward (Håkansson & Snehota 1976 and Håkansson 1982). Much of the customer relationship issues are the concerns of functions other than the traditional marketing function. The interrelationships between functions (Webster 1978) make planning, coordination, and execution tasks much more complicated than what a traditional marketing and sales department can handle. In a service context the situation is often even more complex. Marketing activities—traditional and especially interactive activities—are spread throughout the organization; therefore, the whole organizational structure has to be supportive to marketing. Hence, as Gummesson concludes, "there is extreme interdependence between the traditional departments of a service firm—production, delivery, personnel, administration, finance, etc.—and marketing. Therefore, it is more appropriate in the service firm to talk about *market-oriented management* than to use the traditional label marketing management" (Gummesson 1990, forthcoming).

Top management alone has the overview of the organization necessary, and the authority, to manage the *total marketing function;* therefore, ultimate marketing responsibility has to be sufficiently high up in the organization. A marketing department can plan and execute some of the marketing tasks, but total management of marketing has to be an integral part of overall management. Hence, even for psychological reasons, *market-oriented management* is what it's all about, not marketing in the traditional functionalistic sense. Marketing, therefore, becomes an integral part of service management.

Summary

In service contexts, the marketing function is not restricted to the realm of marketing specialists only. It is spread throughout the organization, and "part-time marketers" frequently outnumber specialists in, for example, market research, market communication, and sales. The traditional models of marketing, therefore, do not fit very well in a service context. The traditional approach to marketing, the so-called marketing mix, is too restrictive to be more than partly useful. Instead, a *relationship approach to marketing* and a relationship definition are suggested. The total marketing function is divided into two distinct parts, the Traditional Marketing Function and the Interactive Marketing Function. Especially during the consumption (or usage) stage of the Customer Relationship Life Cycle, the Interactive Marketing Function becomes paramount. Of course, traditional marketing mix efforts are still important, but predominantly in the initial and purchasing phases of the life cycle. The concept of a marketing strategy continuum is introduced and two distinct marketing strategies, a relationship strategy and a transaction strategy, are analyzed in relation to this strategy continuum. In service contexts the nature of marketing makes this function much more a top management concern than what it is normally considered to be. Hence, it is actually more accurate to talk about *market-oriented management* than merely marketing in the traditional restrictive sense of the term. Therefore, marketing becomes an integral part of any theory of service management.

7
Managing Total Market Communication and Image

Introduction

In this chapter we address the issue of market communication and demonstrate the need for a total communication approach. The *communication circle* concept is introduced, and the impact of various time perspectives on the effects of market communication campaigns is analyzed. Also, some guidelines for managing market communication are presented. In the final sections of the chapter we discuss the concept of corporate and local image. How an image develops is described, and, finally, how to handle image problems is discussed for two situations, when the problem is a real problem and when it is a communication problem.

Market Communication Is a Total Communication Issue

Market communication is, of course, a substantial part of the marketing function. In the marketing model in the previous chapter the Traditional Marketing Function includes market communication activities such as sales, advertising, and sales promotion. Communication is also an integral part of the Interactive Marketing Function. What employees say, how they say it, how they behave, how service outlets, machines, and other physical resources look, and how they function communicate something to the customers. The communication effect may be positive, such as "they really care for me here," "they have modern and efficient equipment," or "they are nicely dressed." It may also, of course, be less favorable, such as "how rude their people are," "what a sloppy office they have," or "how can it always take so long to get things done here."

There is an important difference between the communication of the Traditional Marketing Function and that of the Interactive Marketing

Function. The latter types of communication are related to reality as customers perceive it. They communicate *what really is* as far as consumers are concerned. The former types of communication, such as advertising, are always on an abstract level for customers (and other publics). They involve promises and/or information that may or may not be true; however, as far as the customer or potential customer is concerned, the validity of these types of communication must still be tested. Testing takes place when the customer meets reality. There is an obvious connection here with how service quality is perceived. Market communication efforts like advertising and sales predominantly impact the *expected* service, whereas the communication effects of the buyer-seller interactions of the Interactive Marketing Function influence the *experienced* service. Of course, advertising and brochures may sometimes have some immediate effect on the perception of the interactions, which probably enhances the customer's opinion of the service.

The size of the gap between expectations and experiences determines the quality perception, as discussed in chapter 2. Hence, there is here a truly *total communication impact*; almost everything the organization tells about itself and its performance and almost everything the organization does that is experienced in the buyer-seller interactions has an impact on the customer. Moreover, the various means of communication and their effects are interrelated. Furthermore, these communication effects, together with other factors such as the technical quality of the services, shape the *image* of the organization in the minds of customers, potential customers, and other publics. We shall return to the issue of *image management* in a later section of the chapter.

Types of Communication

As demonstrated in the previous section, there are a range of situations where communication effects occur and thus a number of different types of communication. For instance, the following four broad categories can be distinguished (see, for example, Grönroos & Rubinstein 1986):

1. Personal communication (not related to the interface between service production and service consumption);
2. Mass communication (impersonal);
3. Direct communication; and
4. Interactive communication.

In addition to these types of communication, which are more or less actively used as means of communication, there is a fifth type of communication, which must also be taken into consideration when planning total communication:

5. Absence of communication

When a firm decides not to inform its customers about, say, a delay or quality fault, this is *not* lack of communication. Instead, there is a distinct piece of information involved. This is perceived either immediately on the spot or later on. Moreover, absence of communication is frequently perceived as negative communication.

Personal communication that is not related to the interface between service production and consumption includes, for example, sales by professional or other salespersons that do not take place as part of normal service production. Impersonal *mass communication* includes, for example, advertising, brochures, and mass-distributed sales letters. *Direct communication* is personalized impersonal communication which is directed to named receivers. An example is sales letters addressed to the receivers personally. These three types of communications are part of the Traditional Marketing Function.

Interactive communication refers to the communication effects of customers' perceptions of the buyer-seller interface during service production. Much of this is, of course, personal. But there is a distinct difference between this type of communication and the above-mentioned category of "personal communication." The latter always is, or should be, planned as communication and communication only, whereas the communication effects of personal contacts during service production (part of "interactive communication") are normally pure side effects. Basically what is planned is the production process itself, whereas the communication effects are a second-hand issue, which in reality is equally important. Furthermore, much of the interactive communication effects are due to how customers perceive the physical aspects of the service production process, such as offices, the technology used, the fit of technology and systems to the customer's needs and level of knowledge, and so forth.

From a communication point of view, the challenge is to manage all of the five types of communication and their effects in an integrated way. Otherwise, customers will receive different and sometimes even contradictory signals from the various sources of communication. A salesperson may promise one thing (effect of personal communication), or a personalized sales letter (effect of direct communication) may be somewhat different, and yet a third communication effect may emerge when the customer actually perceives reality in the buyer-seller interactions when consuming the service (effect of interactive communication). And furthermore, somewhere along the line there may be an absence of communication, either deliberate or due to ignorance, which adds to the confusion of the total communication effect.

On the other hand, the organization that masters total communication management can achieve a powerful market communication impact, which adds substantially to the performance of the total marketing function. It is a way of boosting image and has a substantial effect on another phenomenon in the communication area, one that has yet to be added to a discussion of market communication. This phenomenon is *word-of-mouth*.

Word-of-Mouth and the Communication Circle

The marketing impact of *word-of-mouth communication* is almost always huge, frequently greater than that of personal communication, mass communication, or direct communication. Word-of-mouth is the message about the organization, its credibility and trustworthiness, its way of operating, its services, and so on that is communicated from one person, a customer or practically anyone, to another. In the eyes of the receiver, a sender who perhaps has had personal experiences with the organization and who is independent of it is a fairly objective source of information. Consequently, if there is a conflict between the message of word-of-mouth and, say, an advertising campaign, advertising, and all other paid messages as well for that matter, loses, or at least has only a minor impact when the two messages are blended into one communication effect.

We are not going to go into the area of word-of-mouth in any further detail in this context (but see, for example, Arndt 1969, Reingen & Kernan 1986, and Brown & Reingen 1987). Instead, we are turning to what we call the *communication circle*, where word-of-mouth plays a critical role (Grönroos & Rubinstein 1986). This circle is schematically illustrated in Figure 7–1.

The communication circle consists of four parts, Expectations/Purchases, Interactions, Experiences, and Word-of-Mouth/References. A customer or potential customer has developed certain *expectations* and therefore may decide to make a purchase; that is, an ongoing customer relationship continues or new business is created, respectively. Having done so, he or she (or an organizational customer) moves into the consumption stage of the Customer Relationship Life Cycle. At this point, the customer

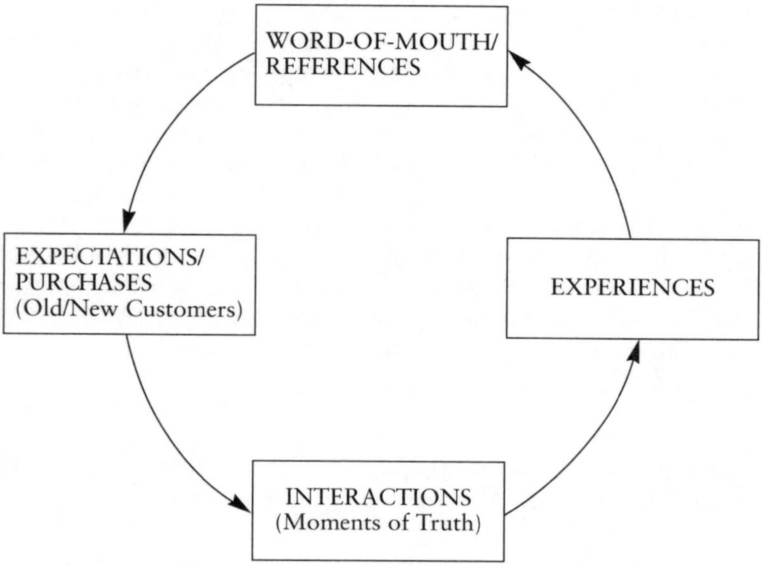

Figure 7–1. The Communication Cycle

gets involved in *interactions* with the organization and perceives the technical and functional quality dimensions of the services rendered. These interactions usually involve a high number of *moments of truth* or *moments of opportunity*. This is where interactive communication effects occur as part of the customer's perception of the interactive marketing performance of the organization.

Now, the *experiences* that follow from the fact that a customer has been involved in buyer-seller interactions and has there perceived the quality dimensions multiply several times by means of *word-of-mouth*. If the message communicated by word-of-mouth is positive, customer expectations develop favorably. The customer with positive experiences is inclined to return or continue to use the services on an ongoing basis. New potential customers get interested in the organization and its offerings as a possible means of satisfying their needs and solving their problems. *References* (and *testimonials*) represent an active way for the firm to use positive word-of-mouth in its marketing, thus capitalizing more effectively on potential sources of good word-of-mouth.

The multiplier effect of word-of-mouth varies very much between industries and situations. And as common wisdom tells us, negative experiences tend to multiply by word-of-mouth quicker and more often than positive experiences do. The multiplier may be any number between, say, three and thirty. An often-cited multiplier in service contexts is twelve; that is, bad experiences are communicated to at least twelve other persons, good experiences perhaps to somewhat fewer. There are no facts to prove this figure, but the trend is clear and sends the marketer a blunt message: *Do not play with word-of-mouth*. Make it work for you in all situations. Always try to capitalize on word-of-mouth (compare George & Berry 1981).

Thus, word-of-mouth has a powerful impact on the formation of *expectations* of existing and potential customers (and other publics as well) and is an important determinant of future *purchasing behavior*. On the one hand, good word-of-mouth has a positive effect on expectations and future purchases. On the other hand, negative word-of-mouth has, of course, the opposite effect.

Market Communication and the Communication Circle

It is extremely important that the existence of the communication circle be understood and its consequences for market communication fully appreciated by the marketer. If the interactions create too much negative experience and negative word-of-mouth follows, a *resistance to actively used market communication* is built up. The more negative word-of-mouth there is, the less effective are, for example, advertising campaigns, direct communication, and sales efforts. More has to be invested in these types of communication if the negative impact of word-of-mouth is to be nullified. And if too many negative messages are communicated by word-of-mouth and the image of the organization suffers severely, no increase in the market communication budget will be enough to save the situation, at least not in the long run.

Positive word-of-mouth, on the other hand, decreases the need for huge budgets for market communication, through, for example, advertising and sales. Word-of-mouth takes care of much of the new business that is wanted. In theory, *excellent interactions*, including good customer perceived quality and interactive communication, *make mass communication less necessary and allow more freedom for pricing*. Only when totally new services are launched may mass communication such as advertising campaigns be needed. There are numerous examples of small local firms that operate successfully in this way. Moreover, larger firms operating in larger areas can do the same. One of the leading banks in Sweden, Svenska Handelsbanken, has since the 1970s pursued such a communication strategy which has worked well. The profitability of the bank has constantly been well above average.

Whatever communication strategy the organization adopts, the key to successfully executed market communication is how the *interactions* between the organization and its customers have been geared to the needs and wishes of customers and to the production of excellent perceived quality and the building up of supportive word-of-mouth. If the communication aspects of the interactions are neglected, the interactive communication impact will probably be not as good; perhaps even negative. As a consequence, more money will be needed for other types of communication. Indeed, even this may not be enough.

If the personal communication, mass communication, and direct communication programs are developed without being geared to the interactive communication effects and word-of-mouth, the risk of overpromising and, consequently, of building up quality gaps grows substantially. Then, customers will meet a reality that does not correspond to their expectations. This, in turn, destroys the communication circle, and three types of consequences follow:

1. The effects of word-of-mouth and references become negative;
2. The trustworthiness and the effects of the organization's market communication suffer; and
3. Corporate and local image is damaged.

On the other hand, if all elements of the communication process and customer perceptions of the buyer-seller interactions fit, the corresponding effect is, of course, the opposite. Good word-of-mouth is built up, and the credibility of the market communication efforts increases and image improves.

To sum up, only a *total communication management* approach will be effective and justified from a management point of view. The effects of all types of communication, including that of absence of communication, have to be taken into consideration and put to work in a *total communication program.*

Planned and Unplanned Communication

There is another aspect of total communication, which is far too often neglected yet frequently imperative to the communication effects achieved.

This is the notion of *unplanned communication*, as opposed to planned communication (Calonius 1989). Just as absence of communication has a distinct communication effect, there are often a number of situations where communication effects occur, although these situations have not been planned from a communication point of view.

As Calonius (1989) defines it, "planned communications means communications with goals." However, he continues, "planned communications need not be strictly formal or structured—of the 'canned sales talk' type" (p. 543). Communications that go unplanned easily have a negative impact on customer perceptions. Therefore, it is important to analyze all sources of communication and their possible effects, planned as well as unplanned. In Table 7–1 examples taken from the airline business illustrate how communication effects may occur.

In practical situations it is, of course, seldom possible to exclude all sources of unplanned communication. However, successful total communications management requires that as many as possible of the potential communication situations be planned and the risk for unfavorable unplanned communication at least minimized.

Table 7–1
Planned and Unplanned Communication

	Planned	*Unplanned*
Personal Communication	Good travel plans Good advice	Sloppy dress
Mass Communication (Impersonal)	Target-group directed advertising Informative menus	Rude collection letter
Direct Communication	Correct address Personalized content in letter	Irrelevant information
Interactive Communication	Good manners Pleasant premises Effective systems	Snooty "Next window!" Badly maintained premises
Absence of Communication	"We won't give any information unless it is correct"	Neglecting to inform about delays and connections

Source: Based on two tables in Calonius, H. (1989): Market Communications in Service Marketing. In Avlonitis, G.J., Papavasiliou, N.K. & Kouremeos, A.G., eds., *Marketing Thought and Practice in the 1990's.* Proceedings from the XVIIIth Annual Conference of the European Marketing Academy, Athens, Greece

Short-Term, Medium-Term, and Long-Term Effects of Market Communication

Very frequently market communication is used to achieve short-term goals only. Sometimes efforts are taken to create more enduring effects, for example, so-called corporate advertising campaigns or image communication programs. Too often, however, such long-term efforts are planned separately from other campaigns. In fact, every communication activity, short-term or longer-term in scope, has its effects on customers, as well as on potential customers, employees, and other publics in a number of time perspectives.

We are here going to distinguish among *three* time perspectives and their impacts on how an organization is perceived in the marketplace:

1. A *market communication impact* in the short run;
2. A *marketing impact* in the medium run; and
3. An *image impact* in the long run.

Every communication effort, such as an advertising campaign, the behavior of customer service personnel, or the ease with which an ATM is operated, has an instant, *short-term communication impact as a communication activity*. This may be very effective as a means of communication; for example, a well planned and executed advertising campaign that makes potential customers believe in the promises given. However, in a longer time perspective the effects may be less clear, even negative.

In Table 7–2 quite possible effects of such a per se effective advertising campaign (or any type of communication effort) are illustrated. "+" denotes a favorable effect, "-" a negative effect, and "0" a neutral effect, that is, no effect at all. Three target groups for this campaign, customers, potential customers, and employees, are identified and the impact on these groups indicated.

The hypothetical advertising campaign obviously includes promises that cannot be fulfilled. For potential customers and even for existing customers the effects of this campaign may be positive in the short run, if it is well executed. However, the employees, who know they cannot possibly fulfill such promises, react differently. If this is the first time such overpromising takes place, they will probably react in a neutral way. The campaign has no effect. However, if such overpromising has continued for some time, their reactions will change.

In a somewhat longer time perspective, as customers and potential customers get involved in interactions with the organization, the perception

Table 7–2
Effects of an Effectively Executed Communication Campaign Involving Overpromising in Three Time Perspectives at Three Levels

Effect/ Time Perspective Level	*Target Groups*		
	Existing Customers	*Potential Customers*	*Employees*
Short term: Effect of campaign *as communication*	+ or 0 "Maybe they really mean it!"	+ "This sounds good!"	0 "I doubt it!"
Medium term: Effect of campaign *as part of marketing*	– "I should have known better! Cheated again!"	0 or – "Wasn't it more than this?" or "This is not at all what I expected!"	– "It's as I thought and I have to explain why we cannot fulfill our promises!"
Long term: Effect of campaign *on image formation*	– – "They never do what they say they are going to do!"	– – "They just talk and promise."	– – "I'm looking for another employer."

of this campaign changes. They realize that reality did not meet their expectations and the promises given by the campaign. The combined impact of the advertising campaign as a traditional marketing effort and the interactive marketing effect of the buyer-seller interactions, which are inconsistent with the campaign, thus changes the per se positive effect of the campaign. This combined effect is the impact of the total marketing performance, including traditional as well as interactive activities, and it is most probably negative. The customers feel cheated, and justifiably so. Hence, in a somewhat longer time perspective, in the medium run, *the marketing effect of a campaign, which judged in isolation may seem quite good and effective, can be poor or directly negative.*

As far as the employees are concerned, the medium-run effect is definitely negative, because they will have to cope with customers with unrealistic expectations who probably get angry and sometimes even nasty toward the employees. The personnel is put in an awkward position, which damages motivation for quality behavior and good interactive marketing performance.

Finally, we can stretch the time perspective even more, and observe possible long-term effects of this advertising campaign. If the campaign runs for a longer period of time, or is followed by other campaigns, which also overpromise or in any other aspect are too far from reality, customers and potential customers through word-of-mouth will learn that the organization is not trustworthy. In the long time perspective single communication campaigns that, *again judged in isolation, look like good communication may have a fatal impact on the image of the organization.*

Of course, employees react as strongly or even stronger. Unsatisfied customers can normally leave with short or no notice, whereas it may be less easy for many employees to find a new employer. In the long run employee motivation goes down the drain.

The effects of a trustworthy communication campaign that does not involve overpromising are, of course, totally different. Table 7–3 illustrates effects that can be expected to occur when, for example, an advertising campaign is run which in an effective manner gives realistic promises. Customers exposed to the messages of this campaign experience a reality that corresponds to the promises, if they decide to buy and consume services provided by the organization.

The effects demonstrated in Table 7–3 are totally different when compared with Table 7–2. In the short run, existing and potential customers as well as employees can be expected to react positively. This initial favorable effect is enhanced by the fact that the service production process is perceived to be in line with the campaign. Interactive marketing in the buyer-seller interactions and the market communication campaign support each other. In the long run, image is improved by the fact that the organization consistently gives a good impression, by market communication as well as by reality and interactive marketing performance. The employees react in a similar manner. In the longest time perspective, they will probably consider their employer the best possible, if other internal activities by management do not destroy this impression.

As these hypothetical examples demonstrate, it is imperative that every communication effort is judged not for its virtues as a communication

Table 7–3
Effects of Realistic Market Communication

Effect/ Time Perspective Level	*Target Groups*		
	Existing Customers	*Potential Customers*	*Employees*
Short term: Effect of campaign *as communication*	+ "They have something new to offer."	+ "It sounds interesting."	+ "We are prepared!"
Medium term: Effect of campaign *as part of marketing*	+ + "What a good service!"	+ "They really fulfilled their promises."	+ "It works out well."
Long term: Effect of campaign *on image formation*	+ + "That's my service provider!"	+ + "You really can trust them."	+ + "This is the best employer I've ever seen."

effort only, but in a much larger perspective. Otherwise unwanted effects may occur. And today, far too often this holistic approach to marketing communication is more or less lacking.

Guidelines for Managing Market Communication

Some general guidelines or rules of thumb for managing market communication can be identified. George and Berry (1981) have presented six guidelines for the advertising of services. Although they only consider advertising, the rules of thumb they suggest are equally applicable in most market communication contexts. The six guidelines are (George & Berry 1981):

1. Direct communication efforts to employees
2. Capitalize on word-of-mouth
3. Provide tangible clues
4. Make the service understood
5. Communication continuity
6. Promise what is possible

To this list we would like to add a seventh and an eighth item:

7. Observe the long-term effects of communication
8. Be aware of the communication effects of absence of communication

Direct Communication Efforts to Employees. All advertising campaigns and most other mass communication efforts, at least, which are planned for various segments of existing and potential customers, are also visible to employees. They are therefore an important "second audience" (George & Berry 1981, p. 52) for this campaign. Promoting the position of employees in external communication campaigns is a way of internally enhancing the role of the employees and adding to their motivation.

Capitalize on Word-of-Mouth. As demonstrated by the discussion of the *communication circle* and the vital role of word-of-mouth and references, good word-of-mouth makes customers more receptive to external market communication efforts, and vice versa. Moreover, good word-of-mouth can be considered the most effective communication vehicle. Therefore, if the organization has created good word-of-mouth, which is a message from an objective source (satisfied customers), using this objective nature of word-of-mouth in market communication is a good idea. Testimonials are examples of this.

Provide Tangible Clues. As services are more or less intangible, communicating about a service, especially to an audience of potential customers, becomes very difficult. The intangible service easily becomes even more abstract. Therefore, it is frequently a good idea to try to make the service more concrete. For example, a firm may illustrate or demonstrate tangible items that are either involved in the service production process or in one way or another relate to the service. This is a way of demonstrating the quality of the service. Showing the physical comfort of first-class travel on an airline in a advertisement may be a more effective way of giving potential customers something more tangible to relate to and remember than a more abstract visualization of luxury.

Make the Service Understood. Because of the intangible nature of services, special attention has to be paid to making the benefits of a particular service clearly understood. Too abstract expressions and excessive use of superlatives may not lead to a good communication effect. The service and what it can do for the customer remain unclear. Therefore, it is important to find good metaphors that in a concrete way communicate the service.

Communication Continuity. Once more, because services are intangible, and because mass communication about services especially are therefore difficult for the audience to grasp, there has to be continuity in communication efforts over time. A common tune in a TV or radio commercial or a common layout, picture, or phrase in a newspaper ad, which continues from one campaign to the next, may be a way of making the audience realize more quickly what is advertised and what the message is.

Promise What Is Possible. If promises given by external market communication are not fulfilled, the gap between expectations and experiences is widened, and customer perceived quality decreases. Berry (1988) claims that the research into the facets of service quality he and his colleagues have been engaged in demonstrates that keeping promises is the most important single aspect of good service quality. As George and Berry (1981) conclude, "since service buyers have only fulfilled promises to carry away from the service transaction, it is especially important that service firms deliver on advertising promises" (p. 56). Clearly, avoiding overpromising is essential in managing market communication. This has a clear connection with the next and last guideline.

Observe the Long-Term Effects of Market Communication. As the discussion in the previous chapter demonstrated, a communication campaign which seems very effective may have unexpected, negative effects when viewed in a longer time perspective. If promises that cannot be fulfilled are given, the short-term effects on sales may be good, but customers become dissatisfied as they perceive reality and do not return and create bad word-of-mouth. In the longest time perspective, the image of the organization is damaged. The effects on the employees are similar. Hence, a long-term perspective must always be taken when external market communication is planned and executed.

Be Aware of the Effects of Absence of Communication. If there is no information available in a stressful situation, customers often perceive this as negative information because they lose control of the situation. Frequently, it is better to share bad news with customers than to say nothing.

In the earlier discussion on the effects of market communication, the longest perspective was related to how the image of an organization is formed. We are going to address this issue in the following sections.

Managing Image

The image of an organization, international, nationwide, or local, represents the values customers, potential customers, lost customers, and other groups of people connected with the organization. The image may vary depending on which group of persons is considered, and it may even vary between individuals. However, there is some kind of common perception of the organization, which may be either very clear and well known to some group or diffuse and not very well known to another group.

Image exists on several levels. A large network organization, for example, a restaurant chain, has a corporate image. But in addition to this, a local organization, for example, a local restaurant, has a local image. If many outlets or offices belong to the local organization (for example, a range of car rental locations belong to the same local franchisee, which, in turn, is part of a nationwide car rental organization), each individual outlet may very well have an image of its own, in addition to an overall local image.

The images on different levels are interrelated. The corporate image influences the perception of the local organization, that is, the local image;

and the image of an individual office or outlet to some extent depends on the local image. Moreover, the way in which the various images affect each other depends on whom we are talking about. Very large customers, for example, financial organizations, are more inclined to be influenced by corporate image. Smaller and local customers, as well as local publics such as local politicians and opinion leaders, are more interested in local image. For a local firm, corporate image and local image may be very much the same thing.

It is important from a management point of view to note that a local unit is inevitably affected by the corporate image of the bigger organization which it is a part of. On the other hand, service operations in many respects are local, which presents a good opportunity for a local organization to develop a local image of its own among its local customers and other publics. For example, if a hotel chain in one sense or another has, on the corporate level, a bad reputation, a local unit may nevertheless develop a strong and favorable local image, which helps attract customers. This is probably most effective from a local perspective and in relation to enduring customer relationships, whereas customers who perhaps visit the town only once or very seldom are more likely to be influenced by corporate image when making their purchasing decisions.

From the corporation's point of view, a distinct and different local image may be tolerated within limits, whereas too-different local images may be harmful as far as the pursuit of a corporate strategy is concerned. If the images of local units are too diverse, it may be difficult to maintain a clear corporate image. This is, of course, a very industry-specific, and even company-specific, issue.

However, again, services are local, and most customer relationships and relationships with many other publics are local. Therefore, corporate-level management should not automatically try to streamline the images of all local units. Local business environments and local societies are different, and a too-streamlined local image may hurt business. The issue of streamlining or differentiating local images in relation to a desired corporate image is a management concern, where the strengths of disparate local images should be compared to the need for a clear image on the corporate level. Sometimes there is a conflict involved, sometimes not.

The Importance of Image

A favorable and well-known image, corporate and/or local, is an asset for any firm, because image has an impact on customer perceptions of the communication and operations of the firm in many respects. The role of image is at least threefold. For the sake of simplification, no distinction between corporate and local images is made here.

First of all, *image communicates expectations*, together with external marketing campaigns such as advertising and personal selling and word-of-mouth communication. Here we consider only customer relationships, but image works in a similar manner in relation to other publics as well. Image has an impact of its own on expectations. Moreover, it helps people screen information, market communication as well as word-of-mouth. A positive image makes it easier for the firm to communicate effectively, and it makes people more perceptive to favorable word-of-mouth. Of course, a negative image has a similar effect, but in the other direction. A neutral or unknown image may not cause any damage, but it does not make communication and word-of-mouth effects more effective either.

Second, *image is a filter* which influences the perception of the operations of the firm. Technical quality and especially functional quality are seen through this filter. If the image is good, it becomes a shelter. Minor problems, even occasional larger troubles of a technical or functional quality nature, are easily considered less fatal. However, this works temporarily only. If such problems occur often, the effect of this shelter diminishes. The image has changed. This filter has an effect in the opposite direction as well. An unfavorable image makes customers feel more unsatisfied and angry with bad service than they would otherwise be. A neutral or unknown image does not cause any harm in this respect, but it does not provide a shelter either.

Third, as briefly mentioned already, the *image is a function of the experiences as well as of the expectations of customers*. When customers develop expectations and experience reality in the form of a technical and functional quality of the service, the resulting perceived service quality changes the image. If the perceived service quality meets the image or exceeds it, image is reinforced and even improved. If the firm performs below image, the effect will be the opposite. Also, if the image is not very clear or well known to customers, it is developed and given distinct features by customer experiences.

There is a fourth effect of image which is of importance to management. *Image has an internal impact as well.* The less clear and distinct the image is, *the more this may affect employee attitudes* toward the organization as employer. This, in turn, may have a negative influence on the performance of the employees and thus on customer relationships and quality. On the other hand, a positive clear image, say, of a firm with excellent service, communicates clear values internally and may thus strengthen positive attitudes toward the business among its employees. Such a firm more easily attracts good employees, too.

Developing Image

Frequently we hear managers say that the image of their firm is, for example, bad or not clear or old-fashioned. Far too often they try to solve this problem without really analyzing it and the reasons behind the unfavorable image. This, in turn, easily leads to wrong actions. For example, cosmetic actions—such as corporate image advertising campaigns or actions involving other means of mass communication—are often turned to in situations where they do not solve the actual problem. Such actions have limited effect, or they may even damage image.

As was noticed by Bernstein (1985), *image is reality*. Therefore, image development or improvement programs have to be based on reality. "If the image is false and our performance is good, it's our fault for being bad communicators. If the image is true and reflects our bad performance, it's our fault for being bad managers" (Bernstein 1985, preface).

First of all, one has to analyze why there seems to be an image problem. Basically, there are two possible reasons:

- The organization is known but has, nevertheless, a bad image;
- The organization is not well known and, therefore, has an unclear image or an image based on old customer experiences.

If the image is negative in one way or the other, *the experiences of the customers are probably bad*. There are problems with technical and/or functional quality. In such a situation if management calls upon an advertising agency to plan an advertising campaign offering a message that the firm is service-oriented, customer conscious, modern, or whatever, the result will only be disaster. At best, the campaign is just a waste of money; however, there are cases where such actions have had much more fatal consequences. A nationwide retailing chain in Europe suffered from an image of being less service oriented than the competition. It invested extensively in a corporate advertising campaign which communicated good service, customer-conscious employees, a nice milieu in its retail outlets, and so forth. In the short run, sales improved, but in the long run, sales came down to where they had been and even below. Moreover, its already bad image was damaged.

The lesson is, of course, that because image is reality, if market communication does not fit reality, reality normally wins. An advertising campaign that is not based on reality only creates expectations. If expectations are higher than they used to be, but the experiences of reality have not changed, the perceived service quality is affected in a negative way, and the image is damaged.

If the image problem is a real problem, only real actions help. Real problems with the performance of the firm, its technical and/or functional quality, cause the image problem. Internal actions that improve the performance of the firm are needed if the bad image is to be improved.

If the image is unknown, there is a communication problem. The firm may be entering a new market, where it is unknown, or the nature of the business may lead to sporadic customer contacts only, which means that the customers never develop an in-depth image of the firm based on experience. Also, reality may have changed so that the firm is, say, more customer conscious and service oriented than earlier, but this has not been fully appreciated by its customers yet. Therefore, the image is still negative or not as good as it should be. The image will improve eventually, when enough customers become sufficiently experienced with the new reality; however, if the firm communicates this change to the market by means of, for example, an advertising campaign, this process will probably take less time. In these situations the image problem is a communication problem, and improved market communication offers a solution.

Furthermore, it is always possible, at least marginally, to influence the image using various means of communication. The layout of advertisements, brochures, packages, and letterheads and the design of offices and delivery trucks may support a given image if they are in line with it. On the other hand, modern office design and advertisement layouts do not improve the image if the firm performs in an old-fashioned and bureaucratic manner.

In summary, it is important to realize that image is what in reality exists; image is not what is communicated *if the communicated image does not correspond with reality.* When there is an inconsistency between real performance and communicated image, reality wins. The communication of the firm is perceived as untrustworthy, which damages image even more. If there is an image problem, management has to analyze the nature of the problem thoroughly before taking action. A communication problem can and should be solved with improved communication. However, if there is a real problem, that is, if the negative or otherwise unfavorable image is due to bad performance, the image can be improved only by internal action, the objective of which is to improve performance. Only in a second phase can communication be used, when the real performance-related reason for the bad image has been removed.

Summary

In this chapter we have dwelt upon market communication issues, and have especially argued for a holistic approach to managing communication.

There are a number of main categories of communication, some of which are easily given less or no attention. Moreover, the need for a total communication approach and a sufficiently long time perspective has been discussed at considerable length. Finally, managing image is a complicated undertaking, especially for larger service organizations that operate in a network, because image exists on several levels, corporate as well as local. Moreover, actions initiated by image problems have to be planned carefully, and a clear distinction between real image problems and image communications problems has to be made.

8
Organizing for Market Orientation: Structure and Resources

Introduction

In the present chapter we are going to discuss the difference between the marketing function and the marketing department. A different approach to how to organize for market orientation is required for services. Models for developing appropriate organizations are presented. Moreover, the development of quality-generating resources within the organizational structure is discussed.

The Marketing Function and the Marketing Department

In standard marketing thinking, which is based mainly on experience from consumer packaged goods, a marketing department is offered as the organizational unit responsible for planning and implementing marketing activities. The logic behind this solution is, of course, that marketing can best be planned and executed if all marketing activities are concentrated and taken care of by a group of specialists.

However, such logic requires that marketing as a function be separated from the other business functions and activities of the firm in a logical and manageable way. Today, this way of organizing for marketing is considered the most appropriate one. At the same time, however, there is a small but increasing amount of criticism emerging. As Haller stated it in the early 1980's: "Marketing as we know it will disappear sometime in the 1980's" (Haller 1980). Piercy (1985) concludes, referring to Haller, that "in such a structure, the marketing department would cease to exist" (p. 86). Peters (1988b) argues that "if we are to respond to wildly altered business and economic circumstances, we need entirely new ways of thinking about organizations" (p. 103). He also claims that the military model with its hierarchical charts-and-box structure is old-fashioned in today's business environment.

Haller's vision for the 1980's has not come true, as a brief look at the standard marketing textbooks and marketing journals quickly reveals. The same is true for the practice of marketing. However, when moving the focus from the established areas of marketing, such as consumer goods marketing, and looking at new emerging areas, such as industrial marketing and services marketing, one can see another picture. This is less obvious in the approaches to these areas so far developing in North America, which probably is explained by the dominating role of the established models of predominating consumer goods marketing and of the marketing mix there. Globally, however, the trend is much different. Much of the modern research into services marketing and industrial marketing, in fact, supports the above cited statements by Haller, Piercy, and Peters. The long-term perspective of marketing and the recognition of the characteristics of long-term customer relationships of service firms and industrial firms demonstrate that marketing is not a responsibility for marketing specialists only, but that *marketing activities are carried out throughout the entire organization* (Gummesson 1979 and Grönroos 1983b). As has been pointed out by Gummesson (1979 and 1990), this poses an organizational dilemma: "(This) organizational dilemma is created by the fact that those who produce and deliver services carry out marketing activities for that service, whether they know it or not" (Gummesson 1990, forthcoming).

In Figure 8–1 the position of marketing in a bank, or any service organization, is schematically illustrated. The shaded areas indicate the marketing responsibilities of various functions. For example, the managing director, the regional directors, the director of loans, and the cashiers all have marketing responsibilities, because what they say and do and how they do it may have an important impact on the future buying and consumption behavior of the customers. Simultaneously, they have responsibility for operations as well.

The status of most employees in service operations is complicated. They have dual responsibilities because clearly a cashier or bank teller or a waiter, hotel receptionist, or service technician must first be able to take care of his or her duties in a technical sense. However, at the same time they all have to realize that the way in which they do their duties is a marketing task. Hence, we have a number of *"part-time marketers."* In many service operations these marketers with dual responsibilities outnumber the marketing specialists of the marketing department many times over (see Gummesson 1987a).

The main problem in most situations is the fact that one mistakes the *marketing department* for the much larger concept *marketing function. The*

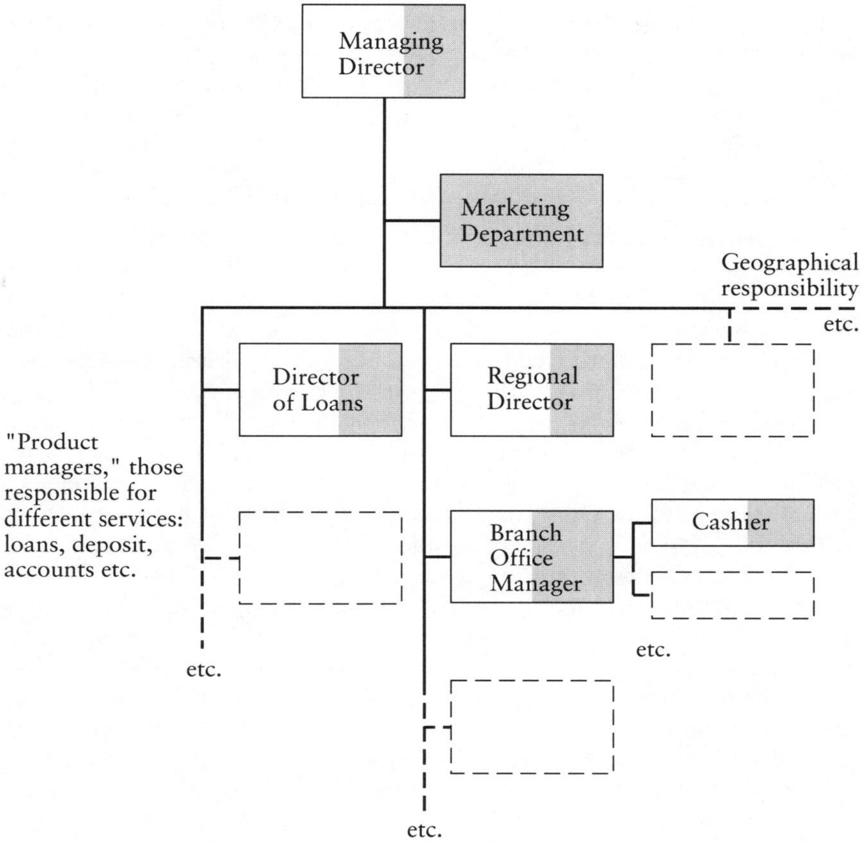

Source: Gummesson, E. (1981): Marketing Cost Concept in Service Firms, *Industrial Marketing Management*, No. 3 (Elselvier Science Publishing Co.): p. 177. Reprinted with permission.

Figure 8–1. The Simultaneous Responsibility for Operations and Marketing among the Personnel in a Service Organization

marketing function includes all resources and activities that have a direct or even indirect impact on the establishment, maintenance, and strengthening of customer relationships, irrespective of where in the organization they are. The marketing department, on the other hand, is an organizational solution which aims at concentrating some or all parts of the marketing function into one organizational unit. Introducing and using a marketing department as an organizational solution to handling marketing may at some stage be an acceptable step. By doing so, management may be able to create an interest in and at least a theoretical understanding of the importance of marketing to service providers. In the long run, however, this solution easily becomes a trap, which psychologically and in practice makes it difficult to make the whole organization think and perform in a true market-oriented manner.

The Marketing Department as an Organizational Trap

In a consumer goods context, mixing the two concepts of the marketing function and the marketing department is not a fatal mistake, because there most of the contacts between the firm and its customers can be taken care of by the marketing department. The preproduced product, which should be geared to information from market research, sales and advertising activities, price, and the distribution channels, is what the customers see and are influenced by. Only some sales responsibilities of top management are normally marketing activities outside the marketing department.

In most service contexts the situation is the reverse. Normally only traditional marketing tasks such as advertising, pricing, and public relations can be handled by a typical marketing department, whereas other marketing activities carried out as part of operations and other functions are outside the realm of this department. In a service firm a large part of the marketing function is carried out by "part-time marketers" outside the marketing department. Nevertheless, growing service firms have, in the best consumer goods tradition, often been inclined to establish a marketing department, in order to maintain or even strengthen the market orientation of the firm. However, the long-term effect may easily be the reverse.

A traditional marketing department usually cannot be responsible for the total marketing function of service firms. The introduction of such departments, on the contrary, easily influences the organization in an unfavorable direction. People working in other departments performing, for example, operations or personnel tasks stop worrying about their customer-related responsibilities and totally concentrate on just handling operations or personnel tasks for their own sake. The reason for this is clear. The firm now has marketing specialists in their marketing department; why should they bother any longer. The result is an increasing production orientation and a less market oriented performance. The marketing department solution becomes *an organizational trap* (see Grönroos 1983b).

Table 8–1 shows the reactions of executives in a range of Scandinavian service firms to the introduction of a marketing department in service organizations. The risk that a marketing department will widen the gap

Type of respondent / Item	Percentage agreeing strongly or partly with item								
	Total	Position in organization			Structure of operations		Structure of customers		
		Top Management	Marketing	Other	Network	Single outlet	Industrial	Households	Both
1. A separate marketing department may widen the gap between marketing and operations	66.7 Percent	72.8 Percent	53.9 Percent	77.4 Percent	67.1 Percent	65.8 Percent	68.1 Percent	64.7 Percent	63.9 Percent

Type of respondent / Item	Percentage agreeing strongly or partly with item								
	Service industry								
	Bank & Finance	Hotel & restaurant	Transportation	Travel agency	Professional Services	Cleaning security etc.	Public sector	Insurance	Misc.
1. A separate marketing department may widen the gap between marketing and operations	57.5 Percent	100.0 Percent	62.9 Percent	25.0 Percent	73.4 Percent	75.1 Percent	62.5 Percent	84.6 Percent	86.7 Percent

Type of respondent / Item	Percentage agreeing strongly or partly with item					
	Size (employees)					
	Less than 11	11 – 50	51 – 200	201 – 501	501 – 1000	More than 1000
1. A separate marketing department may widen the gap between marketing and operations	67.6 Percent	85.2 Percent	90.9 Percent	76.7 Percent	90.0 Percent	76.6 Percent

Source: Grönroos, C. (1983): Innovative Marketing Strategies and Organization Structures for Service Firms. In Berry, L.L. et al., eds., *Emerging Perspectives on Services Marketing*. Chicago: American Marketing Association, p. 15.

Table 8–1. Effects of Separate Marketing Departments

between marketing and operations is considered substantial (see Grönroos 1983b). *Two thirds* of the respondents in this survey stated that a separate marketing department may widen the gap between marketing and operations. As the table shows, top management level persons and other nonmarketing respondents were more inclined to share this opinion than were the marketers. Yet, of the marketers, roughly half agreed with this opinion. The table also demonstrates the percentage of respondents holding this view depending on the structure of the operations of their business, whether the firm serves industrial customers or households or both, which service industry they represent, and finally the number of employees.

As far as working in different service industries is concerned, some interesting discrepancies occur. For example, respondents from travel agencies show an extremely low percentage holding the view that a marketing department may be the cause of organizational problems; only one fourth of them shared this view. Also, in the banking and financial business, the respondents holding this opinion are few, relatively speaking, but nevertheless they represent more than 50 percent. In the hospitality industries (hotels and restaurants) as well as in insurance, the corresponding percentage is, again, very high. It is difficult to say how executives in manufacturing industries would respond to a question like this. Probably the percentage of persons representing consumer goods industries would be very low, whereas it would be on the average substantially higher for manufacturers serving industrial markets.

The problem with marketing departments is very real, however. As one executive of a large insurance company recognized:

> Our corporate marketing department has become an organizational trap. Employees working in the various operational departments and account servicing and administration concentrate on handling operations rather than focusing on their customer influencing activities. These customer influencing activities are thought of as being the responsibility of the corporate marketing department. Although these employees realize that they do have responsibilities of maintaining customer satisfaction, they tend to focus on the technical aspects of their job. Performance is measured quantitatively and quality is enforced by penalties for mistakes.

If the negative effects of a marketing department are further reinforced by performance measurement systems and rewarding systems that focus on aspects of jobs other than customer relationship building and maintaining, the problems increase. In such situations these negative effects are not only psychological, but real as well. Concentrating on the technical aspects of a job instead of giving the customer relationship aspects more attention gives more credit to the employee; the reverse discredits the employee in the eyes of his or her superiors. How often is this not the case?

In summary, in service organizations' marketing departments should not be introduced as *the* ultimate solution to problems where a market orientation is lacking or insufficient. Sometimes it can, however, be used as an intermediate solution. As has been illustrated by Grönroos (1983b), there are some good examples of firms that have either closed down or drastically reduced the size of their marketing departments and become very successful in the marketplace.

Marketing departments may be helpful for planning, market research, and executing corporate campaigns. As much of the marketing effort as possible should, however, as a rule of thumb, be planned and implemented in the line organization, where the immediate responsibility for rendering the service lies. A marketing department should always be introduced very carefully, so that no one in the organization misunderstands the role of that department. And careful attention should always be paid to the measurement and reward systems used for personnel outside the marketing department, the "part-time marketers," when such departments are introduced. *A marketing department is definitely not an excuse for the rest of the organization to stop being responsible for the customers.* But again, how often is this not the case today?

Organizing for Market Orientation—Flattening the Pyramid

A service organization must never be unnecessarily bureaucratic with a large number of hierarchical levels. As was recognized by the President and CEO of SAS Service Partners, Ivar Samrén: "In the service industry I would at any time recommend a horizontal spread rather than an added vertical level" (Samrén 1988, p. 31). Market orientation requires more thoroughly understood and accepted responsibility for customers and authority to take actions to serve them than do large staffs with substantial planning and decision-making authority. This fact is illustrated in a beautiful way by the following case, quoted from Jan Carlzon, President and CEO of SAS (Scandinavian Airlines System).[a]

> A few years ago, Werner Tarnowski was appointed to manage the SAS office in Stuttgart. Inheriting an outmoded organizational structure, Werner set three major goals: (1) to cut costs without sacrificing the

[a] From Jan Carlzon (1987): *Moments of Truth*. Cambridge, Mass.: Ballinger Publishing Co., Harper & Row: 59–61. Used with permission.

quality of service, (2) to increase the efficiency of his staff, and (3) to give the organizational structure more flexibility.

The Stuttgart branch operated out of two locations: a ticket sales office downtown, where Werner and other district managers worked, and the airport itself, where the flight-related personnel reported.

The downtown office served little purpose, aside from being a meeting place for Scandinavians staying at nearby hotels, and yet the sales department located there was unable to handle phone calls from customers and travel agents.

At the airport, meanwhile, the workload for employees was uneven. SAS had only one daily round-trip passenger connection, a flight between Stuttgart and Copenhagen. The plane landed in the evening and took off again in the morning. An SAS cargo plane also made a stopover in the morning. The cargo people in particular had very little to do for long stretches of time.

So Werner decided to consolidate all the employees and services at the airport location and closed down the downtown office. At the same time he rearranged the organization. He had the passenger-service employees from the airport and the sales staff from downtown teach each other how to do their jobs. This reciprocal training program, intended to introduce new work routines, also broadened the employees' knowledge of the overall operation.

Today, a number of SAS functions in Stuttgart are integrated. The sales people are now responsible for both cargo and passenger sales. And everybody pitches in to answer phones, sell tickets, check in passengers, handle customer problems, and conduct load checks.

As a result of Werner's changes, the Stuttgart office now costs SAS less money both because one fewer office is open and because the employees' time is spent more productively. And, most importantly, no services were cut! In fact, service is probably *better* because the organization is more flexible. Now that everyone knows each other's jobs, there is always someone around who can handle the problems of the moment. And for many employees, work has become more fun and challenging.

The Stuttgart story shows that flattening the traditional organizational pyramid works. Any business organization seeking to establish a customer orientation and create a good impression during its "moments of truth" must flatten the pyramid—that is, eliminate the hierarchical tiers of responsibility in order to respond directly to customers' needs. The customer-oriented company is organized for change.

"Managing" is thus shifted from the executive suite to the operational level where everyone is now a manager of his own situation. When problems arise, each employee has the authority to analyze the situation, determine the appropriate action, and see to it that the action is carried out, either alone or with the help of others.

It may seem like a mere word game to call everyone a "manager," but I use the term to remind my staff—and perhaps most those at the upper

> levels of the old pyramid—that their roles have undergone a fundamental change. If the top executives who were once the managers must learn to be leaders, then those people out in the front lines must make all the operational decisions. They are the ones who most directly influence the customer's impression of the company during those "moments of truth."

Organizing for Market Orientation—Turning the Pyramid Upside Down

What was realized by SAS is the fact that the customer contact employees, together with the customers in what they call the "frontline," create value for customers. The rest of the organization, the back-office functions and management and staff, form a support for the frontline activities. This support creates the necessary backup for service production and delivery of the frontline, that is, for a successful handling of the numerous moments of truth and a profitable use of the corresponding moments of opportunity.

Management should not be directly involved in operational decision making on an everyday level, but it should give the strategic support and resources necessary to pursue a service strategy. In a traditional "military structure" top management is often far away from reality. Tom Peters illustrates the classical organizational structure as a wheel with top management as the hub surrounded by staffs. In a military model, where he describes management as "the traditional, invisible, impersonal, generally out-of-touch corporate hub," he criticizes severely the capability of management to make good decisions (Peters 1988b, p. 104). In large companies the abundance of staffs makes accurate and up-to-date decision making even harder. States Peters (1988b): "Then comes the praetorian guards of central corporate staffs. The corporate center is tightly protected . . . by a phalanx of brilliant, MBA-trained, virgin (no line-operating experience), analysis-driven staff. If the isolation of the corporate chieftains in their plush-carpeted executive suites were not enough, this group seals them off once and for all," (p. 105). The situation becomes even worse if interactions with the outside world, consisting of customers, suppliers, distributors, and others are impersonal and highly industrialized. Then, no first-hand information is obtained from the marketplace by frontline personnel to be distorted by the staffs.

The old traditional view of the organization and the new, service-oriented organizational framework of, among others, SAS are schematically illustrated in the form of pyramids in Figure 8–2. The transition in the organizational thinking, which is, of course, the result of a change in strategic thinking according to the principles of service management, means actually three things. First of all, the priorities are changed. This is schematically demonstrated by the fact that the organization pyramid is turned upside down (compare Davidson 1978). The top management level is not the apex of the pyramid and the part of the organizational structure that immediately determines whether the strategy of the firm will be a success or failure. Instead, the frontline, including personnel, physical resources, and operational systems, interacting with customers, is at the top of the organizational hierarchy. The performance of the frontline determines whether the organization will be successful and profitable or not. Staffs and other support functions as well as management are a prerequisite only for excellence.

Second, the responsibility for customers and for operational decisions is moved from staff functions and management to those involved in the buyer-seller interactions and thus immediately responsible for the moments of truth. Third, the new thinking means that the organizational pyramid has to be flattened. This follows from the transition of responsibilities and authority from staff functions to the frontline. Less intermediate levels are needed.

It is fascinating how little has been written on marketing organization. From a general innovative perspective, there is the textbook by Piercy (1985), and from a service organization point of view, this issue has been treated in a comprehensive manner only by Gummesson (Gummesson 1990).

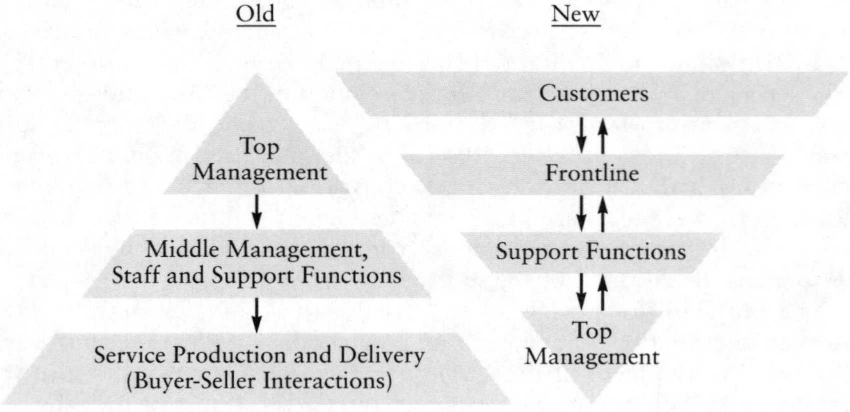

Figure 8–2. Service–Oriented Organizational Structure

Bigness versus Smallness

Flattening the organization pyramid and decentralization of decision-making authority are necessities if service organizations are to become truly market oriented. As Samrén of SAS Service Partners observes: "This enables decision making and problem solving in direct and immediate contact with partners or customers, and our own investigations show us that one of the leading edges we have is this ability to make decisions at every level in the organization" (Samrén 1988, p. 30). However, he continues: "But it *is* necessary to keep *some* functions very central, as otherwise chaos may result"(p. 31).

It could be argued that a service firm that is relatively small on the local level is frequently more market oriented than a big firm. In a smaller organization decisions are made faster and closer to the market. It is easier to develop good interactive marketing performance and to give better functional quality in such situations. Internal marketing (see chapter 10) is less time consuming and troublesome. On the other hand, there is potential strength in large service firms. In a bigger firm more resources can in most cases be used in order to develop the technical quality dimension.

Invisible systems and support functions, to which local branches can easily gain access, can often be developed centrally. This may give economies of scale as well as improve the efficiency of the total service production system. It is also sometimes easier to attract better trained persons to leading positions in a larger organization. Economies of scale can be achieved in such functions related to production, administration, finance, and so on, which are invisible to the market.

Therefore, as Figure 8–3 illustrates, one may argue "that *a growing service firm, in order to remain market-oriented and be successful, will have to be able to combine the strength of being small in a local perspective with the strength of belonging to a large organization*" (Grönroos 1983b, p. 20). However, there is lots of evidence that demonstrates that this may be difficult to do. As an organization grows and tries to achieve the advantages of bigness, far too often it destroys the potential strength of being small locally.

Customer-Oriented Organizational Structures for Services

For developing customer-oriented organizational structures for services, some general tendencies can be observed as rules of thumb. Industries and firms differ from each other, and specific situations require situation-oriented solutions. However, most often a basic structure can be found.

The Strength of Smallness

- Decisions are made near the market
- Decisions are made quickly
- Better knowledge of the desires of the customers
- Good interactive marketing performance is easier to achieve
- Internal marketing is easier
- Quality control, technical as well as functional, is easier to handle

The Strength of Bigness

- Economies of scale can be achieved in functions that are invisible to the customers
- More resources, personnel and technology as well as financial, available for developing technical quality
- Easier to attract personnel to the organization

Source: Reprinted from Grönroos, C. (1983): Innovative Marketing Strategies and Organization Structures for Service Firms. In Berry, L.L. et al., eds., *Emerging Perspectives on Services Marketing*. Chicago: American Marketing Association, p. 20.

Figure 8-3. The Strength of Bigness versus the Strength of Smallness

As noted previously, the marketing department may, at some stage in the process, be useful, although this is not quite clear. In the long run the separate marketing (and sales) department easily becomes a burden, which hinders market-orientation efforts. Only if the marketing manager's personality is such that he or she manages to overrun the formal organization can a customer-oriented development be expected. Otherwise the marketing manager is likely to be overrun by the organizational constraints. The result is bad or nonexistent interactive marketing and low functional quality, and in the long run, deteriorating image and lost customers. Yet, the traditional marketing mix elements of marketing may be well taken care of, and this may, therefore, especially in the short time perspective, give an impression of a well-managed marketing function. However, what easily happens and often goes unnoticed is the fact that the firm loses potential profits by managing its market share only, *and not its customer base*. Simultaneously, especially if too much overpromising is involved in external market communication campaigns, customer perceived service quality is deteriorating, bad word-of-mouth is slowly building up, and eventually management finds that the organization has an image problem. The organization then often gets profitability problems as well.

The responsibilities for planning and executing both the traditional marketing function and the interactive marketing function should be delegated toward the frontline of the organization as much as possible, for example, to a regional manager or a branch manager who is also responsible for operations. It seems reasonable to also give such a person the responsibility for the management of the personnel on his or her level. Such a regional or local unit could be a profit center.

Because service quality is produced locally, the local manager is also responsible for producing good technical as well as functional quality. The latter quality dimension emerges when there is good interactive marketing performance in the organization. In a decentralized organization, the local manager thus has dual responsibilities. In Svenska Handelsbanken, these dual responsibilities for the local manager, the head of a branch office, are formulated as follows: The branch manager is required to be *responsible for service quality toward the customers of the branch and responsible for profitability toward the corporation.* For almost two decades Svenska Handelsbanken, operating nationwide, has had one of the most decentralized organizations that can be imagined and continues to be among the most profitable banks in Sweden.

Furthermore, on the head-office level, some kind of marketing coordination and marketing planning and support may be needed. Such staff offices can be very small, including only a few persons. Their main duty is to give assistance in marketing planning, to plan corporate advertising and market communication programs, to help the regional or local managers to develop and execute their own local traditional marketing activities, if needed, and to assist them in developing interactive marketing performance on the local level. Internal marketing planning may also be part of their duties. This office could be labeled *market coordinator,* or the marketing and customer contact or service coordinator.

Finally, because the market coordinator supports all kinds of marketing activities on the local level and coordinates the traditional and interactive marketing functions as well as internal marketing throughout the organization, he or she is actually engaged in planning the total performance of the organization. As we have noticed, the interactive marketing concept requires that marketing on the interactive level is not separated from operations and the use of technology and other physical resources. Consequently, the marketing coordinator should be responsible for developing *market-oriented corporate action plans,* which cover traditional marketing as well as interactive marketing, and which, therefore, also take into account operations, personnel, internal marketing, and the development of new technology.

This customer-oriented organizational structure for services is schematically illustrated in Figure 8–4. In the figure the functions of the firm are divided into three categories: *traditional (mass) marketing activities, interactive functions, and noninteractive functions*. In order to develop a customer-oriented structure, the noninteractive functions, such as finance and accounting, R&D, and centralized support functions, form one category. Another category is formed by the interactive functions, which include operations and production, personnel, and technology on the local level. Starting from the service concept of the firm and its local unit, the frontline employees (contact persons) and the systems and physical resources must be developed and used in contact with the customers so that an acceptable, and preferably excellent, perceived service quality is achieved. If the firm is successful in this respect locally, the interactive marketing is good. The interactive marketing activities must, however, be coordinated with centrally located support functions, and with traditional marketing activities. Most of these are planned and executed locally, but some may be implemented on a regional level or at the head office. This means that the local manager is responsible for total marketing on the local level.

On the corporate level, only the top manager can be responsible for total marketing, in principle. In a growing organization a *market coordinator* may be needed. This individual coordinates all marketing activities throughout the organization. Moreover, this office can be responsible for centralized internal marketing planning, market research and so forth.

Successful Organizational Development: A Bank Case

This case has been adopted from Grönroos 1983b. The bank is a major bank. It suffered from low profitability and production-oriented attitudes among its personnel including branch managers and other middle management executives. The marketing function was handled by a large marketing department on the head-office level. In order to turn the bank into a market-oriented and profitable firm, it was decided that the bank should concentrate on profitable services and profitable market segments. Moreover, an organizational development process was initiated. This process included several stages, where each stage was caused by problems in relation to the market orientation of the bank perceived at the previous stage.

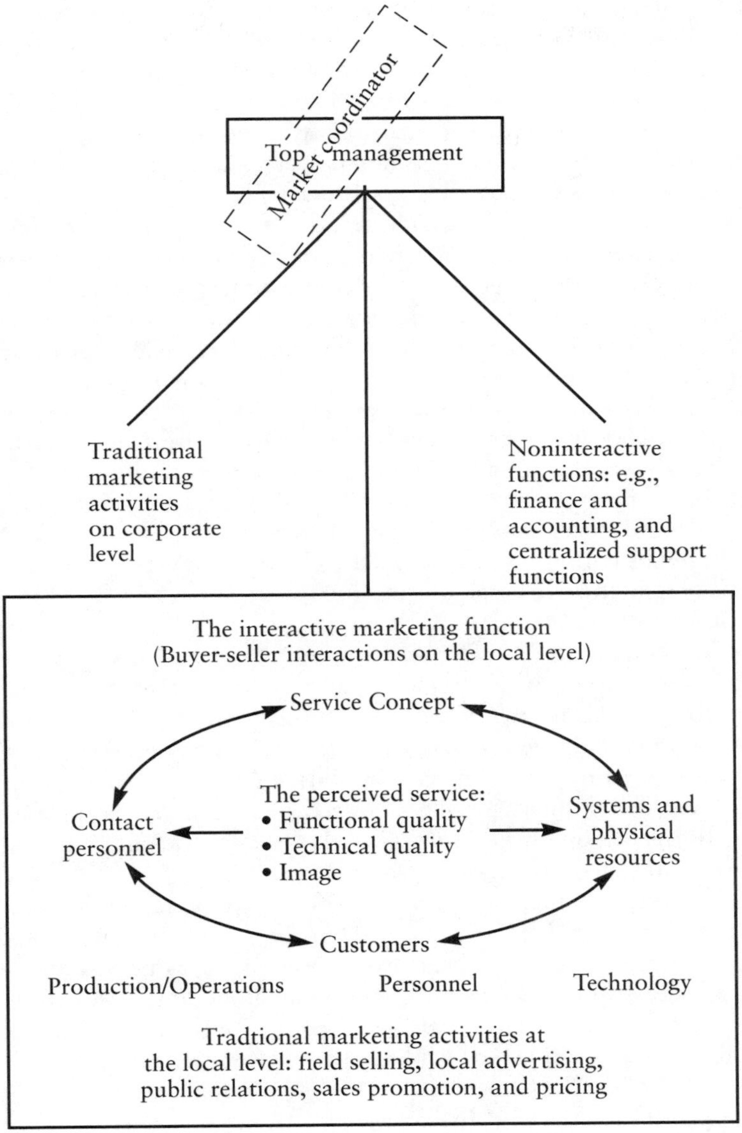

Source: Grönroos, C. (1983): Innovative Marketing Strategies and Organization Structures for Service Firms. In Berry, L.L. et al., eds., *Emerging Perspectives on Services Marketing*. Chicago: American Marketing Association, p. 18.

Figure 8–4. A Customer–Oriented Organizational Structure for Services

At the first stage, the central marketing department was closed down. Instead, a *customer contact development office* was established. This office was staffed by only a few people, and reported directly to the president. The bank was divided into regional banks, and the responsibility for marketing, including field selling in industrial markets, was given to local branch managers. Marketing consultants were located at the regional level. Their duty was to give marketing assistance to local managers. At the same time the bank stopped all corporate advertising on the national level, because the people in charge felt that purchase decisions are made locally and are influenced by the performance of the local branch offices.

However, the local branch offices remained quite production oriented, and they did not actively take over marketing tasks. When the branch manager felt he should do some marketing, he called upon the regional marketing consultant. When the regional marketing consultants left the local office, the interest in market-oriented activities decreased again. Nevertheless, the situation was better than before, because the customer contact development office created guidelines for local advertising and sales campaigns and developed training programs for employees. Specifically, these training programs were intended to help employees handle customer contacts and interactive communication.

In order to improve market orientation on the local level, the regional marketing consultants were removed, and the total responsibility for marketing was given to the branch managers. At the same time the bank started to turn the local offices to profit centers one by one. When the regionally located marketers were gone, and there was no central marketing department to turn to, the interest in marketing and customer consciousness among the branch managers started to increase. The profit center responsibility accompanied by a very large decision making authority obviously supported this tendency.

The customer contact development office supported the branch office managers in training their personnel and in developing advertising and sales efforts locally. Slowly, the market orientation and sales mindedness among the employees improved. The bank also became one of the most profitable, and has remained so. In fact, over the years its profitability has always been above the average of all major banks in the market it serves.

Interactions and the Service Production System

In this and the following sections of the present chapter we move the focus from the structural approach to organizing to a more detailed discussion of how to manage the moments of truth in the interactions of the service production and delivery system.

The most central cornerstone of service quality is the interactions between the organization and its customers, where the moments of truth occur. As discussed in the present chapter, the resources used by the organization to product and deliver a certain quality have to be directed toward supporting customer perception of these moments of truth. These buyer-seller interactions have to include a process quality dimension, the *functional quality*, in itself, and they have to enhance the rendering of the outcome quality dimension, the *technical quality*, as well.

The customer impact of the buyer-seller interactions is not only a function of the customer orientation and the service mindedness of the resources directly involved in these interactions; it depends just as much on the support given by other resources and functions, which are less visible to customers. If, for example, in a warehouse the delivery truck is not loaded carefully and according to schedule, the delivery function will not be able to interact positively with its customers. The term *back office* is sometimes used in connection with such invisible parts of the organization (see, for example, Eiglier & Langeard 1976 and Normann 1984).

Consequently, when the service orientation of the interactive part of a firm is planned and managed, one has to go much deeper into the organization in order to strengthen the moments of truth of the interactions. This means that the whole system for producing and delivering a service has to be managed as a total function. Looking only at the interactions themselves and the resources involved easily misguides management.

In this connection the terms *service delivery system* and *service production system* are used. The former term is definitely too narrow in scope, because it only focuses on the delivery of the service, which more or less equals the interactions with the customers. The latter term is more inclusive, because producing a service includes by definition delivery of that service. This, of course, follows from the fact that a service is not finished until it has been fully delivered to the customer. (Langeard and Eiglier have suggested the term "servuction" as an abbreviation of service production; see Langeard & Eiglier 1987.)

In the following discussion of the system where the service is produced and delivered we prefer to use the term *Service Production System.* If this total system is well designed and functions well, the experiences of the moments of truth will be favorable and the perceived service quality will be good. The service concepts of the firm will be transformed into concrete, high-quality service offerings.

Managing the Service Production System

Managing the Service Production System includes two main areas:

1. Developing service-generating resources, and
2. Coordinating the interaction of these resources.

Thus, developing and managing the system requires, first of all, that the amount of resources are determined. These *quality-generating resources* are the human (personnel and customers) and physical resources needed to produce a certain predetermined level of service quality.

Second, these resources have to be *coordinated into a functioning system,* which turns the service concept into services with the desired quality. If the organization has invested correctly in resources, but the interactions of the resources are badly managed or not managed in a servicelike manner, the service concept does not hold. On the other hand, if the interactions are managed in a servicelike way, but the resources are insufficient or otherwise less adequate, it will also be difficult to produce the desired service quality.

Managing the service-generating resources and the Service Production System starts with the *business mission* of the firm. The quality-generating resources and their use should always be geared to clearly stated *service concepts.* Moreover, these concepts must be derived from the business mission. A service firm should not go into areas of service production other than those that are within the scope of the firm's mission. Otherwise, for example, competence problems may occur. By the same token, a manufacturer of goods should not add services to its customer relationships that are not clearly part of the overall mission of the firm.

When deciding upon the service concepts and the quality-generating resources, *market research* is required in most cases. Otherwise the needs and wishes of the potential customers may be misinterpreted and wrong steps taken in the planning process. For example, research concerning the following issues is essential: which segments of potential customers are there, how big are they, what are the needs, wants, and wishes of potential customers, and what are the corresponding benefits from a service offering sought by these customers. In addition to using information from external market research, management should also tap internal sources of information. For example, people involved in producing a service and in interactions with customers are often invaluable sources of relevant information.

The Quality-Generating Resources

As indicated in the previous section, a clear strategic base is needed when the Service Production System is developed. This, of course, is a prerequisite for achieving a certain desired service quality. Figure 8–5 illustrates in a simple but useful way the quality-generating resources in their strategic setting. If the central elements of the strategy model of this exhibit—service concept, systems, personnel, and customers—are properly interrelated, and if they, moreover, are adequately based on the business mission, so that a desired total service quality is achieved, the organization probably has a winning *service strategy*.

The lines connecting the elements in the figure with each other illustrate the existing interrelationships in the model. The *interrelationship between service concept and customer* indicates that the organization through market research gathers information from the market concerning what

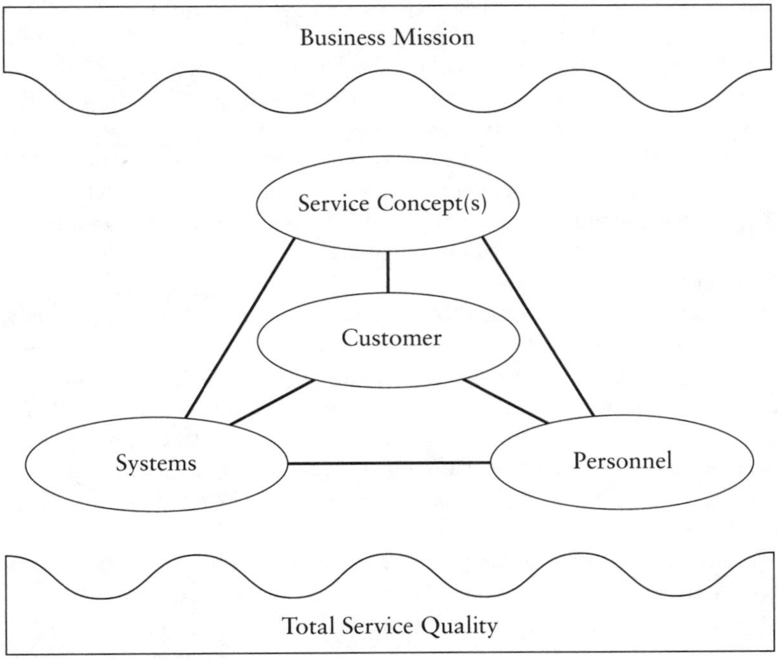

Figure 8–5. A Strategic View of the Interrelationships of the Quality–Generating Resources

potential customers want and how they want to be served. Based on such information the service concepts are developed. Second, in the other direction this line is a recognition of the fact that in most cases the customers themselves actively take part in the service production process. As Normann (1984) states: ". . . the client (customer) appears twice: as a consumer in the market segment and as part of the service delivery system" (p. 51). Because of the double role of customers, it may often be valuable to maintain a sufficiently extended contact with them. "Clearly, many successful organizations have found it beneficial to keep customers in the organization for as long as possible to maximize impulse purchases, . . . or to gain information from the customer that may result in an additional sale now or in the future" (Tansik 1988, p. 9). The service concept guides the way in which customers are supposed to perform. Depending on the service concept self-service activities may be demanded, or abilities to fill out certain documents, give necessary information, or interact with other customers.

In this manner customers as quality-generating resources are made an integral part of the Service Production System. Customers become involved in co-designing and/or co-producing what they get, and the organization has to develop means of facilitating them with the tools and knowledge necessary to handle this role (Bowen, Siehl & Schneider 1989 and Mills & Morris 1986). Customers have to be *guided,* for example, by information in advance, by signs or personal advice from employees, so that quality is added to their service perception. Otherwise the opposite effect may occur. Finally, customers have to feel *rewarded* when they take over production tasks from the firm. Lower prices are usually used as rewards, but they are by no means the only ones.

In conclusion, customers can be expected to do well as co-producers or "partial employees" if they have a (1) *motivation* (feel they are rewarded by their efforts) to take part in the production process, if they (2) *understand the task* they are expected to carry out, that is, if there is a (3) *role clarity*, and have been accurately (4) *informed* about the task and how to cope with it, and finally, if they have the (5) *ability* (the required task-relevant competence) to carry out the task (Bowen, Siehl, & Schneider 1989 and Bowen 1986).

The *interrelationship between service concepts and personnel* illustrates, first of all, the fact that staffing is an important part of service management. Personnel includes frontline customer contact employees as well as back-office employees and staff needed to produce the service. The right number of employees are required, if the service concepts are expected to be transformed into an adequate service offering. Too little personnel, inappropriately trained personnel, or a less efficient distribution of the personnel among various functions may cause quality problems. Moreover, the attitudes of employees and their motivation to perform in a service-oriented manner has to correspond with the intentions of the service concepts. If there is a mismatch between service concepts and personnel, the quality of the service offering will be damaged. The basic service package may be acceptable, but problems with accessibility and interactions with customers may occur. Then, functional quality in particular will deteriorate, because the employees do not have enough time for their customers, they may be rude or lack interest in the customers, waiting times may become long, and so forth.

The *interrelationship between service concept and systems* can be interpreted in a similar manner. Systems include ways of operating, routines, and so on, as well as the technology used and the physical resources involved in the service production process. The way of operating and the appropriateness of the technology and physical resources used determine the extent to which the service concept can be turned into a desired service offering. The better systems, technology, and physical resources are matched to each other and the service concepts, the better a certain service quality can be achieved.

However, internal systems and the way in which such systems are geared to the service concept are important as well. For example, measurement and rewarding systems have an impact on the externally perceived quality. As Donald Myles, Vice President of Information and Service from IBM Canada urges: "Ask yourself, are your measurement systems, what you measure, and your rewarding system, what you reward, consistent with your goals." If the answer is no, the goals will probably not be achieved.

The *interrelationship between personnel and systems* demonstrates that the employees in service organizations and the various systems for operations and administrative routines and the technology used have to match each other. If a customer service routine is too complicated or a system for back-office information check-up takes too much time, employees cannot give good service, even if they would like to and are prepared to do so. As the discussion in chapter 3 showed, a mismatch easily creates gaps in the internal quality production process. The technical quality dimension may not be damaged, but the functional quality easily deteriorates.

Also, the technology used, for example, computer systems for information processing, or other physical resources, for example, documents, may make everyday life unnecessarily complicated for the employees. Problems in maintaining a high service quality will probably follow from this. If systems and technology are considered complicated and inappropriate, and especially if the employees do not realize why they have to be so, the motivation for good service among the personnel may be damaged. On the other hand, if systems, technology, and other physical resources are developed so that they make it easy to give good service, it will be much easier to maintain service-oriented attitudes among the employees.

Finally, there is the *interrelationships between customers and personnel* and *between customers and systems,* respectively. For example, in a bank the attitudes and behavior of the teller may have a critical impact on the service quality as it is perceived by the customer. On the other hand, the customer influences the teller by his or her way of behaving. A tricky customer easily gets a less courteous response than a polite and well-behaving customer. A customer who has complicated problems or who is not able to express his or her demands clearly may get less attention if the teller does not understand what the customer really requests. The customer who wants to operate an automatic teller machine has to know how to use the machine. If the system is unnecessarily complicated, or if the customer just does not know what to do, the service will be bad or nonexistent.

Customers, personnel, and systems, including technology and other physical resources, are sometimes related to each other in a rather straightforward way, but often in a rather complicated fashion. Depending on how well the organization manages to plan and execute these interrelationships, the service will be good or bad. If there is a mismatch, technical quality may or may not be damaged, but the functional quality of the process itself will most certainly be low.

Strategies for Developing the Service Production System

There are a variety of strategies that can be used in developing the Service Production System to achieve a desired level of service quality. The service concept, of course, itself implies some guidelines. However, a similar result may be reached by various combinations of quality-generating resources.

The strategy has to be geared to the needs and wishes of the target customers. Some customers are well prepared and perfectly willing to perform many tasks in the production process. For such customers various elements of self-service can be used. Personnel can to some extent be easily substituted by systems and technology, and customers can be asked to take an active part in the process. Other groups of customers are not interested in such tasks or are not able to interact in this way. Such customers need to get more advice, or want to be served in a personal fashion. A couple looking for a candlelight dinner are, for example, not willing to act as if they were eating in a fast-food restaurant.

Internal Service Providers and Internal Customers

In the previous section we described the quality-generating resources of a service operation and their interrelationships in a simple but illustrative model. In this section we further develop their role in the service production process. Because services are a number of interrelated activities or processes, all parts of the total process, built up by subprocesses, have to match and function in an acceptable way.

Traditionally, customers are thought of as persons or organizations external to a company. This is, indeed, the traditional position of a customer. And, of course, such *external customers* have to be served in such a fashion that their needs are fulfilled and they are satisfied with the firm's way of performing. In the next chapter we will briefly cover the issue of external customers. However, there are user–service provider relationships inside as well. The frontline employees and functions of a firm have to be supported by other persons and functions in the firm, for example, by back-office functions, if they are to give good service to the ultimate, external customers. For example, goods cannot be delivered in a service-oriented way if the warehouse does not supply the truck driver with the correct items, in good condition, and in time.

As a matter of fact, every service operation is full of such *internal service functions,* which support one another and, in the final analysis, the frontline employees and functions interacting with external customers. Frequently, there may be many more internal service functions than external customer service functions.

To sum up, if the internal service is less than good, the externally rendered service will be damaged. However, it is often difficult for persons involved in internal service functions supporting other functions to realize the importance to the final service quality of their performance. They never see "real" customers, and they easily feel that those whom they serve are somehow just fellow employees and that the service they get does not affect the external performance in any way. In a successful service business, the advice of Jan Carlzon of SAS concerns everybody: "If you don't serve customers, you'd better serve somebody else (in the organization)."

A way of tackling the attitudinal problem of those who should serve "somebody else" (other than the ultimate customers) is to introduce the concept of *internal customer* (Gummesson 1987d). This concept brings customer–service provider relationships inside the organization, as is schematically illustrated by Figure 8–6. There may be one or a whole range of internal service functions, each illustrated by a box within the larger box in the figures. These functions are *internal customers* to other internal service providers; they are also *service providers* to other internal

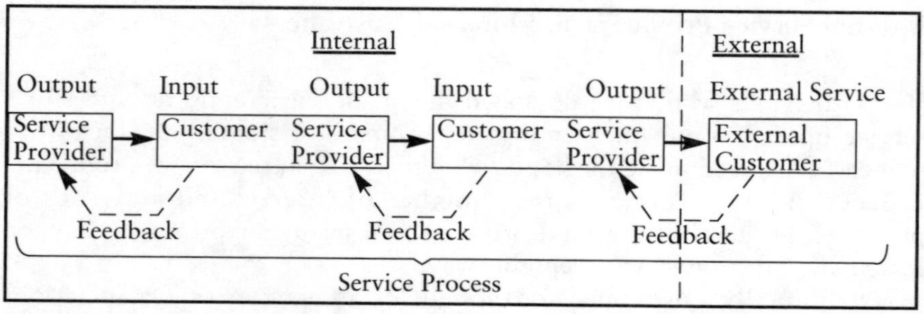

Source: Based on Gummesson, E. (1987): *Marketing — A Long-Term Interactive Relationship: Contribution to a New Marketing Theory*. Stockholm, Sweden: Marketing Technology Center, p. 42.

Figure 8–6. Internal Service Functions and Internal Customers

customers. Finally, in the service process, the ultimate output is the external service received and perceived by the ultimate external customer.

When the existence and importance of internal customer relationships are realized by the personnel, it is much easier to change attitudes among employees. The concept of internal customer gives a totally new dimension to the tasks performed inside an organization. "Only when the customers are satisfied—it is the satisfied customer that counts irrespective of whether he is external or internal—has a job been properly executed" (Gummesson 1987d, p. 42).

Sometimes the internal customer–service provider relationships may be very straightforward. However, frequently they can be very complicated, with relationships in which both parties serve each other, or when the outcome of one function depends on the internal service provided by two or more other functions. It is absolutely mandatory that *such internal customers are served as well as the ultimate, external customers are expected to be served.* Hence, this means that generating quality into services is not the exclusive duty of those functions to which the external customers are visible. For example, the perceived quality of delivery services depends just as much on the performance of the warehouse as it does on the performance of the delivery function itself. Therefore, *the responsibility for producing good service quality is spread throughout the organization.*

A Systems Model of Service Production

In many cases two or more functions may be directly involved with customers. Then it is of vital importance that these parallel processes are coordinated and perceived by customers as *one* single service process. Otherwise service quality will inevitably deteriorate. If there is no one responsible for the customer in such situations, he or she is easily sent from one person to another in an unorganized way. The organization does not take responsibility for the service, and the customer is forced to take over the responsibility for getting service. This is bad quality.

In Figure 8–7 how the service production process is built up by interrelations and interdependencies between a number of subprocesses is schematically illustrated. The external customer gets in touch with part of the subsystems only. As indicated in the figure, there is a *line of visibility* (this concept was introduced in the service literature by Shostack 1984 and 1987) dividing those parts of the process that customers immediately see and perceive from those parts that only indirectly influence the service quality perception. Psychologically, this sometimes causes problems internally.

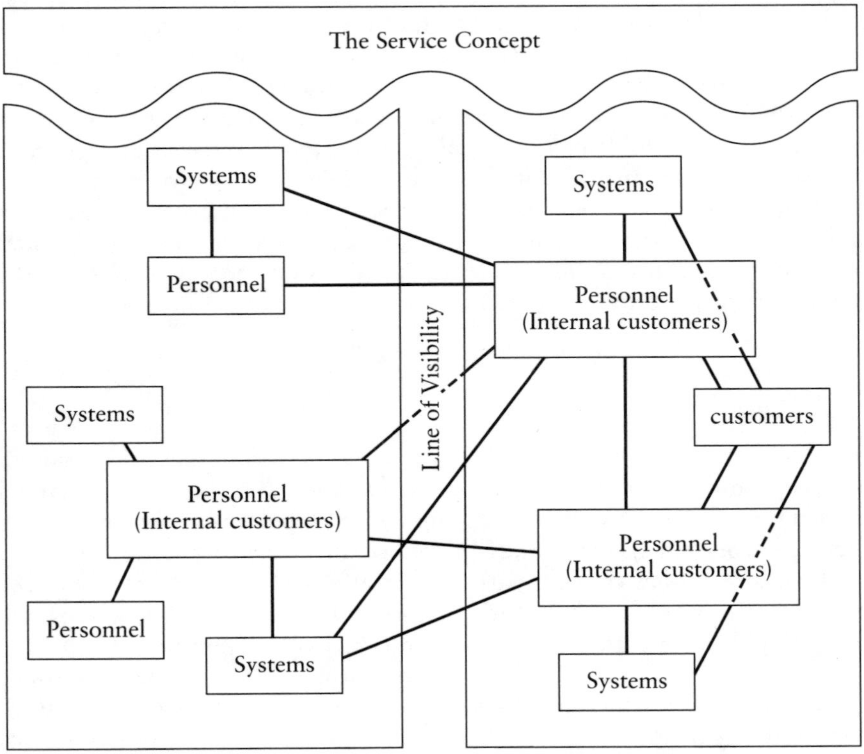

Figure 8–7. The Service Production System as a Function of Subprocesses

Persons behind the line of visibility may misunderstand their role in the service production process. They may feel that what they do and how they do it is of less importance than the performance of those on the visible side of the line. This is a mistake, of course, because the critical importance of servicing internal customers well is forgotten. On the other hand, such a mistake is often understandable, because in many cases these interdependencies are not discussed and stressed enough internally. Figure 8–7 demonstrates the enormous range and impact of the internal customer phenomenon. *Almost everybody has customers to serve, although sometimes most customers are internal ones.*

When developing the Service Production System various strategies can again be used. The part of the total system that is on the visible side of the line can be limited to, say, only one or two persons. Customers get in touch with them only, and most of the service production process is taken care of internally. For example, an insurance company that directs all of its contacts through one single agent is using such a strategy. Such a strategy is applied, of course, to make it as easy and as uncomplicated as possible for customers to deal with the firm. Another strategy is to expose customers to many subprocesses. A restaurant, for instance, is normally forced to apply such a strategic approach. In this case the customer relationship is broader and more vulnerable. Mistakes that may occur do so under the eyes of the customer. Fewer problems can be taken care of as internal affairs. And, of course, there are an unlimited number of options between these two examples. The main thing is that the service production process is designed so that perceived service quality is maximized. Again, the needs and wishes of target customers should guide strategic decisions concerning where the line of visibility is drawn.

Summary

In this chapter we have discussed how to organize for market orientation in a service context. In services, a flat organization that honors the critical importance of the functions and employees in the customer interface is required. Top management, staff functions, and support functions have to be organized so that they support the operations of the frontline. Since the marketing function is spread throughout the organization, a separate marketing department cannot in the traditional sense be responsible for the total marketing function. An organizational innovation is needed. Furthermore, the quality-generating resources within the organization were discussed. Next, more dynamic frameworks for managing these resources are presented in the following chapter.

9
Managing the Moments of Truth: Integrating Service Production with the Consumption Process

Introduction

In chapter 4 we stated that the service as a product is a complicated *service offering* which consists of a basic service package and, in addition to that, accessibility, interaction, and customer participation components. In chapter 8 we observed that the service in a Service Production System is produced by a number of quality-generating resources. The next crucial issue is to identify the resources needed in a certain situation to produce a certain *Augmented Service Offering* with a desired *Total Perceived Quality* to a specified target group of customers. Unless we can do this, it is not possible to develop services in a customer-oriented fashion. In this chapter the customer as an actor in the Service Production System and as consumer will be briefly discussed. Then the issue of how the Service Production System can in detail be understood is addressed. Finally, models for the development of services are presented.

The Consumption Process from the Customer's Point of View

An instrument which can be used for identifying the resources required to produce a service is an *analysis of the consumption process* of the customers. Because of the basic characteristics of services, the process includes a range of activities and subprocesses. The customer perceives these and hence that service consumption itself is also a process. Some production processes, for example, back-office activities, are not perceived directly by the customer, only the result of these activities are consumed. This was illustrated in Figure 8–7 in the previous chapter. However, a certain part, and often a substantial part of the service production process takes place simultaneously with the consumption process. And part of consumption may take place afterward, as is the case with, say, a hairdo or laundry services.

However, from a service quality point of view, that production and consumption are simultaneous processes is of vital importance. In this way the vital functional quality of the process is perceived. And as pointed out earlier, excellent functional quality is a necessity in service competition. The perception of even a very good technical quality of the output of the process is easily destroyed by a bad functional quality impact.

First of all, however, it is essential that the firm knows who its customers in reality are and understands how they make their decisions. It is not enough to have a fair knowledge of the composition of customer segments; more detailed understanding of the individuals that *are* the customer is required. Therefore, we begin this chapter with a brief discussion of who the customers are and how they think.

The Customer as Individual and Group

We are not going to discuss the customer concept, consumer behavior, or organizational buying behavior in any detail. Instead, we will discuss a few important issues in connection with the customer concept. First of all, it is important to realize that the customer may appear either as an individual or in the form of a group. For many consumer services, such as a hair stylists, mass transit, and restaurants, the customer is a single person who purchases and consumes the service. Sometimes, and almost always as far as services to organizations are concerned, the customer is a group of individuals. The service may be purchased by one person, a *purchasing agent* but actually used or consumed by other persons.

The services and the performance of the organization should, of course, be geared to the needs, wants, and wishes of the customers. However, if many persons are involved in the role of customer in the relationship between the service provider and buyer, *the whole group is the customer.* All these actors of the buyer—purchasing agent, users, formal decision maker, and others—together form what is often called a *buying center* in the literature on organizational buying behavior (see, for example, Webster & Wind 1972). Moreover, every single individual involved in the relationship is, in principle and in reality, equally important. Frequently, the purchasing agent, with whom the salesperson interacts, is considered *the* customer. The other persons involved, for example, when the service is used by the buying organization, are easily considered less important.

For example, when a sales representative from a cleaning company negotiates with a buying firm, he or she most often negotiates with a purchasing agent only. If the potential customer is a smaller firm, the sales representative may be in contact with an office manager or even the top person. In any case, he or she hears the views of a person who is not involved in using the service of the cleaning firm. There may be internal differences in the buying firm concerning what is needed. The purchasing agent, however, may not represent all these opinions, and probably not the view of the users. He or she may be more interested in the technical specifications of the service and in price than in how the cleaning firm functions in reality. The sales representative gets the views and perspectives of the purchasing agent, and gives promises that satisfy that individual. However, when the cleaning firm starts to operate the assignment, the users of the service in the offices or in the factories or service locations may be discontented with what the cleaning firm is doing. They perhaps feel that the firm functions in a less appealing way, or they may be dissatisfied with the technical specifications of the service, or they perhaps would like the firm to pay more for a higher level of cleaning service. For one reason or another, the service is considered less good. This opinion eventually spreads to the decision maker and the purchasing agent. The customer is a group, although the salesperson perhaps does not meet anyone other than the purchasing agent. Those providing the service will be in contact with many more representatives of the buyer, and they, too, have an impact on the future purchasing and usage behavior of the customer.

Viewing the customer too narrowly may turn out to be a serious mistake. The users of the service are the persons who perceive the quality of the services. If they are not satisfied with what they get, the whole group, including the purchasing agent, may eventually become discontented with the service provider. If and when this happens, it will be difficult, probably impossible, for the salesperson to keep the customer relationship alive. The customer will be lost. And replacing a lost customer with a new customer is almost always more expensive than reselling and cross-selling to existing customers. According to some anecdotal evidence, marketing to a new, potential customer may be six times or more as expensive than marketing to an existing customer. And getting an unsatisfied ex-customer back may cost up to 25 times as much, and sometimes much more.

Needs, Wishes, and Expectations

What makes a given customer want a certain type of service? And what makes the customer purchase it from a certain service provider? The reactions of customers are based on their *expectations*, but these are a function of a whole range of internal and external factors.

The *needs* of a customer form a basic factor, which at least directs expectations toward a certain type of solution. An organization may form its needs in a somewhat more complicated way than a single customer or a household. In principle, however, it is the same kind of phenomenon, that is, some sort of a problem that requires a solution. This solution may be solved in a number of ways. For example, house cleaning can be managed by buying proper equipment and by a do-it-yourself approach. Or one can take care of it by purchasing the service. In both cases there are a number of options available in relation to what to buy, and where to buy the necessary equipment or the service.

It is, however, essential to realize that needs alone do not determine what kind of, say, service a person looks for. The needs determine in a way *what* the potential customer wants, and many service providers can usually produce an acceptable solution in this respect. In addition, customers also have certain *wishes* in relation to *how* they want the service provider to treat them. This normally narrows the scope of options available. For example, almost any retailing bank can provide an individual with the services he or she may need, but not every bank manages to treat customers in a fashion they are pleased with. (Compare the *technical* and *functional* dimensions of customer perceived service quality introduced in chapter 2.) To sum up, both the *needs*, which mainly determine what customers are looking for, and the *wishes* in relation to how they want the service provider to perform are of vital importance in the development of *customer expectations*.

Expectations, however, are also formed by external factors. This has been discussed in more detail in previous chapters. For example, what family acquaintances and business associates say about a given service provider, word-of-mouth communication, has an impact on the formation of the expectations. This is often of great importance. Moreover, the market communication activities, such as personal selling and advertising campaigns, influence expectations. Finally, corporate and local image influences expectations as well.

Customer Segments and Target Groups

Customers have differing needs and/or wishes concerning how they want to be treated. An organization can, therefore, very seldom satisfy the needs of every potential customer in a similar manner. And it should not try to solve everyone's problems. Customers have to be divided into *segments* which are homogeneous and which are sufficiently different from each other. One or a few such segments are then chosen as *target groups* of customers. In service contexts it is often difficult to satisfy target groups of customers with too different needs and wishes. Because customers frequently meet and interact with each other, they influence fellow customers' perception of the service. For example, a family having a picnic on a Saturday afternoon in the park does not mix very well with a bunch of beer drinkers. If the firm goes for segments that are different from each other, it is normally a good idea to keep them apart. Finally, it should be noticed that a Service Production System in and of itself normally cannot take care of the tasks of satisfying too-diverse needs and wishes. This follows from the fact that services are complicated phenomena and service production is a complicated task.

Relating the Service Package to the Consumption Process

Having discussed the nature and driving forces of customers in the previous sections, we now turn to the issue of how the customer and the consumption process can be incorporated into the service production process. Doing this is of utmost importance because of the nature of services and the inseparability of large and critical parts of production and consumption. To analyze the service consumption process in a systematic manner, one can use the conceptualization suggested by Lehtinen (1983 and 1986). Following Lehtinen, the consumption process can be divided into three phases:

1. The joining phase
2. The intensive consumption phase
3. The detachment phase

The *joining phase* is the first stage of the consumption process, where the customer gets in touch with the service provider in order to buy and consume a core service, for example, elevator maintenance. In this phase mainly facilitating services are required, for example, telephone contact to the elevator maintenance firm in order to get hold of a service technician. Some supporting services may sometimes be used, for example, a toll-free number or an easy-to-use telephone directory which makes it easy for the customer to know where to call.

The *intensive consumption phase*, or just *consumption phase*, is the main stage of the total service consumption process. In this phase the needs of the customer have to be satisfied, or his or her problem has to be solved.

Hence, the core service or services are consumed at this stage. For example, the elevator is serviced. Furthermore, there may be some facilitating services, for example, a shelter surrounding the work space, and supporting services, for example, instructions to persons normally using the elevator directing them to the stairs and telling them when the job is expected to be finished. In the *detachment phase* the customer leaves the Service Production System. This often requires some facilitating services, for example, the service technician fills in a report and hands it over to the janitor or another representative of the customer. Supporting services may be used here, too.

In Figure 9–1 the service consumption process and the various types of services related to the three phases of the process are schematically illustrated. If, for example, we look at a full-service restaurant, the *joining phase* may include table reservations (F1) and cloakroom services (F2) as facilitating services, and valet parking (S1) as a supporting service. During the *consumption phase* the core service, which may be a three-course dinner, is consumed. The table setting (F3) and the performance of the waiters (F4) are facilitating services, and live music (S2) may be a supporting service. In the *detachment phase* when the customer leaves the restaurant, some facilitating services are needed, for example, paying the check (F5) and again the cloakroom services (F6). Valet parking (S3) may be used as a supporting service again at this stage.

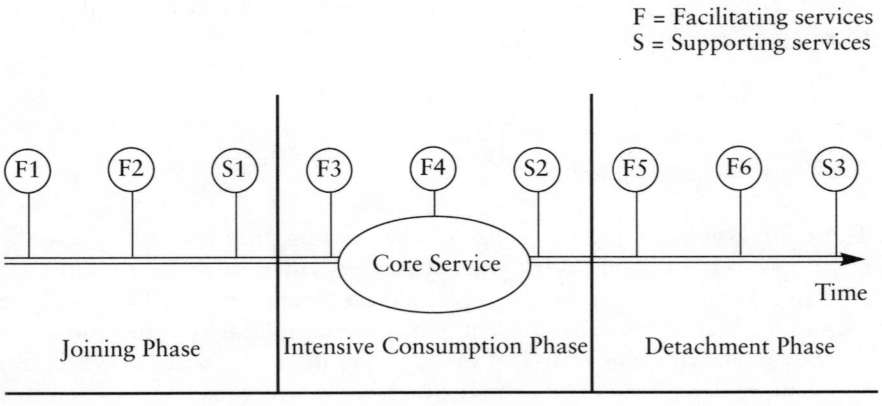

Source: Based on a figure in Lehtinen, J. (1986): *Quality Oriented Services Marketing*. University of Tampere, Finland, p. 38.

Figure 9–1. The Service Package and the Service Consumption Process

It should be observed, however, that this model takes into account the components of the basic service package only. The next step is to take the components of the Augmented Service Offering, that is, *accessibility*, *interactions*, and *customer participation*, into account so that the functional quality dimension of the process is covered as well.

The Service Production System

The Service Production System illustrated in Figure 9–2 can be used for analyzing and planning service production. In the figure the various quality-generating resources are combined in a systematic way. The large central square illustrates the service-producing organization from the customer's point of view. From the producer's point of view there may be several functions or departments involved, but the customer sees it as one integrated system. The customer is located inside the square because, in fact, he or she is a resource engaged in service production. Yet, "most service organizations are managed with an operating bias that treats the customer as being isolated from the organization's core technology, and as only a consumer rather than a co-producer of the organization's output" (Tansik 1988, p. 1). This, of course, is due to a manufacturing-oriented view of the role of the customer (see Chase 1988 and Normann 1984). Customers are not distant and totally outside the organization as they are in a mass-manufacturing context. Instead, they interact with other parts of it.

The *line of visibility*, to use the concept introduced by Shostack (1984 and 1987), divides the part of the organization that is visible to customers from the part that is invisible. To the right, outside the main square, the means of influencing the *expectations* of customers are illustrated, such as their needs and wishes, their previous experiences, corporate and local image, word-of-mouth, external market communication, and also absence of communication.

To the left of the square are the *business mission* and the corresponding *service concepts*, which like umbrellas should guide planning and managing the Service Production System. At the bottom of the main square is the *corporate culture* that is, the norms and shared values that determine what people in the organization think and appreciate. The culture is always present. Sometimes it has a substantial impact on the employees, sometimes it is more vague. If the culture is not service oriented, it creates problems for an organization providing services. We shall return to this issue later on in chapter 11.

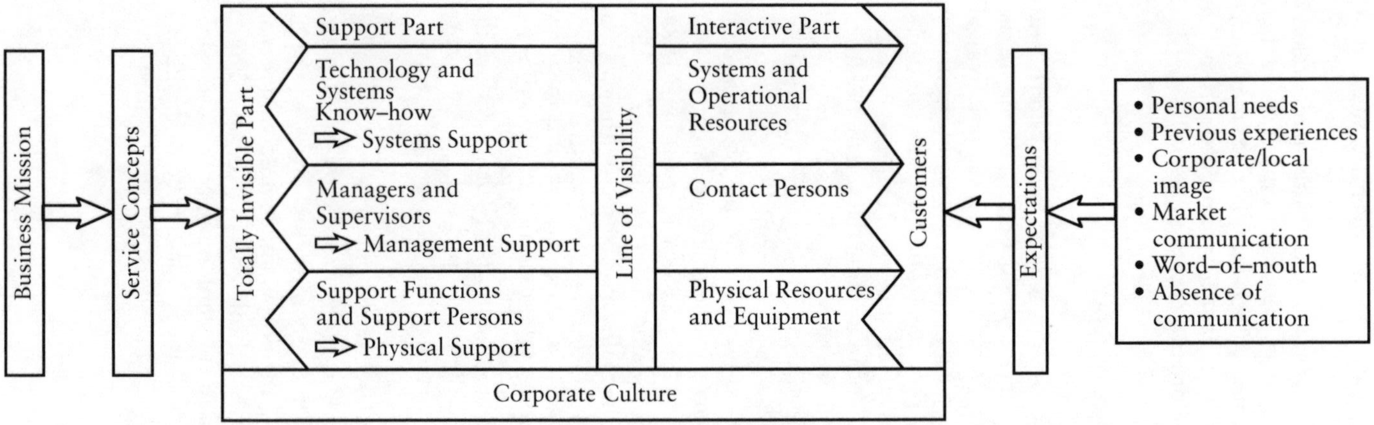

Figure 9–2. The Service Production System

The Interactive Part

In immediate contact with customers is the visible or *interactive part* of the Service Production System (see Figure 9–2). It consists of customers and the rest of the quality-generating resources which the customers interact with directly. These are the direct buyer-seller interactions where the *moments of truth* take place. The quality-generating resources in the interactive part are:

- Customers involved in the process;
- Contact persons;
- Systems and operational routines; and
- Physical resources and equipment

Customers are directly involved in the Service Production System as a quality-generating resource. Because of the nature of service production and consumption, customers are not just passive consumers. At the same time they consume the service, they also take part in production of that service in an active way; sometimes more as when getting a hairdo or having a three-course dinner at a gourmet restaurant, sometimes less as when using a freight forwarder's service. In some cases customers interact with a large Service Production System when staying at a hotel, whereas in other situations they are in touch with only a limited subsystem, as when operating an automatic teller machine. Irrespective of the nature of the situation, customers, however, actively take part in the Service Production System.

Employees directly interacting with customers are called *contact persons* or *contact employees*. Sometimes other concepts such as customer contact employees, service employees, or frontline personnel are used. Anyone can be a contact person, irrespective of which position or job he or she may have in the hierarchy. The interactions that take place may be face-to-face contacts or interactions over the telephone or even by telex, telefax, or letter. A manager or supervisor may also be a contact person if direct customer contacts, on a regular or irregular basis, are part of his or her job. Frequently, the contact personnel is the most crucial resource for a service provider. Systems, technology, and physical resources are a valuable support, but most service organizations depend more on its contact persons than on other resources. The contact persons are in a position to recognize the wishes and demands of customers in the moments of truth by watching, asking questions, and responding to the customers' behavior. Furthermore, they are able to instantly followup on the quality of the service rendered and undertake corrective actions as soon as a problem occurs and is observed.

Systems and routines consist of all operational and administrative systems as well as work routines of the organization. Queuing systems, how to cash a check in a bank, or how to operate a vending machine are examples of such systems. In fact, there are a vast number of systems and routines that influence the way of consuming the service and performing various tasks. The systems can be more or less service oriented. A complicated document which customers are supposed to fill in forms a system that is not service oriented. This normally means that the perceived service quality is less good than it otherwise would be. A manufacturer of goods has a range of such systems, which may be performed as administrative tasks without taking the customer into account, or turned into service-oriented procedures. Such systems are, for example, research and development, installation of machines and equipment, deliveries, customer training, quality control at the customer's premises, claims handling, billing, or telephone receptionist's services.

The various systems and routines have an impact on service quality which is twofold. First of all, they *directly influence the quality perception of customers*, because customers have to interact with the systems. If they feel comfortable with a certain system, it is probably service oriented. If, on the other hand, they feel that they are forced to adjust to a system, it is not as it should be. Quality is destroyed or at least damaged by the system. Second, the systems and routines have *an internal impact on employees*. If a certain system is considered old-fashioned, complicated, or in some way not service oriented, the employees who will have to live with the system will get frustrated. This, of course, influences motivation in a negative way.

Physical resources and equipment (which in the service strategy model in chapter 8 were grouped together with operational and administrative systems) include all kinds of resources used in the Service Production System. Computers, documents, and tools belong to this category. Some of these physical resources are a prerequisite for a good technical quality of the output. They influence, however, the functional quality as well, because customers may find it more or less easy to use them in self-service tasks and they give a favorable or less favorable impression on customers. Other physical resources have an impact on functional quality only. The interior of waiting rooms is an example of such physical resources. Physical resources and equipment used in the service process have an internal effect on employees similar to that of the systems. Contact persons, systems, and physical resources form an integral, visible Service Production System in the minds of the customers. Every single part has to match the total system, including the customers.

The Impact of the Support Part

Behind the interactive part, where the customer directly encounters the service organization, there is the *line of visibility* (see Figure 9–2). Customers seldom see what is going on behind this line, and they often do not realize the importance of the service production that takes place there. This causes at least two types of problems for the service provider. First of all, what takes place behind the line is not always appreciated as much as it should be by customers. Because of this fact, customers do not realize how much the service production there contributes to service quality. Irrespective of whether good quality, especially good technical quality, is produced in these back-office areas, customers probably perceive a bad service quality if the interactive part adds mediocre or worse quality. *What often happens is that good technical quality produced behind the line of visibility is damaged by bad functional quality produced in the service production process in front of the line.*

Second, customers may not understand why a given service has a certain price, because they do not realize how much is done behind the line. It may be difficult to explain why the price is so high, although the visible service production process seems uncomplicated and therefore in the minds of customers should not justify the real cost and price level.

Components of the Service Production System Behind the Line of Visibility

What happens in the supporting and totally invisible parts of the organization has an impact on what can be accomplished by the interactive part. This support is sometimes a major prerequisite for good service. There are three kinds of support to the interactive service production (see Figure 9–2 and Grönroos & Gummesson 1985c):

- Management support;
- Physical support; and
- Systems support

The most important type of support is the *management support* which every single manager and supervisor provides their subordinates with in their everyday job as managers and leaders. Managers and supervisors maintain the culture, and if the firm wishes to be characterized by a *service culture* (this concept is discussed in detail in chapter 11), they will have to keep up the spirit and support the norms and values of such a culture. They are responsible for the shared values and ways of thinking and performing in their work groups and departments. If employees are to be expected to keep up service-oriented attitudes and behaviors continuously, the manager is the key to success. The manager is the leader of the troops. If the boss does not provide subordinates with good examples, and if he or she is not capable of encouraging them to be service minded and customer conscious, the organization's interest in its customers and in giving good service will decrease. From this follows deteriorating functional quality of the service production process and perhaps even difficulties in maintaining the technical quality of the outcome of the process.

Contact persons often have to rely on *physical support* provided by functions and departments invisible to the customers. These *support persons* or *support employees* will have to consider contact persons their *internal customers* (see Chapter 8). In the supporting part there may be a range of support functions, for example, behind each other. Support persons have to be treated as internal customers by support functions further behind in the Service Production System. Internal customers have to be treated equally as well as external customers. The *internal service* has to be as good as the service to ultimate customers is supposed to be, otherwise the perceived service quality will be damaged. Information from registers of some sort, processing checks in the back offices of banks, loading trucks in warehouses, and decisions necessary to execute a service are examples of physical support.

The third type of support is *systems support*. This is of a somewhat different nature. The investments in technology, for example, computer systems, buildings, offices, vehicles, tools, equipment, and documents, form the systems support from behind the line of visibility. If the organization invests in a computer system which does not permit prompt answers to customers' questions or rapid decision making, the Service Production System lacks a good systems support. If a contact person is forced to deny a customer good service because of existing management regulations, there may be another type of inadequate system support—rules and regulations that are too rigid.

There is also another kind of systems support. The knowledge employees have of operating various systems can be called *systems know-how*. The organization must also invest in employees who know how to operate and make use of the systems and technology.

Behind the support part is the *totally invisible part* of the organization. This part is in a way outside the Service Production System. It consists of functions that do not influence the service offering and service quality either directly or indirectly. Internal bookkeeping is an example. Frequently, an analysis of the organization shows that there are surprisingly few parts that are truly totally invisible in this respect.

The Service Production System in a Network of Systems

In the previous sections the Service Production System has been viewed as one single organizational unit. This is, of course, not always the case. Frequently a total system is built up through a network of separate Service Production Systems. This, in the minds of customers, is normally perceived as *one* Service Production System.

For example, a hotel chain may have a hotel reservation system of its own, which is geographically located apart from the hotels. The customers who make their reservations themselves through this system at one point in time and stay at a hotel at a later date do judge the two Service Production Systems (the reservation system and the hotel's production system) separately, but they also view the reservation system as a part of the hotel's system. If the reservation system fails, the customer will not make a reservation at the hotel, and consequently, the total Service Production System (reservation and hotel together) fails. In principle, the same holds true if the customer makes his or her reservation through a travel agent not affiliated with the hotel chain. From a management point of view, it will probably be more complicated to manage the total Service Production System, since the other system of this *network*, reservation through an independent travel agent, is an independently managed organization.

Often the situation becomes even more complicated because the relationships between the parties in a network are often mutual. In the previous case, the hotel's Service Production System depends on that of the travel agent. But the Service Production System of the latter depends just as much on that of the hotel. If the travel agent directs a customer to a hotel that turns out to be less than satisfactory, the customer will blame not only the hotel but also the travel agent. In this situation the hotel can be considered a subcontractor of the hotel. However, they are both part of a network that consists of the Service Production Systems of both parties, and the customer will judge not only the systems of the two parties separately, but the total Service Production System of the network.

In manufacturing, firms often use various types of subcontractors to carry out service activities. For example, independent delivery firms take care of transportation of goods to customers, and independent firms are used to handle installation, technical service and repair, and customer training. In these situations similar networks emerge, where the manufacturer is often judged by the performance of the Service Production Systems of its subcontractors.

From a management point of view, it is essential, often crucial, to observe the existence of these networks of independent or affiliated Service Production Systems, and to realize the impact of one system on the other and on the success of the total system. For example, bad performance by one party, say an insurance broker, in the network may hurt, or even destroy, the other party, in this case the insurance company. On the other hand, an excellent service quality provided by a subcontractor in the network, say, by a delivery and transportation firm, may substantially enhance the image of the manufacturer in the minds of its customers.

Analyzing and Planning the Service Production System

As can be seen in Figure 9–2, a large part of the organization is involved in service production in one way or the other. When analyzing the Service Production System, the first task is to identify the *interaction resources* as well as the various kinds of *support* required from behind the line of visibility. A major mistake is to consider too much of the support part as totally invisible to customers. In fact, most of the organization is involved in the system and in producing service quality.

Next, the *quality-generating resources* and the support should be geared to the phases of the *service consumption process*. To this end, a *Service Production/Consumption Scheme* (Grönroos 1987c) is developed. This scheme consists of all customer contacts, the components of the basic service package, and all resources in the interactive and support parts. The Production/Consumption Scheme is developed in two steps. The first step includes an identification of customer contacts and the moments of truth, as well as core, facilitating, and supporting services during the service consumption process. It is essential that every customer contact and all activities that form the components of the service package are observed. Figure 9–3 illustrates a visit to a dentist as the first step of the scheme. In the column on the left-hand side a sample of service components forming the service package is illustrated. Diagnosis, treatment, and perhaps information about further actions form the core service, whereas dental care information and listening to music are supporting services. The components of the joining and detachment phases are either facilitating services (registration and payment) or supporting services (reading magazines). In the column on the right-hand side contacts between the

Consumption Phase/ Service Component	**Customer Contacts/ Encounter**
Joining Phase	
Arrival	Location
Registration	Registration office formalities
Waiting	Other patients
Reading magazines	Waiting room facilities
	Magazines
Intensive Consumption Phase	
Diagnosis	Dentist and nurse
Treatment	Dentist's room
Information about further actions	Equipment
	Milieu
Dental care information	Music
Listening to music	Information material
Detachment Phase	
Registration for next visit or	Registration office and formalities
Payment	Systems for paying
	Receipt

Figure 9–3. A Service Production/Consumption Scheme — Step 1

patient and the dentist's Service Production System are listed. In this way one gets a list of service components and the contacts emerging to facilitate them. Figure 9–3 is intended to be illustrative only; it by no means tells the whole story. Step 2 in the development of the Service Production/ Consumption Scheme involves identification of the resources required to produce the service package. In Figure 9–4 the dentist example is extended to the second step. The resources needed to produce one component in the basic service package, registration (a facilitating service), are identified. The example is, of course, simplified. The other components of the package will be analyzed in a similar manner.

When the two steps of the Service Production/Consumption Scheme are accomplished, what follows is the issue of *how* the quality-generating resources involved have to be used so that a desired total service quality is produced. The *accessibility* of the basic package, the *interactions* between

- Phase in consumption process: joining Phase
- Type of service component: facilitating service/registration
- Encounter: registering for visit

Identifying Resources			
Systems	Personnel	Physical Resources	Customer
Queuing system Computer system or register	Nurse	Office Computer Documents	Understands how to live up to other customers and their behavior
Line of Visibility			
System for keeping computerized register	Personnel controlling the system Maintenance personnel	Computer paper Maintenance tools	—

Figure 9–4. A Service Production/Consumption Scheme — Step 2

customers and the organization, and the *customer participation* impact have to be planned. When this has been accomplished, an *Augmented Service Offering* emerges.

Fitting the Performance of the Quality-Generating Resources to the Service Consumption Process

The quality-generating resources, that is, personnel, systems including physical resources, and customers, have to be carefully planned so that the emerging buyer-seller interactions produce a competitive functional quality. If this is achieved, an excellent interactive marketing impact is created as well. In Figure 9–5 the nature of this issue is schematically illustrated.

The model demonstrates the need for achieving a fit between the resources involved (see Lehtinen 1983). As we look at the buyer-seller interface and its moments of truth, *contact personnel* emerges as one critical resource. Every contact person has a specific way of performing, which can be called *style of performance*. For example, the dental

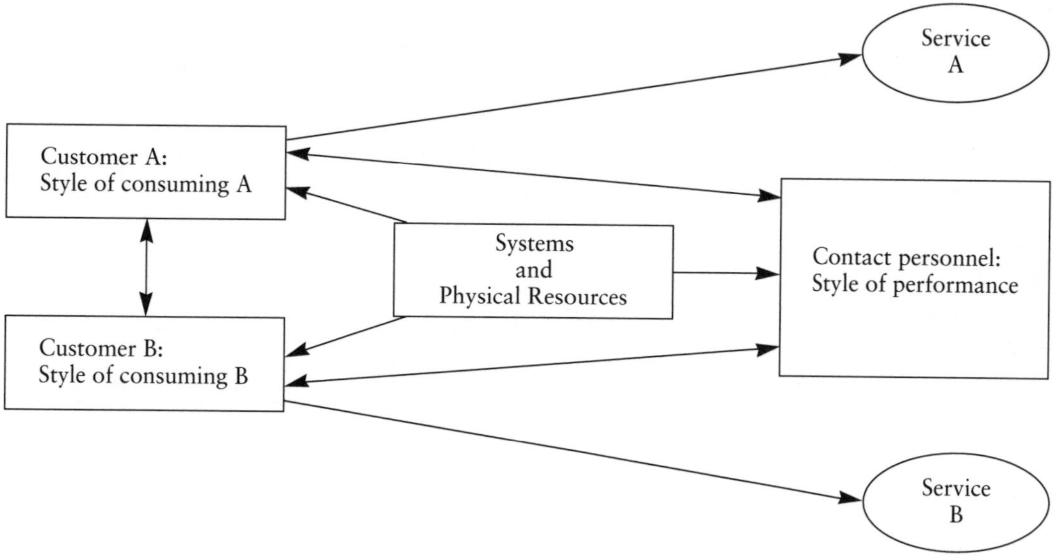

Source: Derived from a figure in Lehtinen, J. (1983): *Asiakasohjautuva palveluyritys* (Customer–Oriented service firm). Espoo, Finland: Weilin+Göös, p. 81.

Figure 9–5. The Content of the Buyer–Seller Interactions

receptionist and the dentist have their own way of doing and saying things and of performing their tasks. This style is, of course, partly due to their professional skills, but partly also due to their attitudes toward the patients.

This style of performance has to be geared to the corresponding *style of consuming* of the customers, the dentist's patients. If there is a misfit between these two styles, the perceived service quality will probably be damaged. Since many different customers are frequently present at the same time, their styles of consuming must fit as well. For example, a nervous patient in the waiting room may scare other people waiting to see the dentist. In a restaurant beer drinkers and a family having lunch may not get along very well in the same place. The perceived service quality deteriorates.

Furthermore, the *systems and physical resources* used in the service production process will have to fit the style of performance of contact persons as well as the style of consuming of customers. Inappropriate systems make it unnecessarily complicated and maybe even frustrating for contact persons to do their job. Moreover, if there is a misfit between the systems and the customers' style of consuming, they will not want to adjust to the systems or they will find it awkward to take part in the process. The perceived service quality is again damaged. For example, the treatment procedures and the equipment of the dentist, as well as registration and recall systems and waiting room facilities, have to fit the dentist and the other contact persons as well as the patient. The circles "Service A" and "Service B" indicate that Customers A and B may perceive slightly different services, irrespective of whether the basic service package is the same or not. In conclusion, the availability of quality-generating resources as such does not automatically lead to good customer perceived service quality. Sufficient and properly designed resources are a prerequisite, whereas the fit between them determines success. As de Brentani (1989) in a study of the development of new industrial services concludes: "The findings show, however, that it is not the basic character of the interface (with customers)—that is, its extent or whether it is equipment- or personnel-based—but the perceived quality of the customer experience that makes some new services winners while others fail" (pp. 31–32).

Figure 9–5 illustrates a case where ultimate, external customers are involved. The same goes for internal customers as well. The style of performance of supporting persons will have to match the style of consuming of contact persons as internal customers. If there is a misfit, the internal climate will suffer and the contact persons will feel that they get bad support, that is, insufficient internal service, from the support function. Moreover, the systems and physical resources of the support function will have to fit into the process in a similar manner.

Proposal for a Course Offering to
Swedish Students

TITLE OF COURSE: Special Topics in Services and Nonprofit Marketing

INSTRUCTOR: Linda Morris, Associate Professor of Marketing

Textbooks: Selected Readings in the Service Marketing (Kinko's package)

In recent years there has been a growing interest in how marketing of intangible services differ from marketing tangible goods. In the U.S. service businesses, e.g. health care, hospitality, home and child care, financial, and fast food service, has surpassed the growth in manufacturing. In addition to the for-profit service businesses there are many non-profit organizations that are interested in ways of improving customer service.

Services marketing is rapidly becoming an interest of Swedish marketers. I had the opportunity a few years ago to meet Christian Gronroos, a professor who is well known in the services marketing literature. Professor Gronroos has recently published a book, **Service Management and Marketing** (1990), which I plan to use in my Business 327-Services Marketing course this Spring, 1990 semester.

PURPOSE AND OBJECTIVES OF THE COURSE:

The purpose of this course is to examine the marketing theories and implementation of marketing strategies as they apply to health care, hospitality, financial, home/child care and other for-profit and non-profit services. More specifically, the course will focus on the traditional marketing mix elements (product, price, distribution, and promotion), the service process (i.e., steps and procedures in providing the service), customer service training and evaluation, and the physical

The objectives of the course are as follows:

1) compare the impact of services on the economies of the United States and Sweden
2) develop the student's understanding of the unique marketing problems faced by various types of service organizations and the service marketing mix elements;
3) develop the student's understanding of the relationship between service operations management and the service marketing activities through the servuction model; and
4) develop the student's understanding the consumer service orientation in the design and implementation of the service marketing activities.

SPECIAL TOPICS TO BE COVERED:

1) The Servuction Model of Service: Services operations management and marketing
2) Dimensions of Service Quality and How to Measure Service Quality
3) Training and Evaluation of Customer Service Personnel
4) The Psychology of Wait Times and Methods for Enhancing Customer Service
5) Service Blueprinting: Analyzing the Service Process
6) Enhancing the Physical Environment to Alter Perceptions of the Service Encounter
7) Supply and Demand Strategies for Service Inventories
8) Pricing and Promotion of Services
9) Distribution of Services

The Blueprinting Model

An engineering type of approach to developing the Service Production System has been proposed by Shostack (see, for example, Shostack 1984 and 1987). According to this *service blueprinting model*, every task needed to perform a service and the relation between the tasks involved in the process are drawn on a blueprint chart. A blueprint should thus document all steps and points of divergence in a given service. This should be carried out on the level of detail needed for the specific purpose. Especially, the difference between the focused service and competing services should be detected from the blueprint. From the service blueprint it is possible to analyze how changes in the use of resources will affect the service process and its outcome (Shostack 1987). The blueprint should also reveal *fail points* where mistakes may happen and perceived quality may be damaged, so that precaution can be taken in the planning process. More detailed information about service blueprinting can be found in publications by Shostack (1984 and 1987).

Summary

As service consumption and production are partly inseparable processes it is important that the development and execution of production resources and activities are closely geared to the whole consumption process, from the beginning to the last moment of truth. Otherwise customer perceived quality deteriorates and moments of opportunity are badly utilized. It is not enough to develop a well-functioning, high-quality operation to meet the demands of the intensive consumption phase of the total consumption process. If the joining and/or detachment phases are less well taken care of, the total perceived service quality suffers. The first and last series of moments of truth are frequently of more importance, relatively speaking, than what happens in between. The beginning of the interaction process sets the tone for the rest of the process, and the interactions in the detachment phase leave the customer with a last impression of the service and its production process.

In some cases, where a large part of service production takes place behind the *line of visibility*, the importance of the joining and detachment phases to perceived quality increases enormously. For example, when using the services of a auto repair shop, the customer may not see what is done to his or her car, or may not understand any more afterward than that the car has been fixed. This has no major impact on the customer's quality perception. The joining phase, when the car is taken in by the garage, and the detachment phase, when the car is delivered back to the customer, include a range of moments of truth where the customer interacts with the garage. These interactions in the beginning and at the end of the total process, then, become the main ground for quality perception, unless there is something wrong with the car. In that case the technical quality of the outcome has a negative impact on the perceived service quality as well. However, the car may have been serviced very well, but the customer is nevertheless unsatisfied with the service received and chooses another service provide the next time.

It is essential to plan for excellence and good service very thoroughly. Quality problems of strategic importance may occur any time during the total consumption process and be caused by mistakes made or a lack of interest in the ultimate customer in the interactive part of the organization as well as far back behind the line of visibility in the supporting part.

10 Managing Internal Marketing—A Prerequisite for Successful External Marketing

Introduction

In this chapter we are going to discuss one of the phenomena that have been highlighted by the research into service marketing, that is, *internal marketing*. The term itself has been coined as an umbrella concept for a variety of internal activities, which as such are not new, but which focused upon in this way offer a new approach to developing a service orientation and an interest in customers and marketing among the personnel. Internal marketing starts from a notion that the employees are a first, internal market for the organization. If goods, services, and external communication campaigns, cannot be marketed to this internal target group, marketing to ultimate, external customers cannot be expected to be successful either.

What Is Internal Marketing: A Summary

During the past fifteen years the concept of *internal marketing* has emerged first in the literature on services marketing and later in the service management literature (see, for example, Grönroos 1978, 1981, and 1985, Berry 1981, Normann 1984, George 1984 and 1986, Compton et al. 1987, and Carlzon 1987). Without using the concept itself, Eiglier and Langeard (1976) discussed the need for marketing services internally in organizations. Recently, this concept has also entered the literature on industrial marketing (see, for example, Grönroos & Gummesson 1985a). In the literature on service management, the internal marketing concept has been included as well, for example by Normann (1984) and, in the context of managing services in the public sector, by Grönroos (1987b) and Grönroos and Monthelie (1988). Heskett (1987) touches upon this phenomenon as well, observing that successful service firms have achieved their position ". . . by turning the strategic service vision inward (p. 120)"; they target key employee groups *and* customers, rather than customers only.

An increasing number of firms have recognized the need for internal marketing processes, again first in the traditional service sector, whereas manufacturers of industrial goods have followed somewhat later. The perhaps most spectacular internal marketing process is the one successfully implemented by SAS (Carlzon 1987), but there are a growing number of North American examples as well. Today, internal marketing is considered a prerequisite for successful external marketing performance (see, for example, Grönroos 1985 and Compton et al. 1987).[a]

Internal marketing is a management strategy. The focus is on how to develop customer-conscious employees. *Goods and services as well as specific external marketing campaigns have to be marketed to employees before they are marketed externally.* Every firm, or any organization, has an *internal market of employees*, which must first be taken care of. Unless this is done properly the success of the firm's operation on its ultimate, external markets will be jeopardized. To put it in the words of Heskett (1987): "Effective service requires people who understand the idea" (p. 124). And an understanding of the business and what is expected of people in the organization and why this is expected of them is not achieved without effort.

A current example of the need for internal marketing relates to the idea of *service guarantees*. Assuring potential customers that a service will work or otherwise corrective actions will be taken is becoming a means of attracting customers. In theory this concept is good. However, in practice it will backfire unless internal marketing is properly taken care of. If there is no understanding and mental readiness among employees for fulfilling in a proper manner what a service guarantee promises to customers, this per se excellent means of competition will become a means of disaster instead.

Internal marketing operates as a holistic management process to integrate multiple functions of the firm in two ways. First, it ensures that the employees at all levels in the firm, including management, understand and experience the business and its various activities and campaigns in the context of an environment that supports customer consciousness. Second, it ensures that all employees be prepared and motivated to act in a service-oriented manner. The premise of internal marketing is that the internal exchange between the organization and its employee groups must be operating effectively before the firm can be successful in achieving its goals regarding its external markets.

---

[a]The author has, together with William R. George, written a chapter on *internal marketing*, "Developing Customer-Conscious Employees at Every Level: Internal Marketing," for Congram, C.A. & Friedman, M.L., eds., *Handbook of Services Marketing*, New York: AMACON, 1990. The present chapter, and to some extent the following one on managing a *service culture*, are partly based on this presentation of internal marketing.

The Internal Marketing Concept

The increasing need for internal marketing is due to the renaissance of man in business in today's competitive climate. There is an ongoing movement from the industrial era to the new competition of the service economy, where the logic of the manufacturer has to be replaced by a new logic which we have called "a service know-how." The emerging importance of services to almost every business has enhanced the notion that a well-trained and service-oriented employee, rather than raw materials, production technology, or the products themselves, is the most critical scarce resource today. These employees will be even more critical in the relevant future in an increasing number of industries.

With the development of services marketing theories marketing is changing (compare also the more general views of the changing role and focus on marketing in Webster 1988). More emphasis is now being placed on keeping customers and cross-selling to existing customers (see, for example, Berry 1983, Grönroos 1983a, Levitt 1983, Jackson 1985a, and Gummesson 1987c). The concepts of *relationship marketing* and *interactive marketing*, which have already been discussed, were developed to describe marketing programs directed toward the existing customers of an organization.

Here the role of the employees is vital. Moreover, the marketing specialists of the marketing department are not the only human resource in marketing; often they are not even the most important resource. During customer contacts these marketing specialists are often outnumbered by a variety of employees whose main duties are production, deliveries, technical service, claims handling, and other tasks traditionally considered nonmarketing. However, the skills, customer orientation, and service mindedness of these persons are critical to the customers' perception of the firm and to future patronage behavior.

The *internal marketing concept* states that *the internal market of employees is best motivated for service-mindedness and customer-oriented performance by an active, marketinglike approach, where a variety of activities are used internally in an active, marketinglike and coordinated way* (see Grönroos 1983a).

The need for internal marketing is certainly not entirely new. Certain aspects of internal marketing programs and activities have been used in many firms for a long time. What is new with the internal marketing concept as described in this chapter is the introduction of a unifying concept for more effectively managing a variety of interfunctional and frequently well established activities as part of an overall program aiming at a common objective. *The importance of internal marketing is the fact that it allows management to approach all of these activities in a much more systematic and strategic manner.*

Two Aspects of Internal Marketing: Attitude Management and Communications Management

Internal marketing means two types of management processes, attitude management and communications management. First of all, the attitudes of employees and the motivation for customer consciousness and service-mindedness have to be managed. This can be called the *attitude management* aspect of internal marketing. This is often the predominant part of internal marketing for an organization that strives to develop a competitive edge by pursuing a service strategy. As Edvardsson, Edvinsson, and Nyström (1988) observe: ". . . there is a need for a more pro-active mental management view where service companies create the future rather than adapt to existing conditions"(p. 12).[b]

Second, managers, contact persons, and support persons need information to be able to perform their tasks as leaders and managers and as service providers to internal and external customers. They need information about job routines, goods and service features, promises given to customers by, for example, advertising campaigns and salespersons, and so forth. They also need to communicate about their needs and requirements, their views on how to improve performance, and their findings of what customers want. This is a *communication management* aspect of internal marketing.

Both attitude management and communication management are needed if good results are to be expected. Too often only the communication management aspect is recognized, and maybe only as a one-way information task. In such cases, internal marketing typically takes the form of campaigns and activities. Internal brochures and booklets are distributed to the personnel, and personnel meetings are held where written and oral information is given to the participants and very little communication occurs. Also, managers and supervisors typically take limited interest in their subordinates and do not recognize their need for feedback information, two-way communication, and encouragement. The employees receive an abundance of information but very little mental encouragement.

---

[b]Edvardsson, Edvinsson, and Nyström (1988) introduce the concept of *mental management*, which we here have changed to *attitude management*. We prefer to use the latter term in this context, since the expression "mental management" seems to lead to unnecessary negative connotations.

This, of course, means that much of the information has no major impact on the receivers. The necessary change of attitudes and enhancement of a motivation for good service and customer consciousness is lacking, and the employees are, therefore, not receptive to the information.

If the need for and the nature of the attitude management aspect of internal marketing is recognized and taken into account, internal marketing typically takes the form of an ongoing process instead of a campaign or series of campaigns, and the role of managers and supervisors, on every level, is much more active. Also, much better results are achieved. As Nils Divert, former CEO of a Scandinavian savings bank where internal marketing has been successfully implemented states: "Internal marketing is like a marriage. Once you start it, you live with it every day, it never ends." The internal marketing process and the development of SAS Scandinavian Airlines System is a good example of a process, where attitude management and communications management go hand in hand and support each other (see Carlzon 1987).

In conclusion, a successful internal marketing process requires an *attitude management impact* as well as a *communication management support*. Attitude management is a continuous process, whereas communication management may be more of a discrete process including information activities at appropriate points in time. However, these two aspects of internal marketing are also intertwined. Naturally, much or most of the information shared with employees has an effect on attitudes; for example, contact persons who are informed in advance about an external advertising campaign develop favorable attitudes toward fulfilling the promises of that campaign. Moreover, the tasks of managers and supervisors include, as integral and often inseparable parts, both communication management aspects and attitude management aspects. We will return to that later on.

Overall Objectives of Internal Marketing

The overall objective of internal marketing is twofold (compare Berry 1981 and Grönroos 1983a):

1. To ensure that the employees are motivated for customer-oriented and service-minded performance and thus successfully fulfill their duties as "part-time marketers" in their interactive marketing tasks; and
2. To attract and retain good employees.

The main objective is, of course, to manage the personnel and implement internal action programs so that the employees feel motivated for "part-time marketing" behavior. However, the second objective follows from the first one. The better its internal marketing works, the more attractive the firm is considered as an employer. These overall objectives can be developed into more specific goals depending on the situation at hand. In the following sections we will discuss different situations where the goals are different, generally speaking. Of course, in any specific situation such generally formulated goals have to be specified to meet the requirements of that situation.

Three Levels of Internal Marketing

In principle, three different types of situations can be identified where internal marketing is called for:

1. When *creating a service culture* in the firm and a service orientation among the personnel;
2. When *maintaining a service orientation* among the personnel; and
3. When *introducing new goods and services as well as marketing campaigns and activities* to the employees.

These situations represent three levels of internal marketing. Each of the situations will be discussed.

Developing a Service Culture

As will be discussed in more detail in the next chapter, a *service culture* exists when a service orientation and an interest in customers are the most important norms in the organization. The Walt Disney organization, SAS, and Nordstrom Department Stores are examples of businesses with established service cultures.

Today, a service culture is lacking in most firms. In such cases internal marketing is often seen as a means of achieving such a culture. However, internal marketing alone is not sufficient. In the next chapter we will show what else is required. It is important to realize that internal marketing programs in a vacuum cannot establish a service culture. Internal marketing can, however, be a powerful means of developing a service culture in connection with other activities. In general, internal marketing goals in this situation are:

1. To enable employees—managers, supervisors, and others—to understand and accept the business mission, strategies, and tactics as well as the goods and services and marketing campaigns of the firm;
2. To develop a service-oriented management and leadership style among managers and supervisors; and
3. To teach all employees service-oriented communications and interaction skills.

It is essential to achieve the first goal, because one cannot expect the employees to understand why services and service orientation and customer consciousness are important and why they have responsibilities as "part-time marketers" unless they are aware of what the firm wants to achieve. The second and third goals are important, because service-oriented management methods and skills are fundamental requirements in a service culture.

Maintaining a Service Culture

The second situation where internal marketing can be useful is when one wishes to maintain a service culture. Once such a culture has been created it has to be maintained in an active manner. Otherwise the attitudes of the personnel and the norms in the firm will easily revert back to a culture where technical efficiency is the main guiding principle. The internal marketing goals for helping to maintain a service culture include:

1. To ensure that the management methods are encouraging and enhance the service-mindedness and customer orientation of the employees;
2. To ensure that the employees get continuous information and feedback; and
3. To market new goods and services as well as marketing campaigns and marketing activities to the employees before they are launched externally.

The most important internal marketing issue here is the management support of every single manager and supervisor. The management style and methods are of extreme importance at this point. Employees seem to be more satisfied with their jobs when supervisors concentrate on solving problems for customers rather than strictly emphasizing existing rules and regulations. There are, of course, other factors involved as well.

Because management does not have the ability to directly control service delivery and the moments of truth, it has to develop and maintain *indirect control.* Such indirect control can be established by creating the atmospherics, that is, climate and ethics, that make employees feel service is the predominant norm guiding their thinking and behavior (Bowen & Schneider 1988). In this never-ending process, every single manager and supervisor is involved. If they are able to encourage their subordinates, if they can open up communication channels—both formal and informal—and if they make sure that feedback information reaches their subordinates, an established service culture can be expected to continue.

Introducing New Goods and Services, and New Marketing Campaigns and Activities

Internal marketing initially emerged as a systematic way of handling problems when firms planned and launched new goods or services or marketing campaigns without properly preparing their employees. Especially contact persons could not perform well as "part-time marketers" when they did not know what was going on, did not fully accept new goods and services or marketing activities, or learned about new services and advertising campaigns from newspaper ads or TV commercials or from their customers.

It should be noted that this third level of internal marketing is interrelated to and reinforces the other two. These introductions, however, form an internal marketing task in their own right. At the same time, they enhance the maintenance of an established service culture or support the establishment of such a culture. The internal marketing goals for helping with these introductions of new goods, services, and campaigns include:

1. To make employees aware of and accept new goods and services being developed and offered to the market;
2. To make employees aware of and ensure their acceptance of new traditional marketing campaigns and activities, which are mostly mass marketing; and
3. To make employees aware and accepting of new ways in which various tasks influencing relationship and interactive marketing performance of the firm are to be executed.

Prerequisites for Successful Internal Marketing

If internal marketing activities are implemented as a campaign only, or, even worse, as entirely separated activities without connections to other management factors, the risk that nothing enduring will be achieved is overwhelming. The organizational structure and the strategy of the firm have to support the establishment of a service culture. Moreover, the management methods and the management and leadership style of managers and supervisors has to be supportive if they are to be expected to fulfill their tasks in internal marketing.

The three prerequisites for successful internal marketing are:

- Internal marketing has to be considered an integral part of strategic management;
- The internal marketing process must not be counteracted by the organizational structure or by lack of management support; and
- Top management must demonstrate constantly an active support for the internal marketing process.

In order to be successful, internal marketing starts with *top management*. Next, *middle management and supervisors* have to accept and live up to their role in an internal marketing process. Only then can internal marketing efforts directed toward contact employees be successful. The employees' ability to function as service-minded "part-time marketers" depends to a large extent on the support and encouragement they get from supervisors. As Berry (1988) concludes: "Only genuine leadership at all levels of the organization can provide the inspiration necessary to sustain committed servers. 'Managing' and 'administering' is not enough" (p. 2).

Finally, all other categories of employees have to be involved as well. The *contact persons* form a natural target market for internal marketing. They have the immediate customer contacts and do the interactive marketing job. However, they often depend on any support they can get from other employees and functions in the firm. Often there is a large number of employees who do not come in contact with customers themselves, but who nevertheless indirectly influence the service the ultimate customers get. The ability of contact employees to perform their interactive marketing task depends to a large extent on their service-mindedness. Such groups of employees, the *support personnel*, should perform in a customer-oriented manner when they serve their *internal customers*. In fact, they are "part-time marketers" as well, although their customers are internal and not external. Thus, support employees should also be included in the target audience for internal marketing programs.

In summary, the four main target groups for internal marketing are:

- (1) Top management;
- (2) Middle management and supervisors; and
- The "part-time marketers": (3) Contact personnel; (4) Support personnel.

It should be noted that the same person may occupy several positions. A support person may sometimes be in the position of a contact person. A supervisor who, for example, is supposed to be able to support and encourage contact persons may be a contact person serving customers, or a support person serving internal customers, regularly or occasionally.

The Internal Marketing Product

In order to make the external market respond, the firm needs acceptable goods or services. Of course, the same goes for the internal market as well. A customer-oriented performance, and thus good interactive marketing, cannot be expected to occur unless the organization has something to offer its employees in return. The simple offering consisting of a job with a salary or a wage is in some cases enough even today. However, in most industries this belongs to the past, at least for most groups of employees.

The organization will have to offer its internal market of employees a "product" which is attractive. *The internal product consists of a job and a work environment which motivates the employees to respond favorably to management's demands for customer orientation and good interactive marketing performance as "part-time marketers" and which, moreover, attracts and retains good employees.* This obviously depends on, among other things, the management methods, the personnel policy, and the nature of the job itself and planning and execution processes (Grönroos 1981 and 1983a). Hence, the internal product must be developed as carefully and market-orientedly as the external goods and services, and this requires strategic decisions by management concerning these issues.

As can be observed, then, internal marketing has to become part of the strategic management philosophy. Otherwise more operational internal marketing activities will be counteracted by demotivating jobs and work environments, caused, for example, by the attitudes and management style of managers and supervisors (compare Schneider 1980), or by a personnel policy that does not support customer consciousness but only other qualities.

Internal Marketing Activities

There is no exclusive list of activities that should belong to an internal marketing program. Almost any function or activity that has an impact, one way or the other, on the service-mindedness and customer consciousness of employees can be included. This, of course, follows from the notion that internal marketing, first of all, is a philosophy for managing the personnel and a systematic way of developing and enhancing a service culture.

However, typical internal marketing activities can be identified. The following list is, by no means, intended to be all inclusive. Nor does it distinguish between activities to be used in developing or maintaining a service culture or in introducing new goods, services, and marketing campaigns internally. Many of the activities are mutual for two or three of these situations.

Training. A lack of understanding of the strategies of the firm and of the existence and importance of "part-time marketer" responsibilities is almost always present. "Service know-how" is lacking in the strategic thinking as well as on the operational level. This is partly due to insufficient or nonexistent knowledge of the content of a service strategy, of the nature and scope of marketing in a service context, and of the employees' role with dual responsibilities in the firm. This goes for contact and support employees as well as for managers.

Partly, this is an attitude problem. Indifferent or even negative attitudes have to be changed. On the other hand, attitude problems normally follow from a lack of understanding of facts. Therefore, the tasks of improving the level of knowledge about reality and of changing attitudes are highly intertwined. As one engineer in Schlumberger's wire-line service said, "Indoctrination is just as important as technical training" (Heskett 1987, p. 123).

Training, either internal or external training programs, are most frequently needed as a basic component of an internal marketing program. Three types of training tasks can be included:

- Developing *a holistic view* of how a service strategy works and what the role of each individual is in relation to other individuals, functions within the firm, and customers;
- Developing and enhancing *favorable attitudes* toward a service strategy and "part-time marketing" performance; and
- Developing and enhancing communications, sales, and service *skills* among the employees.

Training, together with internal communication support, are the predominant tools of the communication management aspect of internal marketing. However, to some extent they are also part of the attitude management process.

Management support and internal interactive communication. No training program alone is enough in an internal marketing program. In order to achieve continuation in such a program, the role of top management, middle management, and supervisors is paramount. As Donald Myles, Vice President of Information and Service from IBM-Canada says: "We believe that effective leadership inspires people to drive towards the goals of the firm."

The management support can be of various types, for example:

- *Continuation* of formal training programs by everyday management actions
- Active *encouragement* of subordinates as part of the everyday management task
- *Involving the subordinates* in planning and decision making
- *Feedback* to subordinates and flow of *information* and *two-way communication* in formal and informal interactions
- Establishing an open and encouraging *internal climate*

Normally, people returning from a course are left almost alone. The supervisor is not very interested in what they have learned and how to make use of new ideas and factual knowledge. The employees are, at best, left alone to implement new ideas. Even more frequently, the returning employees realize that everybody, especially the boss, is totally uninterested in what they have learned. Sometimes they get the impression that the fact that they have been away for training has only created problems, for example, with undercapacity. Nobody seems to care about any positive effects of the course. In such situations, any new idea and favorable-attitude effects are rapidly destroyed.

Instead, the manager or supervisor should encourage the employees to implement new ideas and help them realizing how they could be applied in their specific environment. Moreover, some on-the-premises training is often helpful and encouraging as a continuation of the course or training program.

The management style demonstrated in the daily job by managers and supervisors has an immediate impact on the job environment and internal climate. Says Roger Dow, Vice President of Sales and Marketing Services from the Marriott Hotels and Resorts: "Probably, recognition is the issue that keeps it going. It may sound soft, but it is critical." The mere way of managing is, therefore, an internal marketing issue.

Joint planning and decision making with the employees involved is a means of achieving commitment in advance to further actions that emerge from the planning process. Moreover, as Schneider and Bowen (1984) have observed, the "psychological closeness" between contact persons and customers suggests that frontline employees have valuable information about the needs and desires of customers, so that the involvement of these employees in the planning process leads to improved decision making.

The need for information and feedback has been discussed previously. Here, the supervisor has a key role. Moreover, he or she is responsible for creating an open climate where service-related and customer-related issues are raised and discussed.

Management support and the internal interactive communication are the predominant tools of the attitude management aspect of internal marketing, but they are, of course, key ingredients of communication management as well.

Internal mass communication and information support. Most managers and supervisors realize that there is a need for them to inform their subordinates about new service-oriented strategies and new ways of performing in the buyer-seller interactions, and to make them understand and accept new strategies, tasks, and ways of thinking. However, many persons do not know how to do it. Therefore, it is important to develop various kinds of supporting materials. Videotapes and other audiovisual and written material explaining new strategies and ways of performing can easily be used by managers during meetings with their subordinates. Moreover, brochures, internal memos, and magazines, as well as other means of mass communication, can be used in direct internal campaigns.

Personnel administration tools and human resource management. It is essential to get and keep the right kind of employees in a firm. As Roger Dow from Marriott observes: "We can train people to do any task, but to get people with a friendly attitude, it starts with recruitment and hiring." This, in turn, requires proper job descriptions, where the "part-time marketing" tasks of contact and support employees are recognized. Job descriptions, recruitment procedures, career planning, salary, wage and bonus systems, and incentive programs as well as other personnel administration tools should be used by the organization in such a manner that the internal marketing goals are pursued.

No one of these tasks is new. However, they are often used in a passive way, more like administrative procedures than as active marketinglike tools to achieve internal objectives. Moreover, the external marketing implications of these tasks are far too often neglected, either for "cost efficiency" reasons or because management just is not aware of them. Because of the traditional management approach, most employees are considered costs only, and not revenue-generating resources. As Tansik (1988) observes:

> . . . it is easily noted that in many service organizations the high customer contact jobs are those that are also commonly entry level positions in the

> organization; e.g., counter workers in fast food restaurants, airline flight attendants, bus drivers, office receptionist, etc. Good performance in these jobs often result in a promotion to a low contact (often managerial) job. Two dangers are seen here. First, the organization *places its success in the hands of the newest, least trained employees*. Indeed, in cases such as a fast food restaurant or a local bus system these employees also account for most of the organization's cash transactions. And, secondly, *those who do well* in this line work *are often promoted and removed from it* leaving the less competent employees in the high customer contact jobs [emphasis by the author]. (p. 10)

The lack of logic of this type of staffing and career development strategy is all too evident. Yet, it is all too frequently applied.

External mass communication. The internal effects of any external mass communication campaign or activity is seldom fully recognized. However, the employees almost always form a very interested and responsive target audience for advertising campaigns, public relations activities, and other means of mass communication (see George & Berry 1981).

Advertising campaigns, brochures, and specific ads should be presented to the employees before they are launched externally. This may create commitment and decrease confusion. One step further would be to develop such campaigns in cooperation with the employee groups affected by the external communication effort.

Market research, both internally and externally, can be used to find out, for example, attitudes toward "part-time marketing" tasks and service-oriented performance.

Market segmentation can be applied in order to find the right kind of persons to recruit for various positions in the organization.

In summary, following Ramm-Schmidt (1984), we can divide a continuous internal marketing process into three stages: (1) a profound analysis of the nature of a service strategy and of attitudes among employees and customers, (2) getting people to understand what it is all about to be customer conscious and have an excellent interactive marketing function, and finally, (3) achieving continuous customer-oriented and service-oriented operations.

How to Implement an Internal Marketing Strategy

When starting to plan and implement an internal marketing strategy, a few guidelines should be observed. First of all, the *internal focus* of internal marketing has to be recognized and fully accepted by management. Employees sense that management considers them important when they are allowed to participate in the process; both in an internal research process and in planning their work environment, the goals and scope of their tasks, information and feedback routines, and external campaigns. When employees realize that they are able to involve themselves in improving something that is important to them, they will be inclined to commit themselves to the business and the internal marketing strategy.

However, the *external focus* of an internal marketing strategy and any internal marketing program should never be forgotten. Improving the work environment and tasks for the employees is, of course, an important objective in its own right. It is, nevertheless, the external marketing impact of every employee that is the ultimate focus of internal marketing. The ultimate objective is to improve the customer consciousness and service-mindedness, and thus, in the final analysis, the interactive marketing abilities and the external marketing performance of the personnel. Consequently, the internal and the external focus of internal marketing go hand in hand. None of them should be forgotten.

Furthermore, it should always be remembered that the internal marketing program will fail if it is viewed as being just tactical and initiated only at the customer contact level involving only contact employees. This level alone cannot breed a service culture for the organization, nor reach the many support persons who also have to function as "part-time marketers" internally. Only in a situation where a solid service culture has been established can the internal marketing of, for example, an advertising campaign or a new service be directed toward a specific target group of, say, contact employees in a certain department. In all other situations, internal marketing has to involve, and start with, top management, and also include middle management and supervisors. And, as we have said, a continuous support from management, not only by paying lip service to internal marketing, but by active involvement in the process, is necessary.

Internal Marketing as a Prerequisite for Successful External Marketing—The John Nurminen Case[c]

Internal marketing started in John Nurminen Co. a decade ago with the notion that the employees were a first, internal market of the firm. Service orientation and market-oriented performance of the contact persons were

[c]This was the winning case in the 1986 Internal Marketing Program Competition arranged by the American Marketing Association in connection with its series of conferences on services marketing. The process and this case have been described in Compton, F., George, W. R., Grönroos, C. & Karvinen, M., Internal Marketing, in Czepiel, J.A., Congram, C.A. & Shanahan, J., eds., *The Service Challenge: Integrating for Competitive Advantage*, Chicago: American Marketing Association, 1987.

believed to be at least equally important to market success as sales and advertising campaigns.

John Nurminen is an international forwarding and transportation company based in Finland. In 1986 it had over 600 employees. Billing/sales amounts to approximately half a billion U.S. dollars.

A corporate study in 1979 of users of freight forwarders indicated partly positive results: John Nurminen Co. was considered financially sound, experienced, large, versatile, and good in import forwarding, customs clearance, ocean transport, and warehousing. However, there were important negative findings as well: the firm was viewed as being stagnant, not really providing any value added, old-fashioned, bad in customer service and in giving information, expensive, having rigid credit terms, and bad in some forwarding functions. Management realized that the corporate image was vague and without highlights. Moreover, it noted that the moments of truth where the customers and the employees meet were not handled in a service-oriented and marketinglike manner.

Five overall objectives for an internal marketing process were set forth and eventually achieved:

1. Attitudes: marketing has to be seen as playing a role in everyone's work;
2. Information: internal and external information has to be improved;
3. Corporate image: the firm should be regarded as the best freight forwarder in Finland with a high quality image;
4. Market share: increase of the market share according to plans; and
5. Profitability: ROI should be at least 13 percent before interest and taxes.

These objectives were met before 1984. The interrelationships between the internal and external focus is evident. External objectives and internal objectives are intertwined.

The steps of the internal marketing process included creation of a structure, internal activities, and external activities. Creation of a structure included four parts: organization, guiding principles, definition of marketing functions, and definition of service quality. Sales was decentralized to the line organization. The centralized marketing department became much smaller. As one guiding principle, marketing and personnel policies were combined. Marketing was redefined as a conglomeration of functions in which everyone employed by the firm participate. It was formally stated that *production of the service is part of marketing*. Service quality was defined and the importance of the functional quality of the process was stressed. Every single customer contact was realized to be a "moment of truth" where service quality emerges.

Activities of the internal marketing process included training, internal information, and management support. The training was multifaceted and started off with extensive management training, including four sessions of one week duration each for top management and three sessions of three days duration each for middle management. Business strategy and the scope and nature of service management and services marketing were discussed during these sessions. Vocational training included basic courses on services marketing, professional skills courses, language courses, and special theme sessions. In 1985, for example, 1,000 training days were accomplished. Such training was recognized as investment in the staff.

The marketing courses focused on developing an understanding for the firm as a service business, and on teaching sales and communication skills. However, for psychological reasons, they were labeled "Active Customer Service" courses. These courses were divided into two parts. The first part was a two-day course, including the whole staff from the managing director and his top management team to truck drivers. Lecturing took three hours, with 15 hours of group work. Problems and opportunities related to customer service, handling customer contacts, and operational systems and routines were discussed. The group sessions focused on tracking problems which could be solved immediately and on listing other problems and actions to be attended to in the near future. Deadlines for actions were decided upon. The second part was three-day courses intended for contact employees immediately involved in the "moments of truth."

The internal information element of the internal marketing program focused on internal memos and the internal magazine. These means of information were made less bureaucratic in their layout and content, so that they could communicate messages more effectively. The role of management was very important in this type of communication as well as in the congruence with personnel policy and the integration with external marketing.

Mass marketing was seen as part of internal marketing, because of the need to integrate both the internal and external perspectives. The main vehicle to do this was the *Nurminen News*, which appears six to twelve times a year. It includes mostly facts about the business, international trade, new developments, and so on. It does not, however, include any advertisements. It circulates to 4,000 Finnish import and export companies and also to other potential customers. The customer-oriented information in this magazine was intended to become the best available about import- and export-related issues. This goal seems to have been achieved. Quite often, customers seem to rely more on information in the *Nurminen News* than in official bulletins from, for example, the customs. In addition, advertising campaigns in the press were undertaken.

Moreover, exhibitions were arranged and special events were sponsored. Public relations involving the press was also used. Seminars on special issues were arranged for CEO's. Finally, external marketing included talks in business schools and other colleges of higher education. It should be noted that the external advertising campaigns were directed just as much toward the employees as the customers. The advertising themes used stressed the skills of the employees and their importance to marketing and customer service. The *Nurminen News* could also be expected to have clear internal effects, whereas the other means of external mass communication were more or less external only in their focus.

The impact on corporate image of the internal marketing process was measured by a study done in 1984 and 1985. The following results were obtained: (1) Employee attitudes and customer service skills have improved and are now considered good; (2) John Nurminen Co. was considered the best by far in giving relevant and interesting information to the customers; and (3) the respondents considered John Nurminen Co. the best freight forwarding company in Finland. The market share and profitability objectives were also achieved, which is another indication of the success of the internal marketing process so far. Moreover, in 1984 John Nurminen Co. was awarded the best training organization in the country, and in 1986 the internal marketing program of John Nurminen Co. won the 1986 American Marketing Association Internal Marketing Competition.

In summary, the experiences of the internal marketing process include: (1) Be strong in your faith and secure the continuous support of top management; (2) do your homework well and define the subject comprehensively (a. changing the corporate culture, b. combining and coordinating personnel administration, training, management methods, and the use of internal and external information); (3) make your own applications, do not just imitate the easily implemented components of internal marketing programs run by others; (4) set your planning objectives on a yearly basis, otherwise the process becomes too big, and include measuring of results; and (5) remember, it will take years.

Five pragmatic aspects of the internal marketing program are:

1. Managers: The success or failure of the internal marketing program depends on the change in attitudes and behaviors of the managers. The aspects of service awareness must become part of the daily routines of managers. And just paying lip service to a service strategy is not enough. The behaviors and concerns of managers is quickly reflected in

the attitudes and behaviors of employees. It must be remembered that managers normally get the subordinates they deserve.

2. Circulars and internal mass information: The internal marketing must be reflected in the company circulars. Their layout and the style in which they are written have a direct impact on employee attitudes—an effect which can snowball in time.
3. Management support: The role of top management has been mentioned above, but the role of middle management and supervisors is emphasized here. Giving information, tutoring, advising, helping, encouraging, and controlling is the best way of giving information, and receiving information in return, in a supportive way.
4. Training: The vocational training creates the basic knowledge and skills. After that foundation, it is possible to intensify the change of attitudes. In John Nurminen Co. the whole staff was targeted. Training should include two-way communication.
5. Coordination of subprograms: The coordination of internal and external programs is essential, because of their strong interaction. Coordination also concerns the time span. Although internal marketing is a continuous process, a five-year action plan can never be successful. From the very beginning it is too expensive to be accepted. It is much better to create the long-range structures, define the target, and operate with one year plans within this structure.

Summary

Internal marketing is an umbrella concept for a range of internal activities, the objective of which is to develop a service orientation and customer orientation and an interest in "part-time marketing" behavior among the personnel. It is, therefore, first of all a management philosophy, and secondly a set of tools. As a management philosophy it emphasizes the pivotal role of the personnel as a first internal market. Three levels of internal marketing were discussed, namely, developing a service culture, maintaining a service orientation among the personnel, and introducing new goods and services as well as marketing campaigns and activities to the personnel. Also, a number of typical activities which can be part of an internal marketing process were presented.

11
Managing Service Culture: The Internal Service Imperative

Introduction

In this chapter the concept of service culture will be discussed. First, we present the broader concept, corporate culture, and its importance to the attitudes and behavior of people in an organization. Next, the issue of a service culture and the need for such a culture in a service organization is covered. Prerequisites for a service culture are analyzed and ways of creating such a culture are described. Finally, barriers and opportunities for developing such a culture are discussed.

The Importance of Corporate Culture

The concept *corporate culture* is used to describe a set of more or less common norms and values shared by people in an organization. Hence, culture is an overall concept that explains why people do certain things, think in common ways, and appreciate similar goals, routines, even jokes, just because they are members of the same organization. Corporate culture can, for example, be defined as *the pattern of shared values and beliefs that give the members of an organization meaning, and provide them with the rules for behavior in the organization* (Davis 1985; the importance of corporate culture from a marketing point of view has been discussed by Deshpande & Webster 1987).

Corporate culture can be felt as in internal *climate* in the organization. Bowen and Schneider (1988) observed that service firms have to manage their internal climate for service so that employees who serve the customers develop positive attitudes and behaviors. Because of this, the culture of a firm has a vital impact on how service-oriented its employees are.

Internal activities or even projects, such as training programs or single service courses, do not lead to expected results if they do not fit the existing culture in the firm. For example, a service-oriented training program alone would most probably have no significant impact on the thinking and behavior of employees of a manufacturer where goods-oriented industrial standards are regarded highly. A much more strategically oriented and comprehensive project would be needed, if any results are to be achieved.

A weak corporate culture, where there are few or no clear common values and norms, creates an insecure feeling concerning how to respond to various clues and how to react in different situations. For example, what to do when a customer has unexpected requests may be self-evident, when the culture is strong. On the other hand, if there is a weak culture, such a situation frequently results in inflexible behavior by the contact persons, long waiting times, and a feeling that you really do not know what is going to happen on the part of the customer. This, of course, damages the perceived service quality. In such a culture, employees do not have any clear norms to relate, for example, sales training or a service course to, and hence they do not know how to respond to such activities.

A strong culture, on the other hand, enables people to act in a certain manner and to respond to various actions in a uniform way. Especially in service organizations, clear cultural values are particularly important for guiding employee behavior (Schneider 1986). In many cases newly employed persons are easily formed by the prevailing culture. A customer-conscious and service-minded person who is recruited for a service job may quickly be taken down to earth by his or her new colleagues, who share strong norms and values which do not honor interest in customers and in giving good service. Again, a strong service-oriented culture easily snowballs. Service-oriented persons are attracted by such an employer, and most new employees are formed in a favorable way by the existing service culture.

Schneider and Bowen (1985) have found that when employees identify with the norms and values of an organization, they are less inclined to quit, and moreover, customers seem to be more satisfied with the service. In addition to this, when there is a minimal employee turnover, service-oriented values and a positive attitude toward service are more easily transmitted to newcomers in the organization (Bowen & Schneider 1988).

Moreover, the modern views of quality and productivity, and the relationship between them, "the wheel of fortune" if it can be identified and used by managers, are related to corporate culture. "Improving productivity (and, for that matter, quality) is a matter of infusing a way of thinking into the organization's culture. . . . Behavioral scientists are tentatively concluding that the improvement of both productivity and quality seem to result from or at least be related to corporate culture," (Pickworth 1987, pp. 44–45).

A strong culture is not, however, always good. Especially in situations where the surrounding world has changed and new ways of thinking are called for, such a culture may become a serious hindrance for change. It may be difficult to respond to new challenges. In such a situation a strong culture does not only affect the responsiveness of employees in a negative fashion, it may paralyze management as well. For example, a strong manufacturing-oriented culture may develop into a serious problem for a firm that obviously should respond to service-related changes in the market and in competition. A service strategy is perhaps the obvious solution, but the management team may be too restricted by their inherited way of viewing the business. And if only marginal internal activities to introduce a service strategy are implemented, the equally or perhaps even more old-fashioned ways of thinking among middle management and the rest of the personnel do not permit any major attitude change.

The Importance of Culture in Service Organizations

In a service context a strong and well-established culture, which enhances an appreciation for good service and customer orientation, is extremely important, maybe more so than in a manufacturing environment. This follows from the nature of service production and consumption. Normally service production cannot be standardized as completely as an assembly line, because of the human impact in the buyer-seller interactions. Customers and their behavior cannot be totally standardized and predetermined. The situations vary, and therefore a distinct service-oriented culture is needed which tells employees how to respond to new, unforeseen and even awkward situations (Schneider 1986).

Since service quality is a function of the cooperation of so many resources—human as well as technological—a strong culture which enhances quality is a must for successful management of quality. Moreover, since it is more difficult to control quality in a service context than in manufacturing, very service oriented and quality conscious values are necessary in the organization. In this way management can execute *indirect control.*

Profitability through a Service Strategy Requires a Service Culture

Implementing a *service strategy* requires the support of everyone in the organization. Top management, middle management, contact employees, and support employees will all have to get involved. An interest in service and an appreciation of good service among managers and all other employees is an essential requirement. What is needed is a corporate culture that can be labeled a *service culture*. Such a culture can be described as *a culture where an appreciation for good service exists, and where giving good service to internal as well as ultimate, external customers is considered a natural way of life and one of the most important norms by everyone.* To use the words of Schneider and Rentsch (1987), service has to become "the *raison d'etre* for all organizational activities" and an "*organizational imperative.*"

This, of course, does not exclude other norms from being of utmost importance, too. However, it does mean that service consciousness is not a marginal or even second-level concern, but a top-priority concern in strategic as well as operational thinking and performance. It is one of the, say, three guiding philosophies shared by the people in the organization.

A service culture means that the employees of the organization can be characterized as service oriented. Service orientation has been defined by Hogan et al. (1984) as "a set of attitudes and behaviors that affects the quality of the interaction between . . . the staff of any organization and its customers" (p. 167). They also observe that in several studies service orientation correlates substantially with overall job performance, and they mention as an example "that service-oriented nursing aides relate well with patients, willingly assist other hospital personnel, and communicate clearly and courteously with others" (Hogan et al. 1984, p. 169).

Clearly, a service orientation enhances the functional quality dimension of customer perceived service quality, and it probably also supports the production of good technical quality. As Figure 11–1 illustrates, service orientation among the personnel fuels an important positive process internally in an organization. A service orientation that is a characteristic of

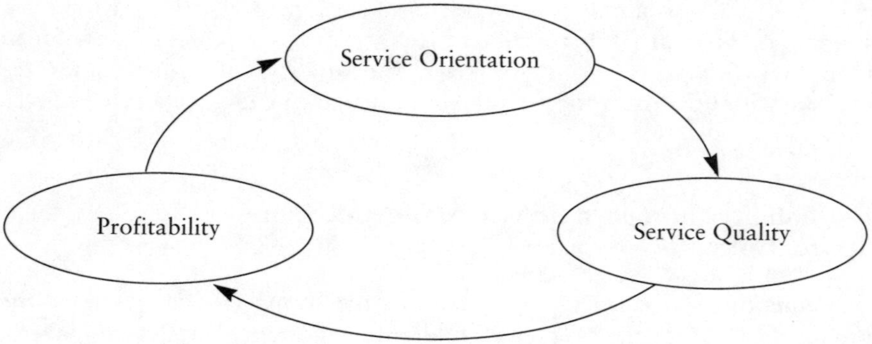

Figure 11–1. Effects of a Service Orientation

a service culture improves service quality as perceived by customers. Service-oriented employees who take an interest in their customers do more for the customers, are more courteous and flexible, try to find appropriate solutions to customers' wishes, and go out of their way to recover a situation where something has gone wrong or an unexpected situation has occurred. Furthermore, we know that customer perceived quality is a key determinant of profitability. Hence, service orientation improves service quality, which, in turn, positively affects profitability. And this favorable process continues as a spiral, because better profitability provides the means to maintain and further improve service-oriented attitudes among the personnel. The process fuels itself.

Shared Values

The values people in an organization have and the prevailing norms are the foundation of the culture. The shared values constitute guidelines for employees in performing their everyday tasks. In an organization with strong shared values three common characteristics are often present (Deal & Kennedy 1982):

- The shared values are a clear guideline for task performance;
- The managers devote much of their time to developing and reinforcing the shared values; and
- The shared values are deeply anchored among the employees.

It has also been found that performance is improved by strong shared values in an organization. Managers as well as their subordinates devote themselves more to issues and ways of performing that are emphasized by the shared values. The performance is better, because people are more motivated. Strong norms and shared values may, however, become a problem, too (Deal & Kennedy 1982):

- The shared values may have become *obsolete* and are therefore not guidelines that are consistent with current strategies and, say, service concepts; and
- Strong shared values may lead to *resistance to change*, which makes it difficult for the organization to respond to external challenges.

In many firms these are highly relevant problems. Even though there may be no service culture, there may be a strong corporate culture. The existing culture may emphasize manufacturing ideals or bureaucratic routines. Today, in many manufacturing firms and institutions within the public sector, a strong culture that does not appreciate service is a major hindrance to change (Grönroos & Monthelie 1988). Challenges from the market and from society may go without notice, or the organization is not capable of adjusting to the need for change. The results are sometimes fatal. The effects of even a single internal activity that does not have a strategic foundation will probably be counteracted by the hostile culture. Internal marketing efforts easily fail if they are not in line with the prevailing culture, or if the objectives of the internal marketing efforts are contradictory to it. On the other hand, a long-term internal marketing process is one ingredient in a process that aims at changing an existing culture. A strategic approach to internal change is needed.

Requirements for a Service Culture

Introducing and implementing a service strategy requires a service culture. In many firms, or organizations within the public sector, a cultural change is called for. Such a change is *a long-range process*, which demands extensive and long-range activity programs. In chapter 10 we discussed one major ingredient in such a process, *internal marketing*. In the present chapter we will with a broader perspective look at general prerequisites for achieving a service culture.

The *requirements for good service* are:

- Strategic requirements
- Organizational requirements
- Management requirements
- Knowledge and attitude requirements

If the four kinds of requirements are not all recognized, the internal change process will suffer and the result will be mediocre at best. The different requirements are intertwined. For example, a complicated organizational structure makes it impossible to implement a good service concept; or a service-minded and motivated contact person gets frustrated and loses interest in giving good service because he or she gets no support and appreciation from his boss, or finds it impossible to be service-minded because the service orientation is not derived from a strategic foundation and therefore sufficient resources are not granted. In the following sections we are going to discuss the four requirements in some detail.

Developing a Service Strategy

By developing a service-oriented strategy the *strategic requirements for good service* are fulfilled. This means that top management *wants* to create a service-oriented organization. The management team is not just paying lip service to service orientation. Here top management may be the CEO and his or her management team, but it may also be the head of a local organization or a profit center which can operate sufficiently well independently.

The *business mission* is the foundation of strategy formulation. Based on the scope and direction of the business indicated by the mission, strategies are developed. A service strategy means that a service orientation, which of course in different industries and even firms means different things, is to be achieved. In this context we will not go into any details in this respect.

However, a service strategy requires that *service concepts* related to the business mission and the strategy be defined. If service concepts are not clearly defined, the firm lacks a stable foundation for discussion of goals, resources to be used, and standards for performance. As previously stated, the service concept states *what* should be done, to *whom, how*, and with *which resources*, and what benefits customers should be offered. If these issues are not clarified, the personnel will of course not understand what they are supposed to do. Moreover, goals and routines do not form a clear and understandable pattern, because there is no clear and well-known service concept to relate them to. If the service concepts are not clearly understood at the middle management level, it will be difficult to perform supervisory duties in a consistent way. Managers as well as the rest of the personnel easily feel a disturbing role ambiguity.

Personnel policy is an important part of the strategic requirements. Recruitment procedures, career planning, bonus systems, and so forth are vital parts of a service culture, as they are of any culture. Good service performance pretty much has to guide the administration of personnel. The more aspects other than skills and service-orientation dominate, for example, recruitment procedures and bonus systems, the less inclined toward service-mindedness employees will be, and a service culture will be difficult to achieve.

Good service has to be rewarded and accomplishments have to be measured in such a way that employees realize the importance of service. However, as Donald Myles, Vice President of Information and Service from IBM-Canada, observes: "Good people are often forced to do stupid things, because the measurement and rewarding systems are wrong." If this is the case, and employees feel they are rewarded for accomplishments other than excellent service quality, any attempts to develop a service culture is bound to fail.

Developing the Organizational Structure

Development of the organizational structure, of course, creates the *organizational prerequisite for good service*. Bowen and Schneider (1988) strongly argue that all the aspects of organization design have to be geared to the creation and delivery of service, if high service quality is to be achieved and consistently maintained. The more complicated the formal structure is, the more problems related to giving good service occur. The organization as such can be a serious obstacle to a service culture. Good service means, among other things, easy access to services and quick and flexible decision making. If the organizational structure does not allow employees to perform in this way, norms and values characterizing a service culture cannot be developed. Good intentions, even when they are based on a strategy, just cannot be implemented. This makes people frustrated and may have a countereffect. Employees easily feel that management demands the impossible, and only negative effects are achieved as far as service-oriented attitudes are concerned.

Good service requires cooperation between various functions and departments in designing, developing, and executing services. However, Peters, who advocates a new partnership mentality internally and externally as a means of achieving excellence, notes that ". . . sadly, we reserve our most virulent adversarial behavior for people *inside* our firms: management versus union, function versus function. And once again, it will not do . . . Partnership must become the dominant mode of daily dealings. For example, manufacturers, marketers, designers, accountants, salespeople, service people (as well as vendors and distributors) must work together," (Peters 1988a, p. 10).

There is also, of course, always the informal organizational structure. People create a value structure and personal contacts, good or bad, which make the formal structure either less complicated or more complicated. In the former case, positive attitudes among the employees involved may make it possible to solve the problems created by a complicated structure. In the latter case, on the other hand, even a service-oriented structure may become an obstacle for good service. If people, for one reason or the other, do not want to collaborate, a service culture is less easy to accomplish.

Normally, a service-oriented firm requires a thin organizational structure with few hierarchical levels (compare chapter 8). Decisions have to be made by employees close to the customers. The roles of managers change. The subordinates get more responsibility and they are expected to perform their tasks more independently. However, this does not mean that the supervisory level loses power, only that the role of supervisors changes. They are not just technical managers and decision makers anymore; instead, they are supposed to be coaches and demonstrate leadership. They will have to assist and encourage their subordinates and create an open climate where good service is a leading shared value among everyone involved.

The role of those in support functions must also be clarified. Often employees in business functions who do not have immediate customer contacts regard themselves as performing passive functions only with some kinds of administrative duties. In fact, the role of those in most support functions is much more active. As we have noted in previous contexts, they should see those in customer contact functions as their *internal customers*, whom they will have to serve as well as these are supposed to serve the ultimate customers.

In many firms, the customer contact functions, the frontline, are too weak and understaffed, whereas various staff functions have grown too much and have become overstaffed. The obvious conclusion is to strengthen the customer contact functions of the frontline and streamline and redesign other functions so that they really support the buyer-seller interactions in an effective and service-oriented way (compare, for example, the SAS case in Carlzon 1987).

Another aspect of organizational development is the development of operational systems, routines, and work flows. Good service normally requires simplified ways of doing things, so that unnecessary delays and information breaks due to a too-complicated operational system or work flow are avoided. The effects of this are twofold. First of all, *customers* perceive such a development as better functional quality of the service. Second, *employees* feel that their job has become more meaningful and motivating when the routines and work flows have been simplified and unnecessary and time-consuming elements of the operational systems have been eliminated.

Developing Leadership

The *management prerequisite for good service* is promoted by establishing a *service-oriented leadership*. This includes managers' and supervisors' attitudes toward their role, their subordinates, and how they act as managers. Jan Carlzon of SAS, says, based on his experience from changing a highly production-oriented culture into a service culture: ". . . management must be supportive, inspirational and adjusted to the individuals it manages" (Carlzon & Hubendinck 1984, p. 15). Without an active and continuous support from all managers and supervisors, the values that characterize a true service culture cannot be spread throughout the organization and maintained once they have been established. Such a managerial impact is of absolutely vital importance if service-oriented values are to be communicated to the employees, strengthened, and made an integral part of everyday corporate life.

Just being a technical manager without taking on the role of coach and leader does not do much in the pursuit of a service culture. A much more wholehearted devotion to the service concepts and the subordinates is called for. Service is to a large extent a human business and the result of interactions between humans internally as well as externally. Inhumane management styles do not fit here.

To a large extent leadership means communication. Berry (1988) puts it as follows:

> The principal tool of leaders is *communication*. Identify a store in a retail chain with particularly outstanding service and you will find one or more store leaders coaching, praising and modeling service excellence. You will find quality 'champions'—leaders who communicate face-to-face rather than by memo; who communicate by example, by deeds *not* just by words; who communicate to inspire rather than to command. (p. 2)

Berry uses retailing as an example, but his view of a leader's communicative impact holds true in any environment.

The importance of leadership and coaching, even mentorship, stresses yet another aspect of today's management—collaboration. This is a major shift for many managers. As Peters (1988a) observes: "Americans thrive on competition. But in today's world, managers must learn to replace antagonism with partnership . . . management and labor must sit on the same side of the table to induce rapid quality and productivity improvement. . . . Our [manager's] role is to garner maximum efficiency and effectiveness in our work places. And that will come only from partnership" (pp. 10 and 12). In some cases, this may mean real partnership, a thing we have seen developing in service organizations, for example, Avis and ARA Services. In other cases, partnership means not de facto partnership but a certain philosophical approach by employees on different levels to interacting with each other in an atmosphere of cooperation and mutual respect. In this respect, most service organizations have a long way to go.

Partnership also implies that everyone in the organization have a sense of fairness. Fairness has to be one of the shared values in the organization. According to Berry (1988):

> Retail executives that engage in phony price promotions, that ask salespeople to mislead customers in sales presentations, that use "bait and switch" tactics, that wink at systematic overcharging of customers on transactions—these executives completely undermine their own credibility on the subject of service quality. Employees learn quickly that management cares not one iota about service and satisfying customers.
> (p. 2)

One of the biggest risks involved in a process toward a service orientation is the risk of ambiguity. If the manager talks about the need of service-mindedness and customer consciousness, but in reality does not pursue a service strategy, he or she *and* the service culture lose credibility. A sense of uncertainty among the personnel is easily created, and the talk about service orientation and a service culture is not taken seriously anymore. Performance that is in line with good quality and the nature of a service culture as expressed by management has to be measured and rewarded. Internal efficiency and manufacturing-oriented productivity measures must not be given priority. Hence, top management and every other manager will have to simultaneously talk about the importance of good service and of pursuing a service culture, *and* demonstrate, in reality in their actions, that this is true. Otherwise, serious damage is easily done to a service-orientation process that may have been initiated in good faith.

The top person in the organization, which may be the entire company, a local unit, a profit center, a strategic business unit, or another well-defined organizational unit, will have to constantly give the service strategy top priority and continuously and actively give it his or her strong support. Furthermore, every manager and supervisor will have to accept the role of coach to their subordinates. They have to be able to encourage people and strengthen their motivation for service-oriented performance.

Monitoring the performance and the results is, of course, still an integral part of management. However, the traditional role of controlling is shifting toward guiding subordinates. Many managers feel that their authority is eroding as a consequence of such a shift, and they cannot "manage" their people anymore. As Carlzon points out, this is not the case: "[The new management philosophy] does not mean that management abdicates but rather that it sets up goals and guidelines and delegates operational responsibility in an extremely strong and clear manner. . . .It requires an open, business-oriented and participative leadership (Carlzon & Hubendinck 1984, p. 15). Hence, the traditional role as mere technical manager is changed to a new role characterized by *leadership* and *coaching*.

Another aspect of a service-oriented management style is the development of a positive communication climate. On the one hand, employees need information from management to be able to implement a service strategy; on the other hand, they have valuable. information for management about the needs and wishes of customers, problems and opportunities, and so on. Moreover, feedback is required so that they see the results of their job. If there is a lack of feedback, employees easily lose interest in what they are doing.

Furthermore, it is a good idea, for example, to get contact employees involved in the planning process and in decision making concerning, say, what new services to offer and how they should be produced and delivered (compare Schneider & Bowen 1984). Overall objectives for a group or a department can be broken down into subgoals for that unit in cooperation with the employees who are supposed to accomplish those goals. This process is, first of all, a way of communicating the strategy and objectives of the firm to the employees, and second, it is a way of achieving employee commitment to the service strategy and to the goals.

Finally, as noted in the previous chapter, management methods and the attitudes of managers and supervisors toward their subordinates are of pivotal importance to the long-term success of an internal marketing process.

Service Training Programs

By training personnel the *knowledge and attitude requirements for good service* can be achieved. Training employees is also an integral part of internal marketing. In organizations where there are distinct nonservice values and the existing norms are not service oriented, an attitude of resistance to change can be expected. A large portion of this resistance can be removed by creating the previously discussed strategic, organizational, and management prerequisites for good service. However, this resistance is also at least partly a question of attitudes. If the firm has always operated in a, say, manufacturerlike or bureaucratic way, it is not easy to make people think in new directions. This goes for management as well as for the rest of the organization.

If top management, middle management, and support and contact employees are expected to be motivated for service-oriented thinking and behavior, *they will need knowledge of how a service organization operates, what makes up the customer relationships, what their role in the total operation and customer relationship is, and what the individual is expected to do*. A person who does not understand what is going on and why just cannot be expected to be motivated to do a good job as, for example, a contact person or an internal service provider in support functions behind the line of visibility.

Jan Carlzon of SAS illustrates the impact on motivation of a holistic understanding of the task by the following anecdote:

> There is no better way to sum up my experience than with the story about the two stone cutters who were chipping square blocks out of granite. A visitor to the quarry asked what they were doing. The first stone cutter, looking rather sour, grumbled, "I'm cutting this damned stone into a block." The second, who looked pleased with his work, replied proudly "I'm on this team that's building a cathedral." (Carlzon 1987, p. 135)[a]

Moreover, every single person should be aware of the firm's business mission, strategies and overall objectives as well as the goals of his or her own department and function and his or her own personal goals. Otherwise, it would be unrealistic to think that an employee understands why he or she is told that it is important to perform in a certain way. This is even more important for persons in support functions than for contact employees.

In training programs knowledge-oriented training and straight attitude training are intertwined. The more knowledgeable a person is, the easier it is for that person to have positive attitudes toward a specific phenomenon. It is essential to realize that attitudes seldom can be changed without knowledge. Pep-talks about service and a lot of hoopla may help in some occasions, but they never create enduring service-oriented attitudes if people do not have the facts: why the firm is a service business, or why as a manufacturer it adopts a service strategy; which requirements for performance follow from this; what is my role in relation to other functions and persons, and what is demanded of me as an individual, and why.

Service training can be divided roughly into three categories:

- Developing a *holistic view* both of the organization and its subfunctions as a service organization and of how it functions in a market-oriented manner;
- Developing *skills* concerning how various tasks are to be performed; and
- Developing specifically *communication and service skills*.

---

[a] It is interesting to note that, in slightly different words, this anecdote is also told by Mikhail Gorbachev in his book on the *perestroika* in the Soviet Union (Gorbachev 1987).

All three types of training are needed. The first type gives a general foundation for understanding a service strategy and how to implement it. The second type provides the skills required so that employees can perform their tasks, which may have been somewhat changed after the introduction of a service strategy. The third type of training provides employees, especially contact persons but also support persons, with specific skills as far as communication tasks are concerned. Courses where the area of service-mindedness is addressed belong to this group, too. A fatal mistake, which is all too common, is to believe that only the third type of training is needed to change the attitudes of the personnel. Such an approach is almost never successful. It may be the easiest, but at the same time it is the least strategic way of addressing the issue of attitude change. Doing so is a pitfall which should be avoided.

In the present chapter we have discussed the nature and importance of a service culture as well as the framework for developing such a culture. When the organizational and strategic prerequisites are present, it is matter of human resource development. Managers and the rest of the personnel will have to get motivated to pursue a service strategy in strategic and operational planning as well as in implementing the strategy. Here substantial help can be provided by the concept of *internal marketing*.

Developing a Service Culture—Barriers and Opportunities

Clearly, the task of changing the corporate culture and creating a service culture is a huge one. And getting started is often a substantial problem. There is an initial barrier to starting the process, and there is a threshold to cross on the way. Before this threshold has been crossed, no major changes in the internal norms and value systems can be seen. However, once the process develops far enough, it usually gains pace; provided it is constantly supported and enhanced, especially by top management. Moreover, a service culture has to be maintained once it has been achieved. Otherwise there is always a substantial risk that the interest in service and in servicing internal as well as external customers will start to deteriorate.

It is not easy to get started, but in some situations it is easier than it otherwise would be. Walker (1986), who has studied the U.S. General Accounting Office, suggests that, generally speaking, fundamental changes in the culture occur only when the professional behavior of the personnel is transformed. Moreover, he claims that such a transformation can occur only if there is a good breeding ground for such a change. Such favorable conditions are: *environmental pressure*, such as increased competition, changes in customer needs and expectations, and deregulation or regulation of the business; *new organizational strategies,* which to a sufficient degree differ from the previous ones; and *new structural arrangements,* such as new management or a sufficient change in the organizational structure.

All or some of these things could, of course, occur simultaneously, which probably would help the process. The "cultural revolution" in SAS Scandinavian Airlines System, and in many other organizations during the 1980's, certainly emphasizes the need for such environmental pressure and new structural arrangements. When times are good, and possible problems seem to be too far into the future or are totally invisible to most people in the organization, it is much more difficult to start to change the existing corporate culture. However, as Zemke (1988b) observes: "While it is possible to change the focus and practices of an organization's culture, it is critical to preserve to a considerable extent what has gone before and build on it to make the change . . . Honoring and learning from the past doesn't mean we have to be trapped by it" (p. 7). He also urges management to move slowly and to make incremental change. Sometimes, however, as in the case of SAS, you do not have time to do that. In most cases there is time, though, and too-quick moves may lead to bad results. A cultural change means that people have to change. The process has to be planned and executed in the same way as any important organizational task. "Make incremental change . . . Set intermediate targets, and realize that as powerful as culture is, it is also fragile" (Zemke 1988b, p. 7).

Summary

The phenomenon of corporate culture and service culture is extremely complicated. Developing a specific culture, therefore, requires that a whole range of internal issues be addressed. Culture is a holistic phenomenon. It cannot exist in isolation from or side by side with, for instance, the organizational structure, the management approaches and methods, or the business mission and strategies of the organization. It is the result of these and other aspects of organizational life.

Hence, culture becomes a strategic matter. It does so in two ways, which are related to each other. First of all, creating a service culture requires a holistic view by the decision makers and the persons responsible for developing the culture, and only top management holds that position. Therefore, it becomes a strategic issue that internal requirements for the creation of a service culture be developed. Second, implementing a service strategy requires, among other things, the kind of people who are to some extent obsessed by service and who consider providing internal as well as external customers with good service a natural way of life. Therefore, if an organization intends to implement a service strategy, it is of strategic importance that it strive towards achievement of a service culture.

12
Conclusions: Quality Management and the Five Rules of Service

Introduction

In this final chapter of the book we are going to summarize the essence of a service strategy. First of all, the scope of *service management and marketing* is summarized in the next section. Then, a service quality management program is presented. In the next sections internationalization problems for service organizations are briefly commented upon. Finally, five rules of implementing a service strategy conclude the book.

An Overview of the Essence of a Market-Oriented Service Strategy

In Figure 12–1 the essence of service management and marketing is illustrated. The core of the process is the *moments of truth* of the buyer-seller interactions, or as they have also been called, "the moments of opportunity," where the employee and the customer meet and interact. In these moments of truth the value to customers is created for them. If they are not taken care of properly, the *Perceived Service Quality*, service quality as perceived by the customers, is damaged, and the service provider may easily lose business. *The main focus in service competition is the management of the moments of truth, and the creation of adequate support from managers, and supporting functions as well as from investments in technology and operations and administrative systems.*

The value for customers is not, of course, totally produced in the moments of truth. Much may have been preproduced by the supporting part of the organization. *From the customer's point of view, however, what happens in the moments of truth counts.* If the customer is not satisfied with what he or she experiences, then the preproduction efforts have been more or less in vain.

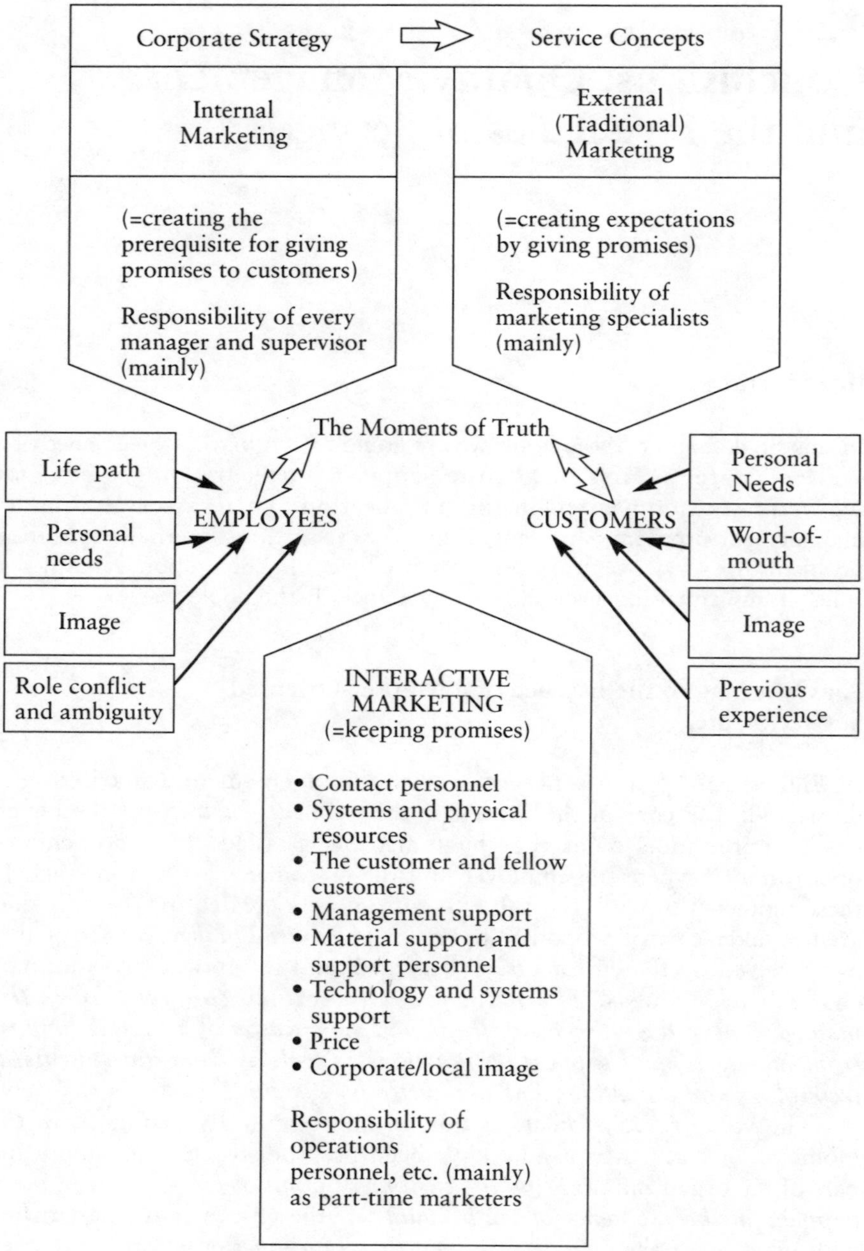

Figure 12–1. An Overview of a Market–Oriented Strategy

Giving Promises: Traditional External Marketing

Customer's experiences of the moments of truth do not take place in a vacuum. They get into them with certain *expectations*, which are partly created by the service provider itself. By its *external marketing function*, involving *traditional marketing* efforts, such as market research, personal selling, advertising, direct mail, sales promotion, pricing, and public relations, the organization *gives promises,* which hopefully correspond with the personal needs and wishes of the target group of customers. *Marketing specialists* inside the organization or outside of it, for example, in advertising agencies and market research firms, are mainly responsibility for this type of external marketing.

These promises are in one way or another, sometimes more, sometimes less, enhanced or counteracted in the minds of the customers by their *previous experiences,* if they have had any, by *word-of-mouth communication*, and by customers' conception of the *image*, corporate and/or local, of the service provider.

Fulfilling Promises: Internal and Interactive Marketing

Employees' abilities and motivation to meet the expectations of customers are backed up by *internal marketing efforts*. By creating and maintaining a service culture, as well as by actively marketing new goods and services, and by marketing campaigns and activities directed toward the employees, the organization may prepare its employees for the moments of truth. Thus, internal marketing is a must for *creating the prerequisite for keeping promises*.

Internal marketing is a *top management* responsibility, but it is also the responsibility of *every manager and supervisor*. Of course, *personal needs* of jobs and *supervisors' encouragement* of employees, as well as their *life path* and their *image of the employer*, also have an impact on employee performance in the moments of truth of the buyer-seller interactions. Moreover, employees are influenced by *role ambiguity*, related to, for example, what they perceive customers on the one hand and the organization on the other expect them to do. Employees are also influenced by role conflicts, for example, when what management says the employees should consider important in their jobs conflicts with the opportunities to live up to these intentions that management provides them.

What actually happens in the moments of truth, where customers and employees meet and interact, determines whether the experience of customers meet their expectations. If experiences equal or are higher than expectations, the Perceived Service Quality is probably good; otherwise there is probably a quality problem. Good quality is a strong basis for a long-term customer relationship, including resales and cross-sales, as well as for favorable word-of-mouth and image.

Thus, *fulfilling promises* in the moments of truth of the buyer-seller interactions is one major aspect of the *interactive marketing function*. The contact persons are most often the key to success. However, the operational systems and physical resources, as well as the customers themselves and their fellow customers, also influence interactive marketing performance. Although the role of the human resource is most often paramount, it should not be overemphasized. First of all, there are a range of situations in which customers interact with systems and physical resources only. Using an ATM and making a normal, local telephone call are examples of such situations. Second, employees need a service-oriented operational system and, for example, proper computer technology and other physical resources to be able to create positive moments of truth. However, one should never forget that if the technology or automatic service production system does not work, breaks down in the hands of the customer, or the customer simply cannot operate it, the key to recovering the situation is a service-minded and customer-conscious employee.

The material support of support personnel and functions, as well as management support, are critical to the service orientation of the contact persons and systems of the visible part of the service production process. Furthermore, the experiences of the moments of truth are influenced by the corporate and/or local image of the service provider in the minds of the customers. Finally, the price level and possible price offerings have an impact on how satisfied with the moments of truth customers are. This is not always altogether true, however. For example, if a manufacturer needs service and spare parts in order to keep the machines running, and if every hour of delay means thousands of dollars of lost production, he or she is probably willing to pay almost anything to get the service.

Interactive marketing and keeping promises is almost totally the *responsibility of operations and other traditionally nonmarketing functions*. Therefore, employees involved in such functions have been called *part-time marketers*, with dual responsibilities—for operations, or whatever their tasks concern, and for the marketing impact of their performance as well. To some extent marketing specialists get involved, too, but their role is mostly marginal. Of course, in most business-to-business relationships the salespersons have continuous responsibility for their customers. They cannot, however, do much to rescue a customer relationship if the organization, in its interactive marketing situations, has made a customer unsatisfied enough with the service quality. In the short run the organization may be able to hold onto the customer's business; in the long run it loses customers.

Principles of Pursuing Service Quality

Producing and delivering excellent service quality has been considered a pivotal issue in service management throughout this book. In the next section we are going to present a Service Quality Management Program. However, before we go into that, we shall present seven principles to guide service providers as they get into improving the quality of their services. These principles have been presented by Berry in a retailing context (Berry 1988), but they seem to be equally valid for most service organizations. The seven principles, which should be considered guidelines only, are listed in Figure 12–2.

All of the principles are equally important and valid. However, the second principle has to be especially emphasized, because it is so often violated. Too frequently management feels, after having completed a quality improvement program, that an ultimate goal has been achieved. Completing the program has been a stressing experience, and it would be easier to concentrate on other issues, which undoubtedly are important as well. But, to quote the words of Lee Iacocca (1988), "It doesn't have a beginning or a middle. And it better not have an end. The quality of a product, and of the process in arriving at that product, has to go on and on to become part of every employee's mind-set. . . . Quality is not something you can buy; it's something you must attain—through people" (p. 253).

A Service Quality Management Program

In chapters 2 and 3 we presented models of service quality and a number of structures for understanding how quality is perceived, how it emerges, and which factors influence the Perceived Service Quality. As a synthesis of a number of studies into determinants of service quality, the Six Criteria of Good Perceived Service Quality were introduced. In the following chapters *principles of service management,* concepts, models, and frameworks for analyzing, planning, and executing a market-oriented service strategy were presented. A common theme throughout this book has been how to create and maintain an excellent total Perceived Service Quality.

In the present section we are going to sum up the hitherto discussed concepts and models in the form of a management-oriented *Service Quality*

1. Quality is Defined by Customers
Quality is conformance to the customer's specifications. Customers decide what they consider good quality, what they consider important, and what unimportant in service production. They also judge the Perceived Service Quality.

2. Quality is a Journey
Formulas for fixing quality quickly once and for all do not exist. Good quality has to be pursued constantly, equally as much when profits are up as when times are bad.

3. Quality is Everyone's Job
Everyone has customers, either external or internal customers. Responsibility for producing quality and for quality control cannot be delegated to one single person or, for example, staff office. Everyone has to consider producing and delivering good quality their responsibility.

4. Quality, Leadership, and Communication are Inseparable
In order to be able to produce good quality people need knowledge, feedback, and support and encouragement from their managers and supervisors. Managers have to show genuine leadership when managing their subordinates.

5. Quality and Integrity are Inseparable
Good quality requires a corporate culture that emphasizes integrity. Fairness in treating customers and employees alike has to be a core value shared by everyone.

6. Quality is a Design Issue
Service quality has to be designated in advance. The use of technology and personnel and the participation of customers in the service production system should be a forethought. Otherwise, the organization is only partly prepared for producing good quality.

7. Quality is Keeping the Service Promise
More than anything else customers seem to expect service providers to do what they have promised to do. If promises are not kept, or if some critical part of the bundle of promises given is not kept, quality deteriorates.

Source: Berry, L.L. (1988): Delivering Excellent Service in Retailing. *Retailing Issues Letter,* No. 4, Arthur Andersen & Co. Center for Retailing Studies: Texas A&M University Press, pp. 1–3

Figure 12–2. Principles Guiding the Improvement of Service Quality

Management Program. This program is intended to help management implement a service strategy so that the challenges of the constantly increasing service competition are properly responded to. If the organization has decided to pursue a service strategy, the Service Quality Management Program should, for managerial purposes, give adequate guidance in what to do.

The Service Quality Management Program consists of *six subprograms* (Grönroos 1986). These are:

1. Service concept development
2. Customer expectations management program
3. Service outcome management program
4. Internal marketing program
5. Physical environment management program
6. Consumer participation management program

1. *Service concept development.* The establishment of customer-oriented service concepts which guide the management of the quality-generating resources and activities is, of course, a first task in service quality development process.

2. *Customer expectations management program.* The traditional marketing activities should never be planned and implemented in isolation. They should always be related to the experiences the service provider is willing and able to deliver to its customers. Otherwise, there will always be a quality problem, irrespective of the other quality development subprograms. Therefore, managing customer expectations is always an integral part of any service quality program. This makes, for example, managing external market communication part of quality management.

3. *Service outcome management program.* The outcome of the buyer-seller interactions, that is, *what* customers get as a *technical quality* of the service, is part of the total service experience. The outcome of the interaction process has to be developed and managed according to the service concepts agreed upon and the specific needs of the target customers. When the concept of product development from the manufacturing-oriented literature is applied in a service context, this aspect of service quality is normally covered, whereas other aspects are perhaps not taken into consideration as much as they should be.

4. *Internal marketing program.* As we have demonstrated, the *functional quality* of the process, that is, *how* the moments of truth of the buyer-seller interactions are perceived by customers, is in most cases the key to an excellent service quality and to achieving a winning competitive edge.

Most frequently this quality dimension is predominantly due to the courtesy, flexibility, and general service-mindedness of the contact persons, and to the ability and willingness of them to perform as "part-time marketers." Hence, the employees, contact persons, managers, and other employee categories alike have to be considered a first, *internal market* of the service provider. A continuous and strategically backed up internal marketing process is, therefore, a vital part of any quality development and management program.

5. *Physical environment management program*. The physical resources, technology, and systems of service organizations are too frequently developed according to internal efficiency standards. The external effects of, for example, a computer system are seldom taken into account to a proper degree. Consequently, these resources, which constitute a technology base for service production as well as the physical environment for service consumption, may have a negative impact on the perception of the buyer-seller interactions. Hence, a physical environment management program should be part of an overall quality program.

6. *Consumer participation management program*. The customers should be advised how to act in the buyer-seller interaction, so that they have a favorable impact on the moments of truth themselves. The service quality can be destroyed by customers who either do not know what to do or do not want to perform according to the service provider's expectations. Negative effects of fellow customers, causing, for example, waiting lines or a dull atmosphere, must also be avoided. Moreover, eliminating unfavorable effects on the moments of truth of a misfit between customer segments or individual customers is also part of a customer participation management program.

Internationalization and International Marketing of Services

In the literature on export and international marketing, usually only tangible goods are considered, while the service sector is neglected. The literature on internationalization and international marketing from a service perspective is very scarce (see, for example, Vandermerwe & Chadwick 1989, Edvardsson, Edvinsson, & Nyström 1988, Riddle 1988, Segal-Horn 1988, Johansson 1987, Sampson & Snape 1986, Edvinsson 1983, 1985, and 1986, Cowell 1983, Edvinsson & Nandorf 1983, and Grönroos 1979b). In addition, there is, of course, a much larger number of industry-specific articles and reports. However, service industries are internationalizing as manufacturers did much earlier. Trade barriers are slowly removed. Although there seems to be no reliable statistics available, the international trade with services amounts to approximately 600 billion dollars. This is somewhere around 25 percent of total world trade (Edvardsson & Magnusson 1988).

There are still, however, substantial barriers making international trade with services a complicated and sometimes even impossible undertaking. Some of these barriers are real, but there are also attitudinal problems. When business executives, customs officials, and others are used to thinking in terms of physical goods, it is not always easy to understand that services are different and should therefore perhaps be treated in a different way.

The following anecdote (which unfortunately is a true story) demonstrates this point: The leading Finnish cleaning and laundry services company, Lindstrom Group, had found a promising business opportunity in exporting laundry services to Swedish hotels in the Stockholm area. The laundry was collected from the hotels by truck and taken by car ferry to Finland, where it was to be processed in the company's large and modern facilities outside Helsinki. The business was perfectly sound, and the service was considered good by the hotels in Sweden, thus giving them value for their money.

The entire undertaking was a flop, of course, because the customs officials in Finland were unable to think in terms of service trade. They only saw textiles—sheets, tablecloths, towels, napkins, and so forth. Hence, every single shipment of dirty laundry was treated as import of textiles, which, of course, added enough additional expenses to make the business unprofitable. Asked whether he could not accept that this was service trade and not import and export of textiles, a high-rank customs official replied: "Of course, this is trade with textiles."

In the next section we are going to very briefly discuss internationalization as an opportunity for service organizations.

Internationalization as a Growth Strategy

In some cases internationalization may be the only growth strategy available for a service firm. In others it may be just one of several possible growth opportunities. However, it is often an alternative that service firms will have to analyze carefully, and it will certainly represent a realistic growth strategy more frequently in the future. Carman and Langeard (1980) compared internationalization with other growth strategies. At the same time they compared goods with services in light of these categories. They concluded that out-of-country expansion is a more risky strategy for a service firm than, for example, concentric diversification and new service development in existing markets.

They also argue that internationalization is more risky for a service business than it is for a manufacturer of physical goods (Carman & Langeard 1980). And certainly for service organizations, internationalization is a tough undertaking, allowing limited time and opportunity for learning in order to understand and get used to the new market. A manufacturer can start its internationalization process by exporting indirectly—for example, utilizing export and/or import agents who are familiar with the foreign market to be penetrated—and then turning gradually to more direct international marketing operations, perhaps with a sales organization or even factories of its own abroad to minimize its risk of major mistakes.

The service firm, on the other hand, has to enter the foreign market all at once one way or the other, starting to produce its services there in more or less direct contact with its customers. The service firm will obviously not have much time for learning to understand the foreign environment, and is thus all too likely to make mistakes. Also, the service firm in such a situation will normally have more trouble with personnel, technological resources, quality control, and know-how than a manufacturer which can move its goods into the new market gradually, thus avoiding a sudden confrontation with all these problems. Here again the marketer of goods has a relatively long learning time; whereas marketers of services are forced, in general, to start finding acceptable solutions to the problems in the new environment practically from their first day there (compare Carman & Langeard 1980).

Internationalization can, therefore, be regarded as a rather demanding growth strategy for service firms, involving a substantial amount of risk. Nevertheless, an increasing number of privately owned firms and organizations within the public sector either will be forced to start looking for international markets or will find it potentially profitable enough to try to find means of satisfying needs for various kinds of services in foreign countries.

Guidelines for Managing Service Competition

In this last part of this concluding chapter we are going to present a set of guidelines for service management. The situation differs, of course, between firms and industries. However, some more or less general guidelines for implementing a service strategy can be put forward. These guidelines start from a notion that men and women are the critical resource and the bottleneck in most service operations. As business is a social phenomenon, it is, of course, not correct to talk about any rules of a service economy in a strict sense. No rules in a positivistic sense can exist. Nevertheless, in order to emphasize the common characteristics of the customer relationships of most organizations in the service economy, we label these concluding guidelines *The Five Rules of Service* (they have also been presented earlier in Grönroos 1988a). We do bear in mind that this is a somewhat inaccurate expression, and also the fact that these rules for some situations overemphasize the role of the employees. The Fifth Rule, however, focuses on other aspects of service management.

The five rules of service are as follows:

First Rule: The general approach
Second Rule: Demand analysis
Third Rule: Quality control
Fourth Rule: Marketing
Fifth Rule: Organizational support

The First Rule: The General Approach

Not only does the importance of service elements in the customer relations grow, the customers—the representatives of organizations as well as individuals and members of households—demand individual and flexible responses from the service provider to an increasing extent. Success in the market requires that the firm can offer advice and guidance concerning big deals, for example, technical advice needed to start operating a paper machine, as well as small details, for example, a quick response on the phone about departure times. If the employees have the knowledge needed, and in addition have a service-oriented approach to their job and to the customers, and if the firm is competitive in other respects, this will give good results in the marketplace. Hence, the *First Rule of Service* can be expressed as follows (compare Mickwitz 1985):

> *People develop and maintain good and enduring customer contacts. The employees ought to act as consultants, who are prepared to do their duties when the customer needs them and in a way the customer wants. The firm that manages to do this best strengthens its customer relationships and achieves the best profitability.*

The Second Rule: Demand Analysis

Services are either rendered directly to people or organizations, or they are services on equipment owned by people (or organizations). In all cases representatives of the customer are present, extensively or occasionally, when the service is produced and delivered. Direct confrontations between contact employees and customers occur, and in such situations immediate actions may have to be decided upon and taken by the contact person. Or the contact person may have to give some information or in some way change his or her way of doing the job according to the action of the customer. Such a reaction may be, for example, a change of level of an ongoing customer training seminar to better meet the requirements or level of knowledge of the attendees, or a quick decision by a telephone receptionist about whom to put on the phone when the person a customer is asking for is absent. Nobody other than the person who produces the service can recognize the maybe unexpected shift in the needs or wishes of the customer, if corrective actions are to be taken immediately. And in such situations prompt actions are called for.

Market demand can, of course, be measured in advance using standard means of market research, and should be done in this way. However, changing needs and wishes of customers at the point and time of service production and consumption cannot be measured in advance. Nor can they be reacted to later on, when somebody else, perhaps based on market research, has detected the changes that took place. The customer relationship was hurt long ago, if a quick reaction did not occur on the spot. Only contact personnel, the contact employees, can do this in a satisfactory manner. Hence, the *Second Rule of Service* can be expressed as follows:

> *The contact persons producing the service in contact with customers will have to do their own analysis of the needs and wishes of the customers at the point and time of service production and consumption.*

The Third Rule: Quality Control

According to traditional quality control models from manufacturing, the quality of a product is controlled by a separate unit, which checks the preproduced goods. In modern quality management (see, for example, Juran 1982, Crosby 1984, Ishikawa 1985, and Gummesson 1987a), this view is not valid anymore. Everyone, in manufacturing as well as in service production, has a responsibility for quality, and producing good quality is based on a notion that things will have to be done correctly the first time. Because of the characteristics of services and the nature of service production and consumption, postproduction control cannot prevent failure, it can only be observed that bad service quality has been produced *and* consumed by the customer. Moreover, if things are not done correctly the first time, the costs of correcting quality problems, which have occurred either in the back office or in the buyer-seller interface, are frequently high. As the quality goal is often less than 100 percent and mistakes are therefore mentally tolerated, these costs easily become "hidden costs" which are taken for granted and not considered unnecessary (Crosby 1984 and Gummesson 1987a). Consequently, it is not possible to have a separate quality control unit only following every production step; rather, everyone has to control the result of his or her job on the spot.

In service operations this is very true, indeed. As Jan Carlzon of SAS puts it in an internal booklet: "Let us state once and for all: *Responsibility for quality in your job is yours and yours alone*. But you do have support" (Our Approach to Quality, 1987, p. 15).

Services are to a large extent the result of cooperation or interactive relationships between representatives of the buyer and the seller, which makes quality management even more complicated than it is in manufacturing. In manufacturing, one has to do things right the first time according to specifications which do not change at the time of production. In service production, *the specifications may change*, as was demonstrated by the discussion of the Second Rule. The customer may change his or her mind or have wishes other than what was originally expected. The technology may break down, or almost anything may happen to unexpectedly change the situation and demand new or unforeseen actions.

The one who renders the service in contact with the customer, the contact person, will have to check the quality of the service on the spot at the time it is produced and delivered. For example, when goods are delivered to a customer, an elevator is repaired, a customer in a restaurant is being served, or a telephone receptionist handles a call made by a customer, the quality of that service operation cannot be controlled and managed by anyone other than the contact person who gets in touch with the customer. As Bowen and Schneider (1988) observe: "There is not a supervisor physically present in the employee-customer dyad who can exercise ongoing, immediate quality control" (p. 65). Afterwards the quality can, of course, be checked, for example, by market research, but then the mistake has already been made and the customer relationship may have been damaged.

On the other hand, the contact person, or support person serving internal customers, must not be left totally alone. "Common sense" may not be enough guidance. Management must provide the employees with the knowledge, skills, and directions needed to manage quality on their own in their customer contacts (internal or external). Moreover, management will have to enhance the attitudes and the mental capabilities of the employees to manage quality. "Management must surround employees with a service imperative by emphasizing and facilitating through all available subsystems" (Bowen & Schneider 1988, pp. 65–66).

Hence, the *Third Rule of Service* can be expressed as follows:

> *The contact person producing the service in contact with customers will have to control the quality of the service at the same time he or she produces the service.*

The Fourth Rule: Marketing

In service competition the nature of marketing changes as well. Although the traditional marketing activities, such as market research, advertising campaigns, personal selling by a professional sales force, and sales promotion, are as important as ever, they are not the only activities to be performed as marketing activities. The *marketing function* is much larger and is spread all over the organization. Traditional means of competition are used mainly to establish new customer relationships, whereas they are of less importance, although not without importance, when ongoing relationships are to be maintained and strengthened. In order to develop already existing customer relationships, exchange of goods, services, and information, as well as financial and social exchange, are of critical importance (compare Håkansson 1982). Personal selling, advertising, and public relations activities are, of course, used in such situations, too, but their impact is often minor. Price is important in all stages of the Customer Relationships Life Cycle.

In service competition every contact between a contact person and a representative of a customer (an individual, a household, or another type of organization) includes an element of marketing. These contacts are the moments of truth or the moments of opportunity where the success of the service provider is determined and resales and cross-sales opportunities can be utilized. If these moments of truth give the customer a favorable impression of the contact person, of the operational systems and physical resources used, and thus of the total organization, the customer relationship is strengthened. The probability that it will last longer and lead to further business increases. On the other hand, the opposite is also true. Badly handled buyer-seller interactions, that is, negatively experienced moments of truth, damage customer relationships and lead to lost business.

Thus, as noted earlier, any service organization has a large number of *part-time marketers*. And marketing is their second responsibility only.

However, the marketing impact of what they do and how they perform their tasks has to be recognized by management and by themselves, because their role in the total marketing function is critical. *If the interactive marketing performance of the part-time marketers fails, the marketing function fails, irrespective of whether the selling efforts of the sales force or the advertising campaigns or other means of competition of the traditional marketing has been successful or not.* This is the essence of services marketing.

Marketing the service as part-time marketer in the interactive marketing sense does not necessarily mean that the contact person would have to actively sell or offer the service, although this may occur, too. Normally good part-time marketing behavior, though, means that the job is done skillfully, in a flexible manner, without unnecessary delays, and with a service-oriented attitude. Hence, the *Fourth Rule of Service* can be expressed as follows:

> *The contact person will have to be a marketer of the service he or she simultaneously produces.*

The Fifth Rule: Organizational Support

The organizational structure of many firms does not support customer-oriented and high-quality service operations today. Contact persons or departments which have to interact with each other in order to produce the service may be far apart in the organization. Often decisions concerning even minor details are made too far away from the service encounter, which, of course, easily has a negative impact on the perceived service. Internal regulations may restrict the flexibility of the contact persons. For example, hotels frequently have their employees say, "No, Sir, we cannot do that—management regulations, Sir" to customers who ask for something outside the normal procedures. Pants cannot be ironed on a Sunday, or pajamas cannot be supplied for a guest whose luggage has been left behind by an airline. Management does not trust the employees to think for themselves and make wise decisions.

Finally, in many manufacturing firms, the service elements are considered less important and without any glamour even today. This means that services are not, like goods, an integral part of the total offering to the market. They get less resources and less of management's time.

The employees, managers, and their subordinates often do not feel that services are important. The organizational structure is not geared to the demands of the new service competition. The result is inevitable, of course. The employees involved in the variety of service operations of the firm feel no pride in their job, nor do they feel motivated to give good service in the customer relations. In order to develop the services into powerful means of competition, the firm will have to adjust the organizational structure so that the organization—the formal as well as the informal one—supports employees in their efforts to give good service. An *organization structure support* is needed.

As previously concluded, technology is not any less important in the service economy than it was before. On the contrary, it may even be more important. A technological solution, or a physical resource that is geared to the needs and wishes of the user and that fits the situation in which it is to be used, may very well enhance the quality of the service. It can improve the efficiency of operations and profitability as well. Even more frequently technological support enables the personnel to produce a better service. Appropriate technology and physical resources, such as computer systems, documents, and tools and equipment, may at the same time improve the working conditions and enhance the motivation of the employees to give good service. In most service operations the employees need an adequate *technological support.*

Finally, there is a third kind of support given to the employees that is essential to good service, that is, *management support.* It is well known that managers and supervisors get the subordinates they deserve. Moreover, they have an important effect on the norms and values that guide the overall way of thinking and behaving in the organization. In service competition this is as true as it ever was, and even more important to realize than before, because of the enormous and immediate impact on demand analysis, quality control, and marketing that contact persons have.

Managers and supervisors will have to be true *leaders*, not mere technical managers. As Albrecht (1988) puts it: "Today's employee is overmanaged and underled" (p. 115). There are too many rules and restrictions which managers and supervisors use as managing devices. This not only damages the service for the customer, in the long run it destroys the employees. People normally are able to think for themselves, act spontaneously and flexibly, and still make good judgments, if they are well informed. Such service-oriented attitudes are effectively damaged by too much rules-and-regulation management and too little leadership.

Today, managers will have to be able to motivate their subordinates to be service oriented and customer conscious, by, for example, their leadership style, their way of sharing information and feedback with people in their organizational unit, and their way of encouraging, supporting, and guiding their subordinates. They will have to demonstrate, by the way they do their job, that they, too, consider good service and satisfied customers important. It goes without saying that this attitude is required of every manager in the firm, irrespective of their hierarchical position and their own personal engagement in service operations.

Finally, unclear visions and/or badly defined or totally undefined *Service concepts* (one or several) make it difficult for managers and their subordinates to decide in which direction they should go, what leads to fulfilling goals, and what is contradictory to the objectives of the organization. If the service concepts are not well stated or not stated at all, no clear and easily acceptable goals can be set. And in such situations chaos occurs both in planning as well as in the everyday implementation of plans.

To sum up, the employees will need the support of the organizational structure and the technology used in service operations, as well as the encouragement of their managers and supervisors, in order to be able to meet the new service competition successfully. Moreover, clearly defined service concepts are a must, if the organization is to avoid a chaotic situation where nobody really knows what to do in certain situations or how to react to changes in the environment and to unexpected behaviors of customers. Hence, the *Fifth Rule of Service* can be expressed as follows:

> *The organizational structure, technology, and managers, as well as explicitly defined service concepts, will have to provide the guidance, support, and encouragement needed to enable and motivate contact persons (and support persons alike) to give good service.*

Five Barriers to Achieving Results

The Fifth Rule can be made more explicit by adding five additional follow-up statements which follow directly from the discussion about this rule. These statements all concern major *barriers to successfully implemented service management*. They are:

Barrier 1 (organizational barriers). *Good service, and sound change processes toward a service culture, are effectively destroyed by an organizational structure inherited from yesterday's society.* If an unappropriate organizational structure is left outside a change program, much of the efforts to achieve better services may be in vain. The organization simply is not suitable for services and, thus, becomes a barrier to change.

Barrier 2 (systems and regulations-related barriers). *Employees normally would like to treat their customers well and give good service, but internal rules and regulations, the systems of operating, and the technology used may make this an impossible task.* It is only natural that most people would prefer to treat their customers well and give good service to them, but if management regulations, operations or administrative systems, or the technology used is counteracting good service, they cannot do this. The internal infrastructure of the organization becomes a barrier to change. This typically happens when only training efforts are used as the predominant means of developing a service culture in an organization, and no attention is given in the change process to this infrastructure provided by regulation, systems, and technology.

Barrier 3 (management-related barriers). *How managers treat their subordinates is the way the customers of the organizations are going to be treated.* If a change process focuses predominantly or only on contact and support personnel and top and middle management is left outside, the risk is all too great that the superiors of those involved in customer contacts will not be totally or at all aware of what should be emphasized in these contacts and how the moments of truth should be handled and managed. Supervisors easily encourage wrong things, and a role conflict emerges for the employees. They would like to implement new ideas, but their bosses have become a barrier to doing this.

Barrier 4 (strategy-related barriers). *If well-defined and easily understood service concepts are lacking, chaos will emerge in the organization, and managers and subordinates alike will be uncertain about how to act in specific situations, in planning as well as in executing plans.* If the organization throws itself into a change process without first clearly analyzing the benefits the customers in the organization's target segments are seeking, and decides what it should therefore do, and how corresponding goals should be accomplished, there is no solid foundation for a consistently pursued change process. A number of projects are initiated and programs started without anyone really knowing why this is being done and what the ultimate objectives are. In short, there is no strategic approach, and this becomes a barrier to change.

All of the four barriers above, as well as the five rules, are easy to accept, and in most practical situations it is not difficult for managers to intellectually admit that these rules are violated and/or several barriers are present in their organizations. However, the step from intellectually understanding a phenomenon and accepting that a problem may exist to really doing something to fundamentally change the situation is often far too overwhelming. Therefore, a fifth barrier is finally offered as the key to real-world success:

Barrier 5 (decision-making barriers). *Good intellectual analysis and thorough planning is of no value unless there is the determination, courage, and strength needed in the organization to implement new visions and intellectually sound plans.* To put this another way, weak management always becomes a barrier to implementing change processes.

Conclusions

In this chapter we have illustrated the essence of managing the moments of truth in a service competition. In the first sections the market-oriented service management framework was summed up and a service quality management program was put forward, and in the following sections five more or less generally applicable guidelines for managing the moments of truth, the Five Rules of Service, were described. Internationalization of service organizations was also briefly touched upon.

The conclusions in this chapter hold true not only for so-called service firms such as hotels and restaurants, banks and financial institutions, insurance companies, transportation firms, and a variety of public services. *They are equally valid for any type of organization.* This follows from the fact that in most industries the importance of service grows dramatically. As stated in the first chapter, *everybody is in the service economy*. Hence, every firm faces, more or less intensely, some kind of service competition. Services can be found in any industry, and they should be an integral part of any firm's offering, irrespective of whether goods or services are the core business of the firm.

The traditional ways of handling demand analysis, quality control, and marketing are not sufficient anymore. The new *service competition* requires a new way of thinking, a *service know-how*. If management cannot adjust its ways of thinking and its actions according to the new situation, the risk that the firm will suffer and lose market share will grow. *The service know-how is a strategic issue as well as an operational one*. The ways in which demand analysis, quality control, and marketing have been done in the past are not necessarily wrong today. Traditional activities may still be efficient and effective, and they should be applied whenever they are appropriate. The main thing is that they are not sufficient anymore. They have to be accompanied by new efforts, and, moreover, they have to be viewed in a new, much more holistic perspective.

In service competition, if the firm fails to understand the characteristics of services and the critical importance of successful management of the moments of truth, the operations of the firm will deteriorate. A number of moments of truth will become wasted moments of opportunity. On the operational level, every employee has to meet the demands that competition makes on them—follow the Rules of Service—all the time. And the support of the Fifth Rule must be present continuously. Of course, this may be impossible to achieve in practice. Mistakes happen. However, *the objective must be to achieve 100 percent excellence*. Otherwise, the battle is mentally lost before it has even begun; the service customers get will be uneven, bad word-of-mouth is created, and the image is damaged.

Unevenness or inconsistency of services is perhaps the severest problem facing service operations today (compare Gummesson 1987a). Most parts of a service production process may function well, but if one or two moments of truth are handled badly, all the good that has been developed may be destroyed by these elements of bad service. Or the customer may get acceptable service by all the normal functions of a service firm, but if he or she has an unexpected wish, no service can be obtained. Whether the customer experiences bad service or a lack of willingness to give good service, the total *Perceived Service Quality* will collapse in the mind of the customer on that one single occasion. The unevenness of the service production process caused by one or a few badly handled *moments of truth* has an immense negative impact on the customer relationship. As Jan Carlzon of SAS states it: "Successful service management is to improve one hundred things by one percent, not one thing by one hundred percent." And in order to do that, consider the advice of Lee Iacocca (1988, p. 74):

> "Start with good people, lay out the rules, communicate with your employees, motivate them, and reward them if they perform. If you do all those things effectively, you can't miss."

Bibliography

Ackoff, R.L., Broholm, P. & Snow, R. (1982): *Revitalizing Western Economies*. San Francisco, Calif.: Jossey-Bass

A Homecoming Lament. *Time* (2 February 1987)

Albrecht, K. (1988): *At America's Service*. Homewood, Ill.: Dow Jones-Irwin

Albrecht, K. & Bradford, L.J. (1990): *The Service Advantage*. Homewood, Ill.: Dow Jones-Irwin

Albrecht, K. & Zemke, R. (1985a): *Service America*. Homewood, Ill.: Dow Jones-Irwin

——. (1985b): Instilling a Service Strategy: Like Teaching an Elephant to Dance. *International Management*, November

Alderson, W. (1950): Survival and Adjustment in Organized Behavior Systems. In Cox, R. & Alderson, W., eds., *Theory in Marketing*. Homewood, Ill.: Irwin

——. (1957): *Marketing Behavior and Executive Action*. Homewood Ill.: Irwin

——. (1965): *Dynamic Marketing Behavior*. Homewood, Ill.: Irwin

AMA Board Approves New Marketing Definition. *Marketing News*, March 1, 1985.

American Society for Quality Control (ASQC). *42nd Annual Quality Congress Transactions*, Milwaukee, Wisc. 1988

Andresen, O. et al., eds. (1983): *Danmark som servicesamfund* (Denmark as a service society). Copenhagen, Denmark: Politikens Forlag

Armitage, H.M. & Atkinson, A.A. (1988): The Choice of Productivity Measures in Organizations: A Field Study of Practice in Seven Canadian Firms. Research Report for the American Accounting Association Conference on *Performance Excellence in Service Organizations*, San Diego, Calif. March

Arndt, J. (1969): *Word of Mouth Advertising*. New York: Advertising Research Foundation

Arndt, J. & Friman, A., eds. (1981): *Ledning, produktion och marknadsforing av tjanster* (Management, production and marketing of services). Malmo, Sweden: Liber

——. (1983): *Intern marknadsforing* (Internal marketing). Malmo, Sweden: Liber

Bateson, J.E.G. (1985): Perceived Control and the Service Encounter. In Czepiel, J.A., Salomon, M.R. & Surprenant, C. F., eds., *The Service Encounter*. Lexington, Mass.: Lexington Books

Bateson, J. (1989): *Managing Services Marketing: Text and Readings*. Hinsdale, Ill.: Dryden Press

Bateson, J.E.G. & Hui, M.K.H. (1987): Perceived Control as a Crucial Perceptual Dimension of the Service Experience: An Experimental Study. In Surprenant, C., ed., *Add Value to Your Service*. Chicago, Ill.: American Marketing Association

Bell, D. (1973): *The Coming of Post-Industrial Society: A Venture in Social Forecasting*. New York: Basic Books

Berekoven, L. (1974): *Der Dienstleistungsbetrieb* (The service firm). Wiesbaden, West Germany

Bernstein, D. (1985): *Company Image & Reality*. Eastbourne: Holt, Rinehart and Winston

Berry, L.L. (1981): The Employee as Customer. *Journal of Retail Banking*, March

——. (1983): Relationship Marketing. In Berry, L.L. et al., eds., *Emerging Perspectives of Services Marketing*. Chicago, Ill.: American Marketing Association

——. (1988) Delivering Excellent Service in Retailing. *Retailing Issues Letter* (published by Arthur Andersen & Co. and Center for Retailing Studies, Texas A&M University), No. 4

Berry, L.L., Zeithaml, V.A. & Parasuraman, A. (1985): Quality Counts in Services. Too. *Business Horizons*, May–June

Bertalanffy, L. von (1950): The Theory of Open Systems in Physics and Biology. *Science*, No. 3

Bessom, R.M. (1973): Unique Aspects of Marketing of Services. *Arizona Business Bulletin*, November

Beyond Customer Satisfaction through Quality Improvement (paid advertisement). *Fortune*, September 26, 1988

Blois, K.J. (1974): The Marketing of Services: An Approach. *European Journal of Marketing*, Summer 1974

Bonoma, T.V. & Mills, M.K. (1979): *Developmental Service Marketing*. Working Paper Series, Graduate School of Business, University of Pittsburgh

Booms, B.H. & Bitner, M.J. (1982): Marketing Strategies and Organization Structures for Service Firms. In Donnelly, J.H. & George, W.R., eds., *Marketing of Services*. Chicago, Ill.: American Marketing Association

Borden, N.H. (1964): The Concept of the Marketing Mix. *Journal of Advertising Research*, June

Boulding, K.E. (1956): General Systems Theory—The Skeleton of Science. *Management Science*, April

Bowen, D.E. (1986): Managing Customers as Human Resources in Service Organizations. *Human Resource Management*, Fall

Bowen, D.E. & Schneider, B. (1988): Services Marketing and Management: Implications for Organizational Behavior. *Research in Organizational Behavior*, 10

Bowen, D.E., Siehl, C. & Schneider, B. (1989): A Framework for Analyzing Customer Service Orientation in Manufacturing. *Academy of Management Review*, January

Bowers, M.R. (1987): The New Service Development Process: Suggestions for Improvements. In Czepiel, J.A., Congram, C.A. & Shanahan, J., eds., *The Service Challenge: Integration for Competitive Advantage.* Chicago, Ill.: American Marketing Association

Brentani, U. de (1989): Success and Failure in New Industrial Services. *Journal of Product Innovation Management,* 4

Brown, J.J. & Reingen, P.H. (1987): Social Ties and Word-of-Mouth Referral Behavior. *Journal of Consumer Research,* December

Brown, S.W., Gummesson, E., Edvardsson, B. & Gustafsson, B.O., eds. (1990): *Quality in Services—Multidisciplinary and Multinational Perspectives.* Lexington, Mass.: Lexington Books

Brown, S.W. & Swartz, T.A. (1989): A Gap Analysis of Professional Service Quality. *Journal of Marketing,* April

Buzzell, R.D. and Gale, B.T. (1987): *The PIMS Principles. Linking Strategy to Performance.* New York: The Free Press

Calonius, H. (1986): A Market Behaviour Framework. In Möller, K. & Paltschik, M., eds., *Contemporary Research in Marketing.* Proceedings from the XVth Annual Conference of the European Marketing Academy, Helsinki, Finland

——. (1988): A Buying Process Model. In Blois, K. & Parkinson, S., eds., *Innovative Marketing—A European Perspective.* Proceedings from the XVIIth Annual Conference of the European Marketing Academy, University of Bradford, England

——. (1989): Market Communications in Service Marketing. In Avlonitis, G.J., Papavasiliou, N.K., & Kouremenos, A.G., eds., *Marketing Thought and Practice in the 1990s.* Proceedings of the XVIII Annual Conference of the European Marketing Academy, Athens, Greece

Campbell, N.C.G. & Cunningham, M.T. (1983): Customer Analysis for Strategy Development in Industrial Markets. *Strategic Management Journal,* 4

Carlzon, J. (1987). *Moments of Truth.* Cambridge, Mass: Ballinger

Carlzon, J. & Hubendinck, U. (1984): *The Cultural Revolution in SAS.* Bromma, Sweden: Scandinavian Airline System

Carman, J.M. & Langeard, E. (1980): Growth Strategies for Service Firms. *Strategic Management Journal,* No. 1

Chamberlain, E.H. (1933): *The Theory of Monopolistic Competition.* Cambridge, Mass.: Harvard University Press

Chase, R.B. (1978): Where Does the Customer Fit in a Service Operation? *Harvard Business Review,* November–December

——. (1988): *Service System Productivity Requires More Than a Stopwatch.* Working Paper. University of Southern California Graduate School of Business Administration

Chase, R.B. & Erikson, W.J. (1988): The Service Factory. *The Academy of Management EXECUTIVE,* No. 3

Cherubini, S. (1981): *Il marketing dei servizi* (The marketing of services). Rome: Franco Angeli Editore

Clement, J. (1985): *Ledelse af servicevirksomheder* (Management of service firms). Copenhagen, Denmark: Civilokonomernes Forlag

Collier, D.A. (1983): The Service Sector Revolution: The Automation of Services. *Long Range Planning,* No. 6

——. (1987): *Service Management. Operating Decisions.* Englewood Cliffs, N.J.: Prentice-Hall

Compton, F., George, W.R., Grönroos, C. & Karvinen, M. (1987): Internal Marketing. In Czepiel, J.A., Congram, C.A. & Shanahan, J., eds, *The Service Challenge: Integrating for Competitive Advantage.* Chicago, Ill.: American Marketing Association

Cowell, D.W. (1983): International Marketing of Services. *Service Industries Journal,* November

Cowell, D. (1984): *The Marketing of Services.* London: Heineman

Crosby, L.A. (1988): *Building and Maintaining Quality in the Service Relationship.* Research Report. QUIS Symposium in Service Quality, Karlstad, Sweden

Crosby, L.A., Evans, K.R. & Cowles, D.L. (1988): *Relationship Quality in Service Selling: An Interpersonal Influence Perspective.* Research Report. 15th International Research Seminar in Marketing, La-Londe-Les-Maures, France

Crosby, L.A. & Giacobbe, R. (1986): Casual Relations among the Components of Service Satisfaction: A Report on Work in Progress. In Möller, K. & Paltschik, M., eds., *Contemporary Research in Marketing.* Proceedings from the XVth Annual Conference of the European Marketing Academy, Helsinki, Finland

Crosby, P.B. (1979): *Quality is Free.* New York: McGraw-Hill

——. (1984): *Quality Without Tears.* New York: The American Library

Czepiel, J.A., Solomon, M.R. & Surprenant, C.F., eds. (1985): *The Service Encounter.* Lexington, Mass.: Lexington Books

Davidson, D.S. (1978): How to Succeed in a Service Industry . . . Turn the Organization Chart Upside Down. *Management Review,* April

Davis, S.M. (1985): *Managing Corporate Culture.* Cambridge, Mass.: Ballinger

Davis, S. (1987): *Future Perfect.* New York: Addison-Wesley

Deal, T.E. & Kennedy, A.A. (1982): *Corporate Cultures: The Rites and Rituals of Corporate Life.* Reading, Mass.: Addison-Wesley

Deshpande, R. & Webster, F.E., Jr. (1987): *Organizational Culture and Marketing: Defining the Research Agenda.* Report No. 87-106. Cambridge, Mass.: Marketing Science Institute

Dixon, D.F. & Blois, K.J. (1983): *Some Limitations of the 4P's as a Paradigm for Marketing.* Report presented at the Marketing Education Group Annual Conference at Cranfield Institute of Technology, U.K., July

Drucker, P. (1973): *Management: Tasks, Responsibilities, Practices.* New York: Harper & Row

Edvardsson, B. (1990): Service Quality in Customer Relationships: A Study of Critical Incidents in Mechanical Engineering Companies. *The Service Industries Journal* (forthcoming)

Edvardsson, B., Edvinsson, L. & Nyström, H. (1988): *Internationalization in Knowledge-Intensive Service Companies.—A Frame of Reference and Some Management Observations.* Research Report presented at the Seventh Annual Conference on Services Marketing, Arlington, Va., October 2–5

Edvardsson, B. & Gustavsson, B.O. (1988): *Quality in Services and Quality in Service Organizations—A Model of Quality Assessment*. Karlstad, Sweden: Center for Service Research

Edvardsson, B. & Magnusson, L. (1988): *Tjänstesverige* (Service Sweden). Lund, Sweden: Studentlitteratur

Edvinsson, L. (1983): *The Development of Service Export. An Overview*. Stockholm, Sweden: Marketing Technique Center

———. (1985): The Export Sales Life Cycle. In Grönroos, C. & Gummesson, E., eds., *Service Marketing. Nordic School Perspectives*. Stockholm University

———. (1986): Organizational Development for International Services Marketing. In Venkatesan, M. et al., eds., *Creativity in Services Marketing*. Chicago, Ill.: American Marketing Association

Edvinsson, L. & Nandorf, T. (1983): The Exporting of Services: An Overview and Presentation of a Case Approach. In Berry, L.L. et al., eds., *Emerging Perspectives on Services Marketing*. Chicago, Ill.: American Marketing Association

Eiglier, P. & Langeard, E. (1976): *Principes politique marketing pour les enterprises des service*. Working Paper. Institute Administration des Enterprises, decembre

———. (1981): A Conceptual Approach of the Service Offering. In Hartvig Larsen, H. & Heede, S., eds., *Proceedings of the EAARM Xth Annual Conference*. Copenhagen School of Economics and Business Administration, May

Ekholm, B-G. (1984): *The Business Idea and Its Lifepath*. Research Report. Fourth Annual Strategic Management Society Conference, Philadelphia, October

European Organization for Quality Control (EOQC). *QUALITY—Challenges and Opportunities*. Proceedings from the 31st Annual Conference, Vols. 1 and 2, Frankfurt am Main, West Germany, 1987

Evans, J.R. & Berman, B. (1987): *Marketing*. 3rd edition. New York: Macmillan

Faes, W. & Van Tilborgh, C. (1984): *Marketing van diensten* (Marketing of services). Antwerpen, Belgium: Kluwer

Falk, B., ed. (1980): *Dienstleistungsmarketing* (Service marketing). Landsberg am Lech, West Germany

Fisk, G. (1967): *Marketing Systems*. New York: Harper & Row

Fisk, G. & Dixon, D.F. (1967): *Theories of Marketing Systems*. New York: Harper & Row

Flocken, B., Gilmour, S., Murphy, M. & Snow-Stegall, M.S. (1988): *The Augmented Service Offering: An Empirical Study—Sonora Laboratory Sciences, Inc.* Unpublished project report. Arizona State University

Fock, H. (1987): *Från produktion till styrning. Om verksamhetsutveckling inom den offentliga sektorn* (From production to management. On the development of operations in the public sector). Stockholm, Sweden: Advisor

Free, C. (1987): Developing a Service Strategy. In *Strategies for Service Management: Marketing in Today's Competitive Environment*. Paris: Esomar

Fuchs, W.R. (1968): *The Service Economy*. New York: Columbia University Press

Garvin, G.A. (1984): What Does 'Product Quality' Really Mean? *Sloan Management Review*, Fall

———. (1987): Competing on the Eight Dimensions of Quality. *Harvard Business Review*, November–December

George, W.R. (1984): Internal Marketing for Retailers. The Junior Executive Employee. In Lindqvist, J.D., ed., *Developments in Marketing Science,* Academy of Marketing Science

———. (1986): Internal Communications Programs as a Mechanism for Doing Internal Marketing. In Venkatesan, M. et al., eds., *Creativity in Services Marketing.* Chicago, Ill.: American Marketing Association

George, W.R. & Berry, L.L. (1981): Guidelines for the Advertising of Services. *Business Horizons*, July/August

George, W.R. & Grönroos, C. (1990): Developing Customer-Conscious Employees at Every Level: Internal Marketing. In Congram, C.A. & Friedman, M.L., eds., *Handbook of Services Marketing.* New York: AMACON

George, W.R. & Marshall, C.E., eds. (1984): *Developing New Services.* Chicago, Ill.: American Marketing Association

Giarini, O. (1990): Notes on the Concept of Service Quality and Economic Value. In Brown, S.W. et al., eds., *Quality in Service: Multi-disciplinary and Multinational Perspectives.* Lexington, Mass.: Lexington Books (forthcoming)

Gorbachev, M. (1987): *Perestroika—New Thinking for Our Country and the World.* New York: Harper & Row

Grönroos, C. (1978): A Service-Oriented Approach to Marketing of Services. *European Journal of Marketing,* No. 8

———. (1979a): *Marknadsforing av tjänster* (Marketing of services). Stockholm, Sweden: Akademilitteratur/Marketing Technology Center

———. (1979b): *Service-Oriented International Marketing Strategies: An Overview.* Working Paper 16. Helsingfors, Finland: Swedish School of Economics and Business Administration

———. (1979c): An Applied Theory for Marketing Industrial Services. *Industrial Marketing Management*, No. 1

———. (1980a): Designing a Long Range Marketing Strategy for Services. *Long Range Planning*, April

———. (1980b): *Marknadsföring av industriella tjänster* (Marketing of Industrial Services). Malmö, Sweden: Studentlitteratur

———. (1980c): *Palvelujen Markkinointi* (Marketing of Services). Espoo, Finland: Weilin & Göös

———. (1981): Internal Marketing—An Integral Part of Marketing Theory. In Donnelly, J.H. & George, W.R., eds., *Marketing of Services.* Chicago, Ill.: American Marketing Association

———. (1983a): *Strategic Management and Marketing in the Service Sector.* Cambridge, Mass.: Marketing Science Institute (In U.K.: Bromley: Chartwell-Bratt and Studentlitteratur)

———. (1983b): Innovative Marketing Strategies and Organization Structures for Service Firms. In Berry, L.L. et al., eds., *Emerging Perspectives on Services Marketing.* Chicago, Ill.: American Marketing Association

———. (1983c): Miten palveluja markkinoidaan (How to market services). Espoo, Finland: Weilin & Göös

———. (1984): A Service Quality Model and Its Marketing Implications. *European Journal of Marketing*, No. 4

———. (1985): Internal Marketing—Theory and Practice. In Bloch, T.M., Upah, G.D. & Zeithaml, V.A., eds., *Services Marketing in a Changing Environment*. Chicago, Ill.: American Marketing Association

———. (1986): Developing Service Quality: Some Managerial Implications. In Möller, K. & Paltschik, M., eds., *Contemporary Research in Marketing*. Vol. 2. The XVIIth Annual Conference of the European Marketing Academy, Helsinki, Finland

———. (1987a): Developing the Service Offering—A Source of Competitive Advantage. In Surprenant, C., ed., *Add Value to Your Service*. Chicago, Ill.: American Marketing Association

———. (1987b): *Hyvään palveluun, Palvelun kehittäinen julkishallinnossa* (Towards good services. Developing public services). Helsinki, Finland: Valtion Painatuskeskus

———. (1987c): *Defining Marketing: A Market-Oriented Approach*. Working Paper 170. Helsinki, Finland: Swedish School of Economics and Business Administration

———. (1987d): *Marknadsföring i tjänsteföretag*. 2. utvidgade upplagan (Marketing in service firms. 2. revised edition). Stockholm, Sweden: Liber

———. (1988a): New Competition in the Service Economy: The Five Rules of Service. *International Journal of Operations & Product Management*, No. 3

———. (1988b): Service Quality: The Six Criteria of Good Service Quality. *Review of Business* (St. John's University Press), No. 3

———. (1989a): Defining Marketing: A Market-Oriented Approach. *European Journal of Marketing*, No. 1

———. (1989b): A Relationship Approach to the Marketing Function in Service Contexts: The Marketing and Organization Behavior Interface. *Journal of Business Research*, 4

Grönroos, C. & Gummesson, E., eds. (1985a): *Service Marketing—Nordic School Perspectives*. Stockholm University, Sweden

———. (1985b): The Nordic School of Service Marketing. In Grönroos & Gummesson, eds., *Service Marketing—Nordic School Perspectives*. Stockholm University, Sweden

———. (1985c): Service Orientation in Industrial Marketing. In Venkatesan, M. et al., eds., *Creativity in Services Marketing. What's New, What Works, What's Developing*. Chicago, Ill.: American Marketing Association

Grönroos, C. & Monthelie, C. (1988): *Service management i offentliga sektorn* (Service management in the public sector). Stockholm, Sweden: Liber

Grönroos, C. & Rubinstein, D. (1986): *Totalkommunikation* (Total communication). Stockholm Sweden: Liber

Groocock, J.M. (1987): *The Chain of Quality: Market Dominance through Product Superiority*. New York: John Wiley

Gummesson, E. (1979): The Marketing of Professional Services—An Organizational Dilemma. *European Journal of Marketing*, No. 5

———. (1981): Marketing Cost Concept in Service Firms. *Industrial Marketing Management*, No. 3

———. (1987a): *Quality—The Ericsson Approach*. Stockholm, Sweden: Ericsson

———. (1987b): Lip Services—A Neglected Area in Services Marketing. *Journal of Services Marketing,* No. 1

———. (1987c): The New Marketing—Developing Long-Term Interactive Relationships. *Long Range Planning,* No. 4

———. (1987d): *Marketing—A Long-Term Interactive Relationship. Contribution to a New Marketing Theory.* Stockholm, Sweden: Marketing Technology Center

———. (1988): Att utveckla servicekvalitet eller "Varför finns det inga servicekonstruktörer?" (To develop service quality or "Why are there no service designers?"). In Edvardsson, B. & Gummesson, E., eds., *Management i tjänstesamhället* (Management in the service society). Stockholm, Sweden: Liber

———. (1989): Nine Lessons on Service Quality. *Total Quality Management,* February

———. (1990): Organizing for Marketing and Marketing Organizations. In Congram, C.A. & Friedman, M.L., eds., *Handbook of Services Marketing.* New York: AMACON

Gummesson, E. & Grönroos, C. (1987): *Quality of Products and Services—A Tentative Synthesis between Two Models.* Research report. Center for Service Research, University of Karlstad, Sweden

———. (1988): Quality of Services. Lessons from the Product Sector. In Surprenant, C., ed., *Add Value to Your Service.* Chicago, Ill.: American Marketing Association

Hackett, D.W. (1976): The International Expansion of U.S. Franchising Systems: Status and Strategies. *Journal of International Business Studies,* Spring

Håkansson, H. & Snehota, I. (1976): *Marknadsplanering: Ett Sätt att Skapa Nya Problem?* (Marketing Planning: A Way of Creating New Problems?). Malmö, Sweden: Studentlitteratur

Håkansson, H. (1982): *International Marketing and Purchasing of Industrial Goods.* New York: John Wiley

Haller, T. (1980): Strategic Planning: Key to Corporate Power for Marketers. *Marketing Times*, No. 2

Harvey-Jones, (1989): *Making It Happen. Reflections on Leadership.* Glasgow: Fontana/Collins

Haywood, K.M. & Pickworth, J.R. (1988): Connecting Productivity with Quality through the Design of Service Delivery Systems. In Thomas, E.G. & Rao, S.R., eds., *Proceedings from an International Conference on Services Marketing.* Special Conference Series, Vol. V. Academy of Marketing Science/Cleveland State University

Haywood-Farmer, J. & Stuart, F.I. (1988): Measuring the Quality of Professional Services. In Johnston, R., ed., *The Management of Service Operations.* Kempston, England: IFS Publications

Hedvall, M-B. & Paltschik, M. (1987): Perceived Service Quality in Pharmacies. In Blois, K. & Parkinson, S., eds., *Innovative Marketing—A European Perspective.* Proceedings from the XVIIth Annual Conference of the European Marketing Academy. University of Bradford, England

Hensel, J.S. (1988): *Service Quality Improvement and Control: A Customer-Based Approach.* Research report from the Seinsheimer Symposium on Business: The Integration of Organizational Behavior and Marketing—Implications for Service Management. Freeman School of Business at Tulane University, New Orleans, November 11–12

Heskett, J.L. (1986): *Managing in the Service Economy.* Cambridge, Mass.: Harvard Business School Press

——. (1987): Lessons in the Service Sector. *Harvard Business Review.* March–April

Hill, T.P. (1977): On Goods and Services. *Review of Income and Wealth,* December

Hirsch, S. (1985): *Internationalization and Forward Market Integration.* Research Report. 2nd Open International IMP Research Seminar on International Marketing. Uppsala, September

Hogan, J., Hogan, R. & Busch, C.M. (1984): How to Measure Service Orientation. *Journal of Applied Psychology,* No. 1

Hutt, M.D. & Speh, T.W. (1989): *Business Marketing Management. A Strategic View of Industrial and Organizational Markets.* 3rd edition. New York: Dryden Press

Iacocca, L. (1984): *Iacocca.* New York: Bantam Books

——. (1988): *Talking Straight.* New York: Bantam Books

Ishikawa, K. (1985): *What Is Total Quality Control? The Japanese Way.* Englewood Cliffs, N.J.: Prentice-Hall

Jackson, B.B. (1985a): Build Customer Relationships That Last. *Harvard Business Review,* November–December

——. (1985b): *Winning and Keeping Industrial Customers. The Dynamics of Customer Relationships.* Lexington, Mass.: Lexington, Books

Johansson, J. (1987): *Japan: The Land of Free Service.* Karlstad, Sweden: Center for Service Research

Johnson, E.M., Scheuing, E.E. & Gaida, K.A. (1986): *Profitable Services Marketing.* Homewood, Ill.: Dow Jones-Irwin

Johnston, R. (1989): A Framework for Developing a Quality Strategy in a Customer Processing Operation. *International Journal of Quality and Reliability Management,* No. 4

Judd, R.C. (1964): The Case for Redefining Services. *Journal of Marketing,* January

——. (1965): *The Structure and Classification of the Service Market.* Diss. Ann Arbor, Mich.: University Microfilms

Judd, V.C. (1987): Differentiate with the 5th P: People. *Industrial Marketing Management,* November

Juran, J.M. (1982): *Upper Management and Quality.* New York: Juran Institute

Keiser, T. (1988): Strategies for Enhancing Service Quality. *Journal of Services Marketing,* No. 2

Kent, R.A. (1986): Faith in Four P's: An Alternative. *Journal of Marketing Management,* No. 2

King, C.A. (1984): Service-Oriented Quality Control. *The Cornell Hotel and Restaurant Administration Quarterly,* No. 4

Kjaer-Hansen, M. (1945): *Afsaetningsokonomi* (Distribution economy). Copenhagen, Denmark: Erhvervsokonomisk Forlag

Klemi, P. (1983): *Sisainen markkinointi* (Internal marketing). Espoo, Finland: Samerka

Kotler, P. (1973): Defining the Limits of Marketing. *Marknadsvetande,* No. 1

——. (1980): *Principles of Marketing.* Englewood Cliffs, N.J.: Prentice-Hall

——. (1986): Megamarketing. *Harvard Business Review.* March–April

——. (1988): *Marketing Management.* 6th edition. Englewood Cliffs, N.J.: Prentice-Hall

Kotler, P. & Bloom, P.N. (1984): *Marketing Professional Services.* Englewood Cliffs, N.J.: Prentice-Hall

Langeard, E. & Eiglier, P. (1987): *Servuction. Les Marketing des Services.* Paris: John Wiley

Langeard, E., Reffait, P. & Eiglier, P. (1986): Developing New Services. In Venkatesan, M., Schmalensee, D.M. & Marshall, C., eds., *Creativity in Services Marketing: What's New, What Works, What's Developing.* Chicago, Ill.: American Marketing Association

Larreche, J-C., Powell, W.W. & Ebling, H.D. (1987): *Key Strategic Issues for the 1990's.* Fontainbleau, France: INSEAD

Lehtinen, J. (1983): *Asiakasohjautuva palveluyritys (Customer-oriented service firm).* Espoo, Finland: Weilin+Göös

——. (1986): *Quality Oriented Services Marketing.* University of Tampere, Finland

Lehtinen, U. & Lehtinen, J. (1982): *Service Quality: A Study of Quality Dimensions.* Research report. Helsinki, Finland: Service Management Institute

Lehtinen, J. & Storbacka, K. (1986): *Palvelujohtaminen* (Service management). Veikkola, Finland: Jarmo. R. Lehtinen

Lele, M. (1986): How Service Needs Influence Product Strategy. *Sloan Management Review,* Fall

Leonard, F.S. & Sasser, W.E. (1982): The Incline of Quality. *Harvard Business Review,* September–October

Levitt, T. (1972): Production-line Approach to Service. *Harvard Business Review,* September–October

——. (1976): The Industrialization of Service. *Harvard Business Review,* September-October

——. (1983): After the Sale Is Over. *Harvard Business Review,* September–October

Lewis, R.C. & Klein, D.M. (1987): The Measurements of Gaps in Service Quality. In Czepiel, J.A. et al., eds., *The Service Challenge: Integrating for Competitive Advantage.* Chicago, Ill.: American Marketing Association

Lindquist, L.J. (1987): Quality and Service Value in Comsumption of Services. In Surprenant, C., ed., *Add Value to Your Service: The Key to Success.* Chicago, Ill.: American Marketing Association

——. (1988): *Kundernas kvalitetsupplevelse i konsumtionsfasen. En studie av tjänstekvalitet* (Customers' quality perception in the consumption phase). With English summary. Helsingfors, Finland: Swedish School of Economics and Business Administration

Lovelock, C.H. (1980): Towards a Classification of Services. In Lamb, C.W. & Dunne, P.M., eds., *Theoretical Developments in Marketing.* Chicago, Ill.: American Marketing Association

——. (1983): Classifying Services to Gain Strategic Marketing Insights. *Journal of Marketing*, Summer

——. (1984): *Services Marketing*. Englewood Cliffs, N.J.: Prentice-Hall

——. (1988): *Managing Services. Marketing, Operations, and Human Resources*. Englewood Cliffs, N.J.: Prentice-Hall

Lovelock, C.H., Langeard, E., Bateson, J. & Eiglier, P. (1981): Some Organizational Problems Facing Marketing in the Service Sector. In Donnelly, J.H. & George, W.R., eds., *Marketing of Services*. Chicago, Ill.: American Marketing Association

Lovelock, C.H. & Young, R.F. (1979): Look to Consumers to Increase Productivity. *Harvard Business Review*, May–June

Lund, K. & Knudsen, K. (1982): *Introduktion til service management* (Introduction to service management). Copenhagen, Denmark: Civilokonomernes Forlag

Lund, K. et al. (1986): Introduktion til intern markedsforing (Introduction to internal marketing). Copenhagen, Denmark: Civilokonomernes Forlag

Lyth, D.M. & Johnston, R. (1988): A Framework for Designing Quality into Service Operations. In Johnston, R., ed., *The Management of Service Operations*. Kempston, England: IFS Publications

Mahoney, T.A. (1988): Productivity Defined: The Relativity of Efficiency, Effectiveness, and Change. In *Productivity of Organizations*. San Francisco, Calif. Jossey-Bass

Maister, D.H. & Lovelock, C.H. (1982): Managing Facilitor Services. *Sloan Management Review*, Summer

Marketing Definitions: A Glossary of Marketing Terms (1960). Committee on Definitions. Chicago, Ill.: American Marketing Association

McCarthy, E.J. (1960): *Basic Marketing*. Homewood, Ill.: Irwin

Mickwitz, G. (1959): *Marketing and Competition*. Helsingfors, Finland: Centraltryckeriet

——. (1985): Arbetstid och service (Working hours and service). *Ekonomiska Samfundets Tidskrift*, No. 4

Mills, P.K. (1986): *Managing Service Industries: Organizational Practices in a Post-Industrial Economy*. Cambridge, Mass.: Ballinger

Mills, P.K. & Morris, J.H. (1986): Clients as Partial Employees of Service Organizations: Role Development in Direct Participation. *Academy of Management Review*, 11

Naisbitt, J. (1982): *Megatrends: Ten New Directions Transforming Our Lives*. New York: Warner Books

Normann, R. (1984): *Service Management*. New York: John Wiley

Orsini, J.L. & Meyer, M. (1987): Services Quality in Teaching: An Exploratory Application of the Disconfirmation Model. *1987 Conference Proceedings*. Western Marketing Educators' Association

Our Approach to Quality. SAS Scandinavian Airline System, 1987

Parasuraman, A., Zeithaml, V.A. & Berry, L.L. (1985): A Conceptual Model of Service Quality and Its Implications for Future Research. *Journal of Marketing*, Fall

——. (1986): SERVQUAL; A Multiple-Item Scale for Measuring Customer Perceptions of Service Quality. *Journal of Retailing*, Spring

Parkington, J.J. & Schneider, B. (1979): Some Correlates of Experienced Job Stress: A Boundary Role Study. *Academy of Management Journal*, June

Peters, T. (1988a): The Great Management Paradox. *Hyatt Magazine*, Summer

——. (1988b): Restoring American Competitiveness: Looking for New Models of Organizations. *The Academy of Management EXECUTIVE*, No. 2

Peters, T. & Austin, N. (1985): *A Passion for Excellence*. New York: Random House

Peters, T. & Waterman, Jr., R.H. (1982): *In Search of Excellence*. New York: Harper & Row

Pickworth, J.R. (1987): Minding the Ps and Qs: Linking Quality and Productivity. *The Cornell Hotel and Restaurant Administration Quarterly*, May

Piercy, N. (1985): *Marketing Organization. An Analysis of Information Processing, Power and Politics*. London: George Allen & Unwin

Pihlgren, G. (1985): *Management i förvalnting: effektivitet och förnyelse* (Management in public administration: effectiveness and revival). Stockholm, Sweden: Liber

Pintak, L. (1988): Beautiful America Keeps Looking Uglier as Attitudes Decay. *Mesa Tribune*, August 8 (America as Bujumbura. *The New York Times*, August 15)

Porter, M.E. (1980): *Competitive Strategy*. New York: The Free Press

Pul-eeze! Will Somebody Help Me? *Time*, February 2, 1987

Quinn, J.B. & Gagnon, C.E. (1986): Will Services Follow Manufacturing in Decline? *Harvard Business Review*, November–December

Ramm-Schmidt, C. (1984): Adapting a Service-Oriented Marketing Strategy in a Service Industry. In Grönroos, C. & Gummesson, E., eds., *Service Marketing. Nordic School Perspectives*. Stockholm, Sweden: University of Stockholm

Rasmussen, A. (1955): *Pristeori eller parameterteori—studier omkring virksomhedens afsaetning* (Price theory or parameter theory—studies of the output of firms). Copenhagen, Denmark: Erhvervsokonomisk Forlag

Rathmell, J.R. (1974): *Marketing in the Service Sector*. Cambridge, Mass.: Winthrop

Regan, W.J. (1963): The Service Revolution. *Journal of Marketing*, July

Reich, R. B. (1987): *Tales of a New America*. New York: Times Books

Reichborn, A.N. & Vifladt, E.H. (1986): *Serviceledelse i offentlig forvaltning* (Service management in public administration). Oslo, Norway: Universitetsforlaget

Reingen, P.H. & Kernan, J.B. (1986): Analysis of Referral Networks in Marketing: Methods and Illustration. *Journal of Marketing Research*, November

Riddle, D.I. (1986): *Service-Led Growth*. New York: Praeger

——. (1988): Cultural Aspects of Service Technology Transfer. In Johnston, R., ed., *The Management of Service Operations*. Kempston, England: IFS Publications

Robinson, J. (1933): *The Economics of Imperfect Competition*. London: Macmillan

Rosenberg, L.J. & Czepiel, J.A. (1984): A Marketing Approach for Customer Retention. *Journal of Consumer Marketing*, No. 2

Salmond, D., ed. (1988): *Business Buying Behavior. A Conference Summary*. Report No. 88-106. Cambridge, Mass.: Marketing Science Institute

Sampson, G.P. & Snape, R.H. (1986): Identifying the Issues in Trade in Services. *The World Economy,* Vol. 8

Samrén, I. (1988): Service Strategies in Practice. *European Research,* February

Sartti, S. (1988): Palveluksia halutaan (Services requested). *Helsingin Sanomat,* August 28

Sasser, W.E. (1976): Match Supply and Demand in Service Industries. *Harvard Business Review,* November–December

Sasser, W.E., Olsen, R. Paul & Wyckoff, D.D. (1978): *Management of Service Operations: Text and Cases.* Boston, Mass.: Allyn & Bacon

Scheuch, F. (1982): *Dienstleistungsmarketing* (Service marketing). Munich, West Germany: Verlag Vahlen

Scheuing, E.E. & Araskog, R.V., eds. (1982): *The Service Economy.* New York: K.C.G. Productions

Schmenner, R.W. (1986): How Can Service Business Survive and Prosper? *Sloan Management Review,* Spring

Schneider, B. (1980): The Service Organization: Climate Is Crucial. *Organizational Dynamics,* Autumn

———. (1985): Organization Behavior. *Annual Review of Psychology,* 36

———. (1986): Notes on Climate and Culture. In Venkatesan, M., Schmalensee, D.M. & Marshall, C., eds., *Creativity in Services Marketing: What's New, What Works, What's Developing.* Chicago, Ill.: American Marketing Association

Schneider, B. & Bowen, D.E. (1984): New Service Design, Development, and Implementation and the Employee. In George, W.R. & Marshall, C.E., eds., *Developing New Services,* Chicago, Ill.: American Marketing Association

———. (1985): Employee and Customer Perceptions of Service in Banks: Replication and Extension. *Journal of Applied Psychology,* 70

Schneider, B. & Rentsch, J. (1987): The Management of Climate and Culture: A Futures Perspective. In Hage, J., ed., *Futures of Organizations.* Lexington, Mass.: Lexington Books

Schoell, W.F. & Ivy, J.T. (1981): *Marketing: Contemporary Concepts and Practices.* Boston, Mass.: Allyn and Bacon

Segal-Horn, S. (1988): Global Service Delivery—Managing Critical Interdependencies. In Johnston, R., ed., *The Management of Service Operations.* Kempston, England: IFS Publications

Shostack, G.L. (1977): Breaking Free from Product Marketing. *Journal of Marketing,* April

———. (1984): Designing Services That Deliver. *Harvard Business Review,* January–February

———. (1987): Service Positioning through Structural Change. *Journal of Marketing,* January

Smith, R. & Huston, M. (1983): Script-Based Evaluations of Satisfaction with Services. In Berry, L.L., Shostack, G.L. & Upah, G., eds., *Emerging Perspectives on Services Marketing.* Chicago, Ill.: American Marketing Association

Stanton, W.J. (1974): *Fundamentals of Marketing.* Tokyo: McGraw-Hill Kogakusha.

Statistical Abstract of the United States 1984. U.S. Department of Commerce

Steedle, L.F. (1988): Has Productivity Measurement Outgrown Infancy? *Management Accounting,* August

Stigler, G. (1956): *Trends in Employment in the Service Industries.* Princeton University Press for the National Bureau of Economic Research

Tansik, D.A. (1988): *Balance in Service Systems Design.* Research report presented at the Seinsheimer Symposium on Business. Tulane University, Freeman School of Business, November 11–12

Tansik, D.A. & Chase, R.B. (1988): *The Effects of Customer Induced Uncertainty on the Design of Service Systems.* Research report presented at the Academy of Management National Meeting, Anaheim, Calif. August

Tettero, J. & Viehoff, J. (1983): *Marketing voor dienstverlenende organisaties* (Marketing for service-providing organizations). Antwerpen, Belgium: Kluwer

Thomas, D.R.E. (1978): Strategy Is Different in Service Businesses. *Harvard Business Review,* July–August

Turnbull, P.W. & Valla, J-P., eds. (1987): *Strategies for International Industrial Marketing.* London: Croom Helm

U.S. National Study on Trade in Services. Washington, D.C.: Office of the U.S. Trade Representative, December 1983

Vandermerwe, S. & Chadwick, M. (1989): The Internationalisation of Services. *The Service Industries Journal,* No. 1

Vicari, S. (1983): *Imprese di servizi e politiche di mercato* (The impact of service on business policy). Universita L. Boconi

Vogels, R., Lemmink, J. & Kasper, H. (1989): Some Methodological Remarks on the SERVQUAL Model. In Avlonitis, G.J., Papavasiliou, N.K. & Kouremenos, A.G., eds., *Marketing Thought and Practice in the 1990's.* Proceedings from the XVIII Annual Conference of the European Marketing Academy, Athens, Greece

Van Tilborgh, C., ed. (1986): *Marketing van Diensten* (Marketing of Services). Antwerpen, Belgium: Kluwer

Walker, W.E. (1986): *Changing Organizational Culture.* Knoxville, Tenn.: The University of Tennessee Press

Webster, Jr., F.E. (1978): Management Science in Industrial Marketing. *Journal of Marketing,* January

——. (1988): *Rediscovering the Marketing Concept.* Working Paper 88-100. Cambridge, Mass.: Marketing Science Institute

Webster, Jr., F.E. & Wind, Y. (1972): Organizational Buying Behavior. Englewood Cliffs, N.J.: Prentice-Hall

Wilson, A. (1972): *The Marketing of Professional Services.* London: McGraw-Hill

Wyckoff, D.D. (1984): New Tools for Achieving Service Quality. *Cornell Hotel and Restaurant Administration Quarterly,* November

Zeithaml. V.A. (1987): *Defining and Relating Price, Perceived Quality, and Perceived Value.* Cambridge, Mass.: Marketing Science Institute

Zeithaml, V.A., Berry, L.L. & Parasuraman, A. (1988): Communication and Control Processes in the Delivery of Service Quality. *Journal of Marketing,* April

Zeithaml, V.A., Parasuraman, A. & Berry, L.L. (1985): Problems and Strategies in Services Marketing. *Journal of Marketing,* Spring

Zemke, R. (1988a): Scandinavian Management—A Look at Our Future? *Management Review,* July

———. (1988b): Creating Service Cultures. *The Service Edge,* No. 8

Zemke, R. & Schaaf, D. (1989): *The Service Edge*. New York: New American Library (NAL Books)

Index

About the Author

Dr. Christian Grönroos was born on January 16, 1947 in Helsinki, Finland. He received his doctorate degree in marketing in 1979 from the Swedish School of Economics and Business Administration in Helsinki, where he has served as professor of marketing since 1984. He has been on the faculty there since 1971. He is former chairman of the Department of Marketing and Economic Geography, former director of the Research Institute, and present chairman of the Management Education Center at the school.

Dr. Grönroos spent the Fall semester of 1988 as visiting professor at Arizona State University and First Interstate Center for Services Marketing in Tempe, Arizona. A Distinguished Fellow of the Finnish Society of Science and Letters since 1986 and a Research Fellow of the First Interstate Center for Services Marketing since 1988, Dr. Grönroos also received the Ahlsell Prize—the most distinguished award in Scandinavia and Northern Europe for research into marketing and distribution.

Dr. Grönroos's research interests include service marketing, service management in the private and public sectors, service-oriented industrial marketing, internal marketing, and quality management. He has spoken and presented papers at numerous international conferences in the United States, Canada, Europe, and Asia.

Dr. Grönroos is a co-founder and member of the board of two consulting firms specializing in service management: Nordic Service Institute Ltd., and Service Consultants Finland Ltd., the former of which he also serves as chairman. He is also a member of Dan Rubenstein Consulting, a firm that specializes in total communications planning; John Nurminen Oy, an international Finland-based forwarding and transportation firm; Kaleva Travel Agency Ltd., the largest privately owned agency in Finland; and Vita Korset, a firm in the consumer packaged goods business. He is an advisor to several major corporations in the service sector and the industrial sector as well as to institutions in the public sector. Dr. Grönroos has been invited as speaker to numerous major firms—AT&T, United Telecom, Dupont, S.C. Johnson & Sons, First Interstate Bank of Arizona, KLM, SAS Scandinavian Airlines System, Volvo Bilmaterial, Saab Scania, Union Bank of Finland, Svenska Handelsbanken, Silja Line, Oslo Sporveier, Varma Ltd.,

Kone Corporation, Finnpap (The Finnish Paper Mills Association), Folksam Insurance, and many others.

The author has written several books and numerous articles on services marketing, service management, and other aspects of marketing and management. Among his books is a volume on the marketing of services. First published in 1983, it has become a classic text both for university students and practitioners of services marketing. Now appearing in several editions in Finnish and in three Scandinavian languages, an edition in English of *Strategic Management and Marketing in the Service Sector* was published by the Marketing Science Institute in 1983 and by Studentlitteratur/Chartwell-Bratt in the United Kingdom in 1984. *Service Management and Marketing: Managing the Moments of Truth in Service Competition,* is Dr. Grönroos's most recent contribution to his field.